o. jects and . mpat y

objects and empathy

essays by arthur saltzman

Mid-List Press
Minneapolis

For the blue light

First printing: June 2001
07 06 05 04 03 02   6 5 4 3 2 1

Printed in Canada.

Library of Congress Cataloging-in-Publication Data
Saltzman, Arthur M. (Arthur Michael), 1953-
        Objects and empathy : essays / by Arthur Saltzman.
        p. cm.
        "First series: creative nonfiction."
        ISBN 0-922811-49-0 (trade paper : alk. paper)
        I. Title.

        AC8.S226 2001
        081—dc21   2001030175

Cover and text design: Lane Stiles
Cover illustration: Joseph Cornell, *Rose des vents,* 1952–1954, box construction, 11–1/2" x 16–1/4" x 4"; photograph by Bill Jacobson, courtesy of PaceWildenstein Foundation/VAGA, New York, New York

Earlier versions of some of these pieces appeared in the following publications: *Florida Review* ("Action Figures"), *Gettysburg Review* ("Incipience and Other Alibis"), *Iowa Review* ("Living Space"), *Ohio Review* ("Objects and Empathy"), *Evansville Review* ("From the Letters to Gamma Man"), *Santa Clara Review* ("Gimme Kilter"), *Contemporary Education* ("Love Among the Stacks"), *The Cream City Review* ("Offerings"), and *Literal Latte* ("The Girl in the Moon," which won the First Annual Roy T. Ames Memorial Essay Award, judged by Philip Lopate).

contents

Preface   vii

Incipience and Other Alibis   1

The Girl in the Moon   11

Gimme Kilter   23

Living Space   31

Action Figures   48

From the Letters to Gamma Man   56

Objects and Empathy   63

How to Play   76

Offerings   87

Call It in the Air   96

Poetasting	106
A Gambler's Chance	119
Tales from the Border Patrol	132
Centers of Gravity	147
Body Language	157
Call Waiting	165
Variations on a Gift Horse	179
Priced to Go	187
The Big Interbang Theory	195
The Poetics of Know-How	201
Primogeniture: 1962	208
Arrangement in Mixed Media	215
The Understory	223
Love among the Stacks	231
Soldiers of Fortune	239

preface

In *Adventures of Huckleberry Finn*, our fledgling narrator announces that the novel that introduced him was "mostly a true book, with some stretchers." In *The Things They Carried*, which bookstores and libraries variously shelve under Memoir, Fiction, Essay Collections, and Nonfiction, Tim O'Brien's "Tim O'Brien" proposes, rescinds, and recombines the components of "story-truth" and "happening-truth," crying wolf so often that by the end of the book the confusion doesn't even raise a bleat from the sheep. In the movie *Casablanca*, Humphrey Bogart's Rick Blaine answers a question about the integrity of Claude Rains's urbanely predatory Captain Renault by saying that he is like other men, only more so. In an interview for *The Paris Review*, novelist Don DeLillo maintains that the writer strives to "place himself more clearly in the world," and "to ride his own sentences into new perceptions." And in an experiment featured on ABC television's 20/20, children who participate with a psychologist in the invention of a make-believe fox succumb to "magical thinking": they come to believe in, then to fear, the creature in the box they *know* is empty. With apologies to those who dread getting a present marked "Some Assembly Required," I submit these fragments because they strike me as analogous to some of the motives and methods on display in this collection.

As to *what* has been collected, I have learned that the terminology itself is still under construction. Once generic
distinctions start to leak, people bring in anything that might
conceivably hold water. "Literary nonfiction," "creative nonfiction," and "lyric essay" are some of the makeshift semantic
hybrids in current use and designed to catch the sort of prose
work which is very like an essay but which exploits the linguistic playfulness, associative logic, and imaginative license of
poetry. It tends to prefer insinuation to insistence, resonance to
resolution. If the critical essay challenges its topic to wrestle, the
lyric essay invites it to dance. (Fact may be its escort, but it is too
flirtatious to stand by Fact all evening.) But even as it dances, it
glances about the room, bumping up against other guests,
angling toward the fresh plate of hors d'oeuvres, spying on
accoutrements and cleavages beyond the shoulder of its chosen
concern. It is ruminative, sly, self-effacing, intimate, sneaky fast,
and (as long as we're breaking in new expressions)
"idiosyncretic." Instead of final findings, it provides an adventure
for the voice and the self's invention.

Basically, working on these pieces began for me as escapes
from, experimental therapies for, or antidotes to the literary critical writing that generally occupies me. While several of these
pieces do employ other literature to some extent, I have found
that they enable me to exercise different muscles and to rummage about with some of the impunity so-called creative writers
assume. (In other words, even when I'm playing hooky, I don't
necessarily stray all that far from school grounds.) They let me
eavesdrop on myself and my experiences from different directions than critical tasks afford. In their roomy, ruminative
spaces—Joseph Epstein once described the essay as "a pair of
baggy pants into which nearly anyone and anything can fit"—
performance is not incidental to the task at hand. They have a
jab-and-feint quality that allows me to move more freely about
the ring. They offer another way to wonder, to sympathize, to
puzzle in, to puzzle out, and to praise.

The authors I most admire enact the belief that every sentence wants to celebrate itself even as it suffers its own insufficiencies. The trick is to look lively on the tightrope. Although readers will likely discover thematic or tonal consistencies among the essays in this volume, as well as detect repeat appearances by some characters in varying degrees of disguise, that is probably the closest I can come to a unifying principle for the volume. Anything more would be an artificial imposition of coherence after the fact-fiction-memoir-anecdote, and hence, another "stretcher" to contend with.

I have the good fortune to teach at a college where more eccentric writing endeavors like these are esteemed along with conventional academic ones. Those friends, colleagues, and family members who have asked after, commented wisely upon, and even listened patiently to my reading of these pieces aloud have made that fortune grow more than they know, and certainly, inexcusably, more than I have let them know before now. I suspect that I am not alone in needing a certain space, time, solitude when I want it, company when I don't. Those closest to me give me leave, and I realize the gift that that represents.

even the smallest presences
take on orientation …
                    —A. R. Ammons, "Enameling"

Everything is more or less in wall building.
  —Steven Allen, champion Cumbrian dry-stone waller

incipience and other alibis

There is not one logic that governs everything, although logic might suggest otherwise. One could choose to look for lost keys where it makes sense to find them or where the light is best. And where is the light best? There is the surgical field, the southern exposure, a dozen matchless Rembrandts. Where best to begin to look? "Our vision is continually active, continually moving, continually holding things in a circle around itself, constituting what is present to us as we are," John Berger explains in *Ways of Seeing*. It is easy to forget how transitive a verb the eye incites.

There is good light in her bedroom. At 5:55 a.m., she is scaling her way out of her last dream of the night to find herself in her bedroom on a Sunday morning and ten years old. There is a gap between dream and alertness lasting long enough—perhaps ten or fifteen seconds—to allow for the completion of the sedimentary process of the ordinary. We say "daybreak," and it is true that the morning is a blow, stunning, and she is young enough to come flailing awake sometimes, as children will, lurching out of the betrayal of their bodies, which let them down when they were determined not to nap. But the day does not break before her eyes. At 5:55 the air is a shimmering, portentous surf, only slowly becoming known as its molecules deploy into nightstand, dresser, doll, and mirror. The breakage

had come with sleep, it seems, but now there is a coalescence
under way, a gathering of features, an assumption of familiar
positions, a taking on of color, contour, presence. In it all comes.

The girl has lately been bothered by God. "Religion," her
religion tells her, "is the vision of something which stands
beyond, behind, and within the passing flux of immediate
things." This passage is from one of the prescribed silent medi-
tations at temple. Along with the rest of the congregation, she
reads that religion is "something which is the ultimate ideal, and
the hopeless quest." When she looks up from those words,
which start to revolve in her hands, pulling her head back
down—the adult service is long for a child—she catches sight of
the older members, who appear to be drifting with the somno-
lence of that doom. Five thousand years of tradition keep them
up and cause them to totter, slightly, quietly, like the candles,
she thinks. When they rise to stage their supplications, they pronounce the heavy, complicated nouns almost dismissively: they
slur past "iniquity," "transgression," "reverence," "atonement,"
"righteousness," "holiness," "redemption," letting the words fall
the way a weight lifter drops the bar after the last repetition, like
an afterthought. They have all been here before, but for the girl,
bunched into a knot against the edge of awe, holding on, some
unprecedented knowledge has begun to dawn.

There is a joke going around the Sunday School: In the
beginning, there was nothing. Then God said, Let there be light.
There was still nothing, but now you could see it.

Now in her bedroom, which she has been filling each night
with prayer, a vision is stirring. Her head is a little troubled pot.
There is a glare above her dresser, which makes a corolla in the
mirror. She wears glasses, and they are within easy reach on the
nightstand. If she puts them on, she thinks, she will see, she will
know. God has come to her to banish the darkness, as the book
says, only not just as a manner of speaking, but waiting silently,
suspended in a molten middle distance, and for her alone. At
5:55 a.m., when everything is tentative and the room looks like

consciousness before it has settled for the mundanities of reference, she puts on her glasses, but she keeps her eyes closed to
pray. A whisper of light is pressing in. She opens her eyes slowly.
   Her hair dryer is on fire.
   And what did she pray for? A sign, perhaps. Logically speaking, she would wish for verification. STOP. YIELD. NO VACANCY. It
is hard to guess what sign would have suited her, playing hide-
and-seek with God when she should have been sleeping, knuckled under the covers, awaiting His "fond Ambush." The phrase
belongs to Emily Dickinson, a connoisseur of rarest light and
homely grails, who also wrote, "It is true that the unknown is the
largest need of the intellect, although for this no one thinks to
thank God." Knowledge is fatal to spectacle. "It is true" and
"thank God" bracket the absence in Dickinson's declaration, but
those phrases are as impeachable as the vagary that like a prime
suspect in a homicide they haul in from both sides. Truth has
never been universally acknowledged, not for long; God is an
elfin divinity, a figment of desire, reputedly given to skulking in
the bedrooms of little girls.
   Perhaps she prayed for the vision to stay. Let God give up
His stick-and-move tactics for a time, at least until she could get
her glasses on. But vision prospers in transition. That is where
Robert Frost cultivates incandescence: "Heaven gives its
glimpses only to those / Not in position to look too close."
Misprision is a gift. Imprecision is. It is essential to poetry that it
not know too much. Not an established figure but ongoing
transfiguration—that is the God she was after to be after her,
ever-arising but not arisen in that granulated first light that is
always building and always failing.
   And if God could accost Moses as a burning bush, who is to
say He could not manifest before her as a burning appliance?
   Matters of fact resolve the issue. Solids occupy the house in
time. The girl tells her mother about the hair dryer, which has
already gone out by the time she gets to it. There is nothing dangerous or marvelous about it anymore. There is no need to rouse

her father, who has had a demanding week of deals and needs his rest. As her mother checks for scorching on the finish of the dresser and considers how best to remove the ruin, the girl enters the extra bedroom that serves as an office, which means that it contains the telephone reserved for her father's business calls. The telephone seems to hold down the desk. It is intransigent and forbidding, a godfather of a phone brooking no approach, completely black. It is one of those old phones that are no longer available, that do not shake from their ringing or budge when the call is taken. It is a moored certainty. There is no hint of the thin pastel priss of the girl's unit, the plastic princess model, which will hardly sustain the coordination of adolescent parties. No, it is a looming thing, fat and massy and truncheon-dark, made to handle bond transactions. On such a phone her father can bring the receiver adamantly down to show his disgust or like the police commissioner in any of a hundred movies to rivet closed a dramatic scene. It is a phone to crush a skull in a detective story in 1947. A weapon to reckon with, to wreak subdural damage with or to fling (use the whole shoulder—there is no wristing this dinosaur) against the wall in a rage and leave permanent scars. It is Saturn to the phones it engendered, and placed next to them would swallow its young. The swim of transcendence stops right then and there at her father's desk, where a telephone that is all business connects her to the unconflicted heft of the world.

Later that afternoon, she discovers that by grinding the heels of her hands against her closed eyes she can almost duplicate the fissiony scrabble of atoms she seemed to see before the routine day set in. In that crushed and blood-soaked light, she imagines, they could at any instant assemble into anything at all.

◻ ◻ ◻

Children have not cornered the market on the romance of revelation by any means. Even as an adult, one has to stay alert for the chance beatitudes.

I myself spend most of my life on one verge or another. I was not aware of this as a child—which I have come to realize, of course, may be the principal advantage of *being* a child—but I now understand that my childhood was a series of near disasters. Everyone's childhood was. Not a week passed without my being spared by some version of a steadying hand taking hold of my shoulder as I was about to follow the fumbled ball into traffic. There were rumors of tetanus lurking in the alleys that seduced all of us with splendid garbage, but I never heard of anyone contracting the disease; despite the warnings, it remained as exotic and irrelevant to us as Communism. Sirens keened regularly in suburban Chicago, but typically beyond the perimeter of any lasting concern. We were middle-class American kids. We took the world for granted because it was given to us daily, sweet and obvious as the same mysteriously colored cereal in the same bowl. Stray dogs and broken glass notwithstanding, everyone we knew survived.

Today, however, the expense of survival is consciousness of survival. When I watch the news, I pay particular attention to where the lightning has struck down power lines and to which states have been hit hardest by the latest outbreak of influenza. How recently did I eat in the restaurant where the cook came down with Hepatitis-B? Was it my brand of packaged turkey that was recalled? Was the victim Jewish? And yet, although the scope of my concern has widened with the onset of adulthood and CNN, I still cannot tell whether or not calamity is closing in. My luck seems to be holding, or at least I am able to believe it is holding as fuses sparkle brightly past my door.

For the daily news that counts as news is proximate. Time does not proceed from one global calamity to the next. Rather, it is marked by quarterly statements from the bank or by lines knifed into the doorjamb to measure the growth of kids too fidgety to appreciate the ritual. We live life close to the vest, meticulously tucking away private histories each day like shirttails. We best attend to detonations nearest our own homes, and we

pore over no one's X-rays but our own. From the first failure of
mothers to urge us to finish breakfast on account of all the
scrambled eggless in Biafra, we sense that things lose gravity as
their orbits around us expand. Real happenings happen *here.*

So even in matters of crisis, we remain homely at heart. Your
three-year-old, who will no longer put up with being clapped in
shopping cart irons, is about half-an-aisle ahead of you in the
grocery store and cornering a second or two before you come
around. He is still in range of your reproof, and you can hear the
squeaks and thawps of his tennis shoes and the reactive clatter
of other carts as he caroms past. Because you stopped to compare jellies, he has slipped beyond the acceptable radius of freedom you allow him, and panic catches fire over your back, and
you are rushing up aisle three and down four and up five,
absurdly caught in the plowman's logic of the supermarket lay-
out, and you come upon a burst jar of pickles he must have set
off like a claymore, and a shiver breaks his name in your throat.
You think you can head off his abductor at the front of the store.
Where are the exits? What must you remember to tell the police
he was wearing? Does he know his own telephone number?
Why did you move here in the first place, so far from any
extended family? How will you tell his mother?

When you finally come upon him at the cage of plastic play-
balls, which he is soberly extracting one by one as though helping some poor animal pass her litter, he looks at you blankly.
Without a word, you sweep him up, tell him you will help him
put back the balls, making that the lesson for now.

Or he decides on an impromptu game of hide-and-seek at
the men's store, and he has gotten too good. He knows how to
hunker down inside the rotating rack of sport coats and muffle
his glee. When else has he ever managed to be so quiet for so
long? It is nearly two full minutes now since you have seen him.
To flush him, you compliment him aloud on his cleverness, his
resolve. Your congratulations begin to clench. You announce that
you give up, that he's won, that he can come out now, so you can

shake him. And the moment the shaking stops, the message ends, as you, who once ran headlong after escaped balls, know.

❐ ❐ ❐

When my daughter was not yet two, I was driving her home with the day's groceries when a white LeSabre left its lane and slammed into us, injuring no one. My daughter, stock-still in her car seat as a section of frieze, did not know what had happened until I removed her from the crumpled car and showed her the damage. It was not until her mother cried that my daughter did, two hours later, awakened to her frailty in that fierce mother-hug. Then *Sesame Street* came on because it was five o'clock, and that was what she knew *Sesame Street* always did, and her familiar day reformed around that.

What made the accident strange was that the LeSabre lost its right rear wheel as it approached, causing it to swerve out of control. The driver confessed to me that her brother must not have taken care to tighten the lugs when he rotated the tires the day before. "Hold that thought," I told her, then phoned the police.

Several days later I was paid a visit by a claims adjustor, who arrived in a powder-blue suit. With the sun directly behind him, it appeared that a graft of sky had alighted on my doorstep. He asked for coffee, and it was not until he was on his second cup that he began to work in earnest. He asked me to reconstruct the accident—he called it an "incident," using the same professional caution that inspires politicians to refer to economic crises as "concerns" and psychiatrists to refer to rampages as "episodes." I complied, having more or less memorized my story after the fourth telling. (The police officer, my wife, my father, and my insurance representative had heard the earlier drafts, with assorted blurbs going out to friends, neighbors, and relatives.) In my kitchen, the suit had turned azure.

"Do you want to see the car?" I asked. When it comes to serious business, I get empirical on people.

"No need," he said.

"Really?"

"Yes. There's no liability here."

"Excuse me?"

"That's all right. No, there's no legal liability. You see, this is what we call 'an act of God.'" He was on his way to the coffeepot for another refill. A cerulean suit moved past me, then resumed the chair. "Say a tree on your property were struck by lightning. If that tree then fell on the car of a friend of yours who had parked in your driveway, well, you could not be held responsible."

"But in this case," I countered, "the tree was traveling at forty-five miles per hour, jumped into my lane, and bit my car!"

"Yes, well … yes. Very good. But we can't expect, you see …" He was looking for the right words, and perhaps a cookie or a doughnut. He was dressed in the raiment of heaven. "An act of God, after all," he reminded me.

"I don't get it. By your definition, *anything* could be called an act of God!"

He regarded me as if I were a beetle trying to make its way up the side of a sink. A seam in his face opened into a wide smile. A moon floating in that dividing and indifferent blue. "You are welcome to sue, of course."

Which is to say that you never know when the odds will gang up. Had I not forgotten the bananas and had to go back to the fruit section before checking out; or had I chosen a check-out line in which no one used a credit card for Doritos and a dozen eggs; or had I in any way made any of a hundred indecisions, visions, and revisions differently before the taking of toasted almonds and Constant Comment Tea, God's act would have been performed on someone else's stage.

On the other hand, my mother-in-law was relieved to hear that the baby was unharmed. ("And you, too, goodness!") She congratulated me on my good luck. "God must have been watching out for you," she concluded, thinking, no doubt, in terms of good fairies rather than deer hunters.

❏ ❏ ❏

In an installment of the television show *All in the Family*, Archie Bunker is nearly crushed at his construction site by a falling bucket of rivets. He buttons his story of this near-death experience by showing Edith, Mike, and Gloria his flattened lunchbox, and he decides that this was a sign from God telling him that—Rilke descending to prime-time Queens—he must change his life. A beat. Another. Then son-in-law Mike breaks the silence: "How do you know God didn't just *miss?*"

A thousand deadly objects dropped from significant heights in the greater metropolitan area today alone, and I escaped unscathed. No stray bullet found me; no meteor crashed through my roof. Indeed, I am a darling of the actuarial tables. Tornadoes have so far kept a civil distance, as have earthquakes and floods, although I know people who know people who have not been so fortunate. If I have been chosen for some elaborate revenge by an industrious mugger or an ex-student nursing a grudge, if there is a cancer plotting against me in an anonymous cell or any of a hundred other subtle horrors homing in, I know nothing about them. My insurance payments are kept up, without my giving them a thought, through automatic withdrawals.

Still, I am not Oedipus, nor was meant to be. Hubris is not in my nature (if it is not arrogant to say so). I believe that the world need not be out to get me for me to be gotten. So I do thank my lucky stars. I act now before the supply runs out and have my ticket ready. I knock whatever wood is at hand and sponsor walkers against muscular dystrophy. I ask forgiveness and ply fate. I beware the stacked deck, the seductive redundancy of the "free gift." I spray with change the homeless who ring Wrigley Field or like ragged insulation plug the crevices of the city. There but for the grace of God go I, I go. Moving through gauntlets of the damaged and the dispossessed, I respect the house odds of existence.

❏ ❏ ❏

Today it is T. S. Eliot. He bids my class enter "a place of disaf-
fection," where a dim light presides. It is "neither daylight /
Investing form with lucid stillness ... Nor darkness to purify the
soul...." Last week it was Frost, and the week before, Dickinson;
now it is Eliot weaving and unweaving deity out of light and
dark, making a sacrament out of the unconsolidatable. "Neither
plenitude nor vacancy." Next week we will come upon another
poet, no doubt, tending the low fires of latency, laboring over
the saying of grace.

All semester the subjunctive mood descends and never dis-
sipates. Foreshadowing is, literally, making the shadows prominent. Meanwhile, a little girl remembers that she had a bad
dream, but she does not remember what the dream was. And
that is all. Light salivates on the windowsill, ripples in faults on
the floor, speculates in the hazy corner, but what of it? Her compensation is getting through the next night, and the next.

And my daughter is now old enough to have no recollection
whatsoever of the accident she was in; we don't even own the car
anymore. Everything and all of us are in conversion, always. For
my part, I tell the story of the car crash in class to illustrate the
ratio between profundity and elusiveness, which I use when I am
teaching Dickinson or Frost or Eliot. I can be pretty practical
when it comes to preparing lesson plans.

Perhaps I have been in the vicinity of something more—I
have seen something moving just out of range, a gathering in a
blind spot, bleeding in an easement of consciousness—but no
one expects me to speak in psalms. Elevation is not really
required of me. If asked, I know how to explain away the contagion of wonder as a glitch in the brain, a logical fallacy, or a trick
of the light. A good teacher lives up to his syllabus; he outlines
and clarifies. A good father strokes his daughter's hair, tells her
there is nothing there, go back to sleep. I do not make the world
whole, but then again, I am not liable.

You are welcome to sue, of course.

the girl in the moon

Beginnings are born in retrospect. They are coercions that let us determine the distance we have come. Beginnings are the first fictions you need to lay more substantial fictions upon. Development is one of these fictions. So is cause. So is prognosis.

Again you wish that you could start again. It is like starting a play with a pause or being seasick still in port. But before you know it, a progress is swelling. "Before you know it"—that is more the way it feels to you than "Once upon a time" or "It all started when." Beginnings are the inevitable blasphemies, the birth of the world sprung by a curse. Before you know it, you are at sea.

Before you know it, then, you are with a doctor who is telling you not to blame yourself. He is a pediatric neurologist, and he speaks with the awful serenity of a man practiced in talking people off of ledges. He is a candid assassin, and you hate him. He comes highly recommended, and he is renowned for being able to find anything there is to find, even to the least scratch in the budding matrix of your daughter. You want to sacrifice the best ram you have to him. The most important thing, he tells you, is not to blame yourself. He thinks that this is the most important thing, that he cannot find any blame. You despise him for what he does find, and you pray for him to be kinder or go blind. You are vexed by the casual drape of the stethoscope over his neck. His martial concision. His scalpeled pleats. And yet, you want this man to diminish you, to dismiss you, to confirm you to be a bother. Disease will shipwreck against the shoals of alphabetized folders on his desk. You are counting on his indifference, his crustacean reserve.

You have brought her in because at sixteen months she is not yet walking. "I don't like the fact that she is not walking yet," the pediatrician told you. John Updike has a story, "The Persistence of Desire," in which a man worries that his recurrent eye problems are an insult to his ophthalmologist: "Clyde always felt unworthy of Pennypacker, felt himself a dirty conduit balking the smooth onward flow of the doctor's reputation and apparatus." Pediatricians may have to content themselves with strep throats and infected ears, but they are just as capable of confronting you with your moral failures, and yours did not like it that your daughter is not walking yet. You prepare to blame the rolling walker she spends hours in each day, scuttling about like a miniature traffic matron and launching herself madly across the linoleum, or thrusting herself with peristaltic resolve—such is the persistence of desire—across what must seem to her a Sahara of living room carpet. She will not surrender that contraption without a fight. But the pediatrician did not blame it or you—you would scour the medical profession for blame and come up empty—he was just unhappy. The words we use.

He referred you to the neurologist to stare your daughter down from a higher altitude. He invites her to play with toys, which are suspiciously simple and clean, Platonic blocks cunningly devised to test muscle groups, dexterity levels. You try to see what he scribbles, then what it is that sets him scribbling, but all you see is your fuddled daughter, who pushes at the bland geometry the doctor has set before her like a dog nosing an egg. He nods, asks you to get her to move across the floor as best you can, as best she can, and he nods again. You are afraid she will let the doctor down, this man with the alien, antiseptic toys, who regards her like a tricky putt.

Still scribbling, he tells you he wants to schedule her for an MRI this week. "MRI" stands for "magnetic resonance imaging," a term which under less anxious circumstances would impress you as almost transcendental. He wants to plumb your daughter for poetry. Resonance. Imaging. The words we use.

Michael Collins: This beast is best felt. . . . I just hope it knows where it's going.

With poetry as with hospital procedures: something lies enchantingly, achingly, disturbingly beyond you. Like poets, doctors "offer their best interventions as works of art," Paul West writes in *A Stroke of Genius: Illness as Self-Discovery*, and you try to synchronize dictions with the neurologist. Language is your operating theater. You bring in Browning, Graves, Rilke for consults: Your reach exceeds your grasp. Your blood runs backwards. You are standing on fishes. The whole world contracts to a little girl trying to navigate the floor of the doctor's office, which is a poem dropped from an impossible height onto your heart.

Buzz Aldrin: During a pause in experiments Neil suggested we proceed with the flag. It took both of us to set it up and it was nearly a disaster. Public Relations obviously needs practice just as everything else does.

You watch them take your daughter away for the MRI. They roll her off in a red wagon, with her clutching a bear they've given her. Really. You sense that you are seeing her from this perspective—seated, departing—for the first time of many times. Dread of the last time descends, and the hallway seems to narrow, the wagon to gather speed, your daughter shrink, but it is a trick of perspective. Science anchors you. You try to summon thoughts of protractors, compasses, beakers, hypodermics. It is late, the night is quiet, and it seems that the staff is allowing itself a collective slouch. From Admissions to Records to ventilation, insouciance pipes through every system in the hospital. A nurse comments on the cop show playing on the uninterruptible complimentary television that flashes benevolently over the empty waiting room. Even an empty room suffers no neglect, and you are steadied. They corner germs like no one's business here, you tell yourself; for deformities they daily drag their nets; mutinous genes are rooted out like the classroom troublemakers they are. Meanwhile the television murmurs placidly on, and you think of test tubes, microscope slides, the vicious precision that shivered your hands in high school chemistry. Professionals coast past you unfazably in shoes that make no sound, while a custodian idly casts a dust mop about the floor for the third time that day. Calibration, you are thinking. Incision. The deft words, steeled against the equally eloquent vocabulary of death.

A panel against the neurologist's office wall shudders with white light—you had not noticed it last time—and you are looking at pictures of your daughter's brain. Phosphorescent. Cold. You are looking at the lunar surface.

Michael Collins: We are in the shadow of the moon now, and the elusive stars have reappeared.

He runs a finger along a line of his notes, transfers his finger to a furrow on the screen, returns it to his notes. You want him to be happier, a director pleased with the day's rushes, but when you look to where his finger lands there is nothing, a lather of grays. He speaks evenly, quietly, the priest at his service pronouncing the Latin stations of your daughter's brain. "Here is the cerebral cortex, this entire convoluted mass, where everything starts," he is saying. "We move up over the parietal lobe. The principal fissures are the darker canals: the transverse fissure, the Sylvian fissure, the fissure of Rolando." The words we use. The ingenious jargon we are.

Buzz Aldrin: In retrospect, we have all been particularly pleased with the call signs that we very laboriously chose for our spacecraft, Columbia and Eagle.

"Here you can see the thinning of the corpus callosum, and you can see where the damage is." He is intent upon a flimmer of cells. You are not fooled. Damage in the brain is brain damage. You are everything but fooled.

You almost did not take off work for that first visit. You figured you knew what he was going to say. You almost did not come at all. But you did come to know, and there was no more past tense, only a relentless present, all dim, insistent middles. There is only now, and again, the next visit, another stymied now. You back away from the future's sheer drop. Nostalgia suggests a time before the adverse brain bled out at you. It sounds like another affected part of her—the nostalgia—or like the new sedative insurance will not cover.

"The brain is very plastic." He is consoling you, teaching you language to hope with. "Its capacity for compensation should not be underestimated. There is so much we don't know about the brain." The doctor sits. Your daughter is sitting, too, playing with the perfect toys she remembers from last time. She has finally found a crack to let her into their pleasures, clever girl. As she plays, the doctor confides to you again the unpredictability of the brain, which he intends as a source of hope. Don't expect anything, and anything can happen. He talks above your daughter, who is hard at the task of entertaining herself, which for children never ends but only changes venue. As he talks, you are looking through the window into her plastic brain, whose gutters running with unparsable oils are halted and flourescent before your eyes: a dreamy hearth, a mind of cloud, the moon basting in light, falling further and further away.

Michael Collins: Despite our concentrated effort to conserve our energy on the way to the moon, the pressure is overtaking us (or me at least) and I feel that all of us are aware that the honeymoon is over and we are about to lay our little pink bodies on the line.

You ask how this happened. Questions are your contributions, things you can do. How, to a child? How, to a child cocooned in your love, cradled there? "It is hard to say," he says. "She had trouble getting her bilirubin count down when she was born, didn't she? That could have been a factor. It may have been an illness sustained by her mother during pregnancy at the critical stage of brain development. Around the third or fourth

month, perhaps? Or it could be something she inherited. Who
can tell what your MRI might reveal?" Beginnings are vanities.
"In any event, your job is to work her body properly, be systematic about her learning processes, watch for milestones, that
she reaches them. Basically, you parent a child with these symptoms the way you parent any child, only maybe a little more
deliberately."

You ask if she will be normal. He asks you what "normal"
means, what you think it means. The words we use. You tell him
he knows what you mean, you do not want to say other words.
Will she be able to go to school and wave to friends as they
depart for their parents' idling cars? Will she be able to run without stumbling, manipulate silverware, live on her own or at all?
He knows what you mean. He cannot help you there. "All we can
do is encourage her. And love her. You have to let her know she
is loved all along the way. She will need that from you if she is
going to improve." If she is not going to improve, he does not say,
she will need that from you, too. The implication is that you will
have to show her how to live as coherently as possible under the
circumstances, whatever they turn out to be, so get a good grip.

Michael Collins: Altitude is holding very well.

HOUSTON: Roger, Mike, just hold it a little bit longer.

Collins: No sweat, I can hold it all day. Take your sweet time.

"We'll keep an eye on her," he says, and he lays his hand
upon her hair. She does not react—she has grown used to being
touched unannounced, having learned to accept grown-up adoration and flares of concern without flinching. Her little diligence endures, but the doctor's touch fires through you.

You look again at that private moon mounted on the wall. It
seems as though you have blasted off for home, and the signals
are breaking up as you escape its orbit. Susan Sontag opens her
book *Illness as Metaphor* with the caution that "illness is *not* a
metaphor, and that the most truthful way of regarding illness—
and the healthiest way of being ill—is one most purified of, most
resistant to, metaphoric thinking." Yet it is hardly possible, you

think ... and she commiserates: "Yet it is hardly possible to take up one's residence in the kingdom of the ill unprejudiced by the lurid metaphors with which it has been landscaped." "Kingdom of the ill"—irresistible.

"When the mind is foiled, it feeds itself some bizarre things," realizes Paul West, for whom metaphor is simultaneously an enlightenment and an anesthetic. West is doubly afflicted: as you discover in an earlier book of his, he has a damaged daughter, too. She does "not grieve over absences," who has nothing much to go on—less than your daughter does, brave man—"but just an assumption of [her] own shrill perpetuality," he explains in *Words for a Deaf Daughter.* Meanwhile, he describes his own mode as "captivated bafflement." Right. So: your daughter is a stowaway, having boarded unbeknownst to you upon your return from the fairy-tale kingdom of the ill. Or she is a replica—you have sat through such movies—who has taken the place of your daughter and who occupies her life now. Your daughter is a metaphor for what she would have been otherwise, if not for the agentless error, the sickness, the accident, the blameless sin that sent her off course.

Buzz Aldrin: Last transmission from Armstrong prior to leaving the pad reportedly was "Oops."

All deliberation, you stare with her into the bathroom mirror, cheek to cheek. You are helping her to move the parts of her mouth properly, engineering language. She is irreflexive, and so she must be made to imitate the movements you make with your mouth. So far, she thinks it is a game, the way you snag her tongue like a slick fish with your fingers and place it behind her teeth or pull her lips clear so that she can do the blends. You have to dig the fricatives out with your own hands because your daughter is stuck with a lazy tongue. Words, words. They catch and cripple in her teeth like chicken bones, and you try to claw them out every morning.

There is also tactility practice. You place bowls of uncooked rice, Jello, sand, coffee beans before her. You lay out fabrics like

a merchant at a bazaar, invite her to fingerpaint or shove wrist-
deep into mud or clay, lift her to rummage in the dresser drawers, soap her hands. Go at it, you say. Dive in. She eyes you
quizzically, somehow already wise to street hustlers like you.
You ridiculously widen your smile, selling, selling.

You encourage her to treat her plate as a palette, to smear
the scrambled eggs and jelly about, to get involved. After lunch
there are large muscle groups to work. You place her on her back
and slowly pump her legs for her; then you stretch her arms over
her head and down to her sides, as though trying to resuscitate
a drowning victim. Move, sweetheart. To keep her on task, you
occasionally get her to giggle by becoming the monster who
feasts on the bellies of little girls. When you push your face into
her, you sometimes hear the seismic efforts inside and stop to
count how many days it has been since she has moved her bow-
els, the most impressive of her blockages. The stalled, hidden
tides within her. (When the moon appears to wobble, it is
because its orbit is not precisely circular, so that from time to
time a few degrees of its far side can be seen. Until the Soviet
spacecraft Luna 3 photographed it in 1959, most of the far side
was completely unknown.) She makes the sound that means she
wants you to make her laugh again the same way, and that you
can do. When the exercise is over, you get on your back and lift
her by the stomach on your shins to play "Rocket Girl" with her,
swinging her about through space. The pressure on her stomach
is good for her. So, actually, is her laughter.

Neil Armstrong: The Saturn gave us one magnificent ride, both in Earth
orbit and on a trajectory to the moon. Our memory of that differs from the
reports you have heard from the previous Saturn flights.

You read up. It cannot hurt. (It hurts.) The corpus callosum
is the sheath that connects the principal halves of the brain.
Activities that require vigorous shifting between them—riding a
bike, climbing—are especially dependent upon the corpus callosum. This is confirmed by studies of subjects who are born
without the corpus callosum. The literature indicates that there

are more cases of this than you might think. (Medical studies are referred to as "literature"—in the end, what we know about ourselves is poetry—or "the literature," which has a soothing ring of consensus to it.) Sometimes, of course, the absence of the corpus callosum has no measurable effect upon the subject, you learn, and after all, who would think to scan a seemingly flawless skull? There is no control group, so to speak. A severed corpus callosum provides the same conflicting data. There is nothing in the literature about the effects of an attenuated corpus callosum like your daughter's. The geneticist opens a massive reference book to indicate where such information would be found, had it existed. You keep reading.

Buzz Aldrin: From space it has almost a benign quality. Intellectually one could realize there were wars underway, but emotionally it was impossible to understand such things.

"Any important disease whose causality is murky, and for which treatment is ineffectual, tends to be awash in significance," Sontag explains, and your daughter's daunting, indefinite status qualifies. It tends to be awash. Beginnings are scandals, they are reproaches and betrayals, but you believe that the etiology of your accommodation begins with the irradiated landscape of her brain.

You want to hold her to you so every resource and errant cell, every escaping bit, stays in place. You want to give her more to exist with. You want to smash the fucking puzzle against the wall.

Neil Armstrong: The exhaust dust was kicked up by the engine and thus caused some concern in that it degraded our ability to determine not only our altitude in the final phases but also our translational velocities over the ground. It's quite important not to stub your toe during the final phase of touchdown.

Her brain is very plastic. You need to cultivate a monkish devotion to the hundred billion neural pathways that require attention. It is a nightmare of civil engineering: any unused synapse will wash away like a bridge left for the weather to rot. Your own awareness must shape itself to the ongoing metamorphic novelty of your daughter. She must be watched. She is an

experiment, a circus of a trillion performing cells—every child
is, but your girl, trammeled in every aspect, is an unprecedented
universe of intimations and subtle eruptions, which the literature
does not cover.

She is a repercussion still spooled, an echo just released.

The lifelong improvisation is now well under way. You are
an expert in your daughter, the spy in her little midst. On her
unsuspecting behalf you are sublimely suspicious of her habits
and gestures. Having explicated her toddles, you now survey
her walk. (Her feet are a bit splayed, but so are yours. Nothing
is more devious than the unremarkable.) Self-consciousness
stabs at the worst days: intestinal troubles, a tumble from a
chair, her backwards z are heavy with latency; they are prophe-
cies or tiny poems to gloss. "Only natural," a relative consoles
you, but you have learned never to trust nature again, to frisk it
after every encounter.

*Michael Collins: My God, the juxtaposition of the incongruous—roll,
pitch, and yaw; prayers, peace, and tranquility.*

You are frustrated and envious that others can look and see
only what is dear, your darling unmarked by anomaly. Her syndrome is nameless and all subterfuge. She looks perfect to your
relatives; they inspect her and grant their sanction, although
they wonder aloud at what your overreaction will do to her.
What do you want to do, debate them, serve as counsel for her
biology and its cruel sense of humor? You have heard the doctors deliver their sentences. Why ruin her amusements with your
perpetual awareness of their context? You have seen the irregu-
larities in stretches of graph paper like read-outs of the pulse of
underground faults; you keep them the way other parents keep
their children's ribbons from athletic competitions. You have
seen the brain's corolla and its warped terrain, the projection of
her destiny. They cannot judge. Discounting, they cannot really love what you love. Nothing is visible to them beyond your
paranoia and your rage, which, in truth, you cannot deny without exposing. Believing in the saving grace of conduct and the

middle-class decency of human reproduction, they plead with and resent you for the way you behave. Only you cannot help yourself because you have learned how to breathe on the moon.

Michael Collins: My God, I never thought of all this bringing peace and tranquility to anyone. As far as I am concerned, this voyage is fraught with hazards for the three of us—and especially for two of us—and that is about as far as I have gotten in my thinking.

Her eyes are still different colors—the green one is browner than it was, while the blue has gone hazel—about which the neurologist is, for once, quite definite: it is invariably a sign of an early neural "glitch." It is often benign, as in the case of Jane Seymour, the actress, whose interview on a late-night talk show you study inches from the television screen, whose picture on the cover of a magazine at the supermarket checkout you treat like pornography or evidence at a crime scene because your daughter's disease, after all, is both of these things.

"When did you first suspect that something was wrong with her?" you ask. "What first gave her away?"

"The first time I looked at her, there was something. I thought I saw something. Just looking at her."

Buzz Aldrin: Beautiful, beautiful. Magnificent desolation.

You press for the thousandth time against the tuck of her ear, the carpentry of her brow. Your father has a jaw like that, does-n't he? Her mother's eyes are close together, too. There may have been an aunt who had a whitish shock of hair, but it disappeared, as did your daughter's, and anyway, that is when the geneticist is considering Wardenberg's Syndrome, which he later rules out. In a museum, you dare not rest on any chair for fear it may be part of the exhibit. How are you supposed to separate your daughter's authentic indications from her false alarms? She does not let you rest.

Strange—a brief spasm of past tense—that you never bothered with Nature in its conventional splendors, never much mentioned its preening. You were never one to grow glad with the sun's ascent nor to compare anyone to a summer's day. You winced at Julie Andrews' joyful whirl upon the mountain in *The Sound of Music;* as far as you were concerned, Gene Kelly sang solo in that benedictory rain. You were never one to look up. But with Nature having gaffed right at your feet, you can never look away.

Buzz Aldrin: We could also look around and see the Earth, which, though much larger than the moon the Earth was seeing, seemed small—a beckoning oasis shining far away in the sky.

It seems as though you move from one waiting room to another while the dossier on your daughter grows. Each revision of her disease creates another alias for her to go by. Devious, that one. Right now she is considering the bright fallopian tangle of wires strung with beads to flick and push along. You will have to tell her one day. You will have to let her in on herself. Even if she clears every milestone, even if she skirts devastation in the end, she will have to know what they've got on her in that folder. What if whatever she has can be passed on to her own children? She is bending down to play—a move she had to be taught to accomplish. It is a trick: there is neither starting point nor destination for the beads, just some arbitrary traffic. So far, she seems occupied. For the time being, while you are waiting, it keeps her happy enough.

HOUSTON: Roger, Tranquility. We copy you on the ground. You've got a bunch of guys about to turn blue. We're breathing again. Thanks a lot.

gimme kilter

Everyone has an acquaintance who brings an almost autistic rigor to breakfast. He arrives at the same coffee shop every Tuesday and Thursday morning at 8:15, takes the paper to the second booth past the counter, and unwaveringly orders a fried egg, hash browns, wheat toast, and coffee. For as long as anyone can remember, he has sat in the same second booth from the door and rotated his plate in the same direction, organizing his bites of egg, potato, and toast in the same sequence. The procedure invariably leaves him with a last crust to dab up the rest of the yolk. Surveillance would confirm that he also drinks his coffee at a predictable pace. His waitress, who is always the same waitress, knows to delay his refill until he turns to the newspaper. He never looks at the bill when he pays, and he always traps his dollar tip under the salt shaker.

This is a man the almanac ignores. The editors at Guinness remain unimpressed. The Chamber of Commerce has not seen fit to depict him in any promotional brochure. He has never graced the cover of the local telephone directory, been noted in the community calendar, or had his likeness hammered into a bit of commemorative tin to decorate the Christmas tree at the county courthouse. Indeed, he waves off any attention at all to his steadfastness. "Nothing remarkable about it," he says. "I like what I like, that's all." Then after a wistful pause, just long enough to look forward to the next inevitable breakfast, he adds, smiling, "I guess I'm just a creature of habit."

It is so casual a phrase that we might miss its essential redundancy. Nothing is more creaturely about us than our habits. They are our fate and our signature. Densely credentialed anthropologists may disagree, but habits link us to one another better than any protocol or bodily function even as they expose the chinks in the species. As we ply our routines, pick and scratch at ourselves, probe our ears and suck our teeth, we reveal our lowest common denominator. Put a chimp in a vest and he'll still dive for his privates. So, too, do we prickle in new Sunday clothes. We are antsy just behind our best behavior; left to ourselves, we beetle about the apartment, anxious and wretched. Core curricula and the literary canon may propose to elevate us, and the National Endowment for the Arts may try to civilize the suburbs, but ultimately we deploy our differentiated forks in vain: none of the forces of social amelioration can contend with force of habit. For in the end, we do not have habits so much as they have us.

Still, there is something whimsical and good-natured about the word, so that even bad habits, like brown shoes, may be worn in public without fatally endangering reputations. For despite their hidden profundities, habits are rather domestic and approachable. The smile that follows the fart of a friend represents commiseration, not superiority. When we say "bad habit," it is the way we say "bad dog" when Tipper tracks dirt on the good rug or drinks from the toilet bowl; the poor, deaf thing is still endearing and, despite everything, unquestionably part of the family.

In this regard, alternative terms somehow miss the mark. "Peccadillo" sounds rather mincing for a grown man to admit to, while a costly aroma rises from "neurosis." "Eccentricity" is a witness that's been bought off, whereas "idiosyncrasy" cleans the living room before company comes. As for "addiction," this unfairly amplifies the crisis; it smacks of smack, and associating gum popping or nail biting with "addiction" is like incarcerating teens caught with joints with hardened criminals. It would be still worse to reverse the construction: there is as much denial in the phrase "drug habit" as there is in the practice it coddles. (As for "nun's habit," the pun so coarsely treats the call to the cloth that, like a giggle at Mass, it is best ignored altogether.) No, we are at home with our habits because of their homeliness, however we try to hide them or apologize. Caught scouring a nostril at the intersection by the driver in the adjacent car, we may hunker down and pray for the green light, but we never think of turning ourselves in to the authorities.

As it happens, my own most consistent habits are not septic, obvious, or (no one having advised me otherwise) especially irritating. I regularly, ritualistically swat my pants pockets—left front, right front, left rear, right rear—assuring myself that my wallet, keys, pens, and change are in place. Whap, whap, whap, whap. At least half a dozen times daily I pat myself down. No worship-driven Muslim more dependably drops to the Meccan dirt; no onanist frisks himself so assiduously as I. When I happen to wear a shirt with a pocket, that, too, is added to the inspection; even empty it earns, like a child at his chores, its tap of acknowledgment. Whap, whap, whap, whap, I do the rounds of my body. I am on my way to class, leaving the bathroom, or about to bowl, but first, whap, whap, whap, whap go my involuntary isometrics. My body's own clownish custodian, I check my premises and jiggle my locks before leaving. I do not deliver before I am edited and proofed, audited and inventoried every thousand steps. Matters of intactness task me—I do not go on before I am all accounted for. In this way I seem to second the anxiety of Holden Caulfield, who in *The Catcher in the Rye* had the sensation of disappearing every time he crossed a road. I am at once the smuggler stuck in customs and the customs officer who sticks it to him. I am the nervous curator of all the quirks I convey.

That is one habit, one drill bit. Another related habit of mine—bad habits tend to propagate while nobler, more attractive ones die childless—is the main theme of a sub-conversation

I seem continually to be having with myself as I walk the neighborhood, shower after the gym, or drive home. I keep myself company with a little catechism: "English, Social Studies, Math, Science." It dates back to junior high school at least, when I used to rehearse my homework. An oral equivalent of whapping and tapping at my chamber doors: "English, Social Studies, Math, Science"—a roll call of bygone classes and song of my former self, which succeeds by more than thirty years its serviceability. Occasionally I will increase my repertoire with itineraries or errands, grocery lists or batting orders, but in stressful times or strange places I always return to the old rundown to steady me, the same meager bleat. And so even in my mantra am I immature. I may be a man of recognized station and advanced degrees, but tune into my mind and what you are likeliest to hear is barely removed from the murmurings of innumerable Boy Scouts committing their creed to memory or of second-graders polishing their multiplication tables before the test.

For if habits have us, they have us early on. From the moment each of us masters the art of dressing himself, his method is either sock-shoe-sock-shoe or sock-sock-shoe-shoe. The choice seems arbitrary enough—it seems a *choice*—and the culture graciously accommodates both approaches. But they are as incompatible as Capulets and Montagues. Religious and political differences may be more substantial obstacles to marital bliss, but a sock-shoe-sock-shoe advocate will watch his sock-sock-shoe-shoe partner get ready for work each day and not even realize how the oddness is nibbling away at his regard. From such small-scale corruptions may love's empire finally fall. Those who must have one foot shod before socking the other and those who need both feet socked before they shoe are the sartorial equivalents of the Big-Endians and their adversaries in *Gulliver's Travels*, whose schism over how best to break their eggs brought war to Part One.

When we watch the child who with plucky diligence insists on carrying his own suitcase through the airport, we can imagine the adult to come who will always refuse to surrender his bags to the Red Cap or his car keys to the valet at the gate. The boy who will not eat his peas if they are touching the potatoes will someday shave in the same direction every morning: north to south over cheeks and chin, then south to north from neck to jaw. And so it goes: in habits extending from the cosmetic to the culinary, the fussy child is father to the finicky man.

Not even the most elegant athletes are exempt from the clutch of small compulsions. However physically gifted, they are still pestered by hiccups and hitches, caught in squalls of itches, winces, and pricks. How many ballplayers must cross and adjust themselves, pluck at their collars and cuffs, or pick invisible nits from their uniforms before each and every pitch? (Scratch and Win, the local ad line urging us to buy lottery tickets, might as well be the motto of the Los Angeles Dodgers.) Joe Morgan would flap his left elbow against his ribs when he batted as though constantly letting himself in on a good joke. Billy Williams made a pendulum of his bat in the on-deck circle, rhythmically scything through some imaginary Nebraska as he waited his turn at the plate. Amidst salvos of sunflower seeds spat by restless teammates from the dugout, Rod Carew stroked his bat with a Coke bottle, always true to the grain. Ernie Banks fingered his bat handle as if trying to coax music from an instrument whose valves were hidden to everyone but him. Mike Hargrove, a first baseman for Cleveland, may have performed less auspiciously than these Hall of Famers during his career, but not when it came to fidgeting: before every single pitch he stepped out of the box to give his best impression of Humphrey Bogart besieged by leeches in *African Queen*. Turning to tennis, I recall that Jimmy Connors never served before contending with his shirt like Hercules being consumed by his poisoned cloak. And in basketball, whenever the peerless Michael Jordan elevated past an opponent, he let his tongue loll as if he were a matador teasing the hopeless bull with his cape.

❐ ❐ ❐

John Updike begins his story "Packed Dirt, Churchgoing, a Dying Cat, a Traded Car" by describing the small blessing of beaten paths. Wherever children day after day decide to cross the vacant lot, wherever their games consistently distill in the playground, their humble passages create sacred grounds. Grace reposes in "these worn, rubbed, and patted patches" that each generation leaves in its wake. They provide "a sense of human legacy," he writes, "like those feet of statues of saints which have lost their toes to centuries of kisses." And what is the written page if not a beaten path? I envision Updike himself scratching in and scratching out words on a page, the way every writer in deft little trenches leaves his mark. In a similar way, as Nicholson Baker reminds us in his essay "Clip Art," a reader will dent the page with a precisely applied fingernail, remembering his place, leaving his impression next to a line that has left an impression on him. "Moreover," Baker notes, "the pressure of a reader's nail, deformed by its momentary trenchancy, against the tender hyponychial tissues it protects, creates a transient thumbwide pleasure that is, or can be, more than literary." Peeled, picked, or bitten nails never claim such elevation, but rest assured, their manicured betters so artfully employed are still consigned to habit. (Taking snuff and chewing tobacco differ in degree, not kind.) Bookish habits are habits still.

To be sure, literary figures, believing that their habits protect them, are in turn notoriously protective of their habits. What the renowned author calls his writing regimen is, after all, basically a batch of habits that we bother to interview. Edward Albee says he stalks his typewriter before he settles down to it "the way a dog before it craps wanders around in circles." James Baldwin claimed he could only write at night, Eugene Ionesco in the morning, John Barth in longhand, Paul Bowles in bed. Guillaume Apollinaire found it liberating to compose in the kitchen, William Faulkner in a brothel, Stanley Elkin in the bathtub. Erskine Caldwell needed his red rug. Truman Capote could not abide yellow roses, but he committed his third drafts exclu-

sively to yellow paper. Robert Graves separated himself from
anything not made by hand. Robert Frost claims he never owned
a table in his life, and he wrote on anything but, including the
sole of his shoe. Joseph Heller found brushing his teeth con-
ducive to the creative process, whereas when he worked at a
newspaper in Bogota, Gabriel Garíca Márquez found the sound
of Linotype machines inspiring. One of Jack Kerouac's unsung
addictions was to candles. Norman Mailer likes a room with a
view, but Blaise Cendrars firmly maintained that "a writer should
never install himself before a panorama." John Steinbeck wrote
only with round pencils, confessing that he was "really a conditioned animal with a conditioned hand." As many writers campaign for background music as for complete silence. Long walks
are popular; so are classical music, masturbation, and the sta-
tionary bike. As for the insistence of so many authors on liquor
and cigarettes, well, these are not clichés for nothing. Nagging
every eminence is some variation on my own basic whap-whap
theme, the metronome of the Muse.

Do they stop to imagine you, the reader who completes the
gentle circuit of consciousness and obsession, as you angle the
lamp, flank your favorite chair with the same salty snack and soft
drink as always, and, settling in, arrange yourself like a bouquet
for their company? Unlikely. Reading is a resonant isolation, but
isolation nonetheless. Even with Virginia Woolf in your lap you
sometimes find yourself squeezing your pimples. "Habit is a
great deadener," said Samuel Beckett's Vladimir, ever-anxious to
be beguiled, while Estragon slept on, heedless of any bad dreams
but his own.

Nor did that noble bricklayer attend to me, the child he hyp-
notized, as he lathered, swept, shaved, and redeposited the
cement with his trowel, in the steady peristalsis of building a wall
in the corner lot of Christiana Avenue. Each situated brick
received a stabilizing *clock* with the trowel handle, so it was
slather, scrape, clock, over and over, gorgeous and indolent and
precise. Intention bent the man entirely to his effort, and slowly

transported me through vivid repetition long before I could read, dissolving both of us into that certain process, that staggered ascent and solid yield. With apologies to Robert Frost, something there is that loves a wall, whose builder, like a writer, like a boy who, running home, still avoids the sidewalk cracks that would doom his mother's back, by increments establishes belief.

Before I knew a lick of Hebrew, I attended services, rising, gazing, lowering my head with the rest of the congregation, going through the motions before I was ever really moved. So reverence promotes habit to ritual. So consecration relies on repeated phrases. Your family always stationed themselves in the same place at shul. The Torah was borne down the aisle. You caterpillared toward it, touched your siddur to it. Then you kissed the book. If your yarmulke dropped to the floor as you edged away again, you picked it up and kissed that, too. Supplication was done according to custom, which, over time, builds a heritage, a retaining wall. By habits we adore.

And so even if the writer, absorbed by his usual functions, loses track of time, time does not forget him; evidence of lost hours compounds in his raw eyes, his aching back. Asked why he writes, he will say he has no choice; glorious prospects may beckon and posterity loom, but on a daily basis it may be mostly a matter of habit that keeps him going. Meanwhile, the reader resists the tug of the upper world as long as he can, making the textured descent down the page the way he long ago rubbed the satin fringe of a blanket like a magic lamp to spring a willing genie. Closing the book ties off the story like a wound; when the reader tries to get up, it seems as if he were climbing out of a well to find it still, impossibly, wordless and expansive day. Automatically, weekend or not, he checks his watch, which he has always worn on his left wrist, facing inward, as custom dictates. It is, as always, three minutes fast, the way he prefers it, the ruse designed to keep him on time, although setting it ahead no longer fools him. He rouses himself, presses up from the chair, slaps all four of his pockets, and gets on with it.

living space

I am moving back into my house again.

Once the place was thick with us, its shelves and cabinets packed like flesh in a fish. With impending company came the controlled havoc of policing the area: giving loitering toys the bum's rush, coaxing mail and lolling magazines into piles to be crammed into already outgrown closets and bulking drawers. Glut was the family genius. Elves filling Santa's bags, hired jammers flanking Tokyo subway trains, knob-knuckled grandmothers stuffing sausage skins—all were kindred spirits of ours. The place was fat with consequence. We lived in a huge digestive system that broke down imports—packages, bills, coupons, party favors, souvenirs, and other burrs brought idly, hourly, in—and distributed them like nutrients through the rooms.

Most infamous was the back bedroom, which we called the Conrad Room for its horrifying, dark heart, where stacks of the latest hasty immigration ("Hurry, they'll be here in ten minutes!") stood on the verge of topple. Beyond them stood other surplus populations of the outdated and forgotten, diaspora'd by other visits. Meanwhile, coats bloated in the hall closet, our resident pashas. The cupboards were crap-stashed as any stretch of Portobello Road. The medicine chest was a munitions plant, which concealed a gunnery of lipsticks and powders in cunning

disks like land mines. The pantry held a hundred cans, and you
could hear bottles in close-order drill shiver against one another
in the refrigerator. Yes, our home was as saturated as cardboard
left in the rain.

Now I stand in the thin midst of what it took a single small
truck but one trip to deliver. I open boxes like a demolitions
expert, suspicious of the meager inventory, but all is secure;
there is not a thrum to wonder about. I begin a tidy, frail occu-
pation. With so much space, anything could go anywhere:
books above the stove, say, or extra batteries in any of a dozen
drawers. Strange that the abundance of space and the arbitrariness of the organization will make it easier to lose things now, as
though I were unpacking starlings in a park.

I put these distractions aside. I need to deploy my forces,
such as they are. I cast about to decide where best to plug in the
lamp, the one lamp.

The floor creaks, and the report runs down the length of the
hall; a dropped penny rattles conspicuously against the tiled
entryway; a spastic light jangles on the kitchen floor. I will have
to close off rooms to stanch the flow. I will work on a hospitable
philosophy for living like Jonah in my own home. The whole
house is in a drowse, but something is quietly proceeding—a
devouring absence, perhaps. A questioning of tenancy. I begin to
plot consolidation against a siege I alone detect.

❏   ❏   ❏

This is the rectitude of emptiness. Getting clean, getting clear,
getting it over and done with, getting down to it. The bone, the
gist, the nub, the mean lean. Assault from a Shaker. A Jack Sprat
rationale. Girding loins, tightening belts. Lessening in stages of
decompression; better, obeying a law of measured jettisons to
move out of a mundane orbit. Shoring up, digging in, laying
low. Architecting essences. Becketting. Speaking in contractions
to minimize the echoes. Making the darkling plain.

❏ ❏ ❏

Pablo Neruda claims in his poem "Investigations" that "nothing is empty— / everything is a box, a train, a boat / loaded with implications."

❏ ❏ ❏

Movies do not prepare us properly. In the movies, a man comes home after a long absence with his arms full of groceries or scrolled documents. Either way, he is visibly a man of substance. He can barely spare three fingers to extract the keys, and he pushes his way in with his hip. A moraine of mail has massed at the door, and the answering machine flashes with persistence. He has been in the hospital or in prison or overseas, but legitimacy still ripples all around him. Clearly he is a man whom the world has not deserted. He is our protagonist, and engagements await him like clamorous fans. He is unabandonable. Such a man can start his car without bothering to insert the ignition key or pick up a telephone at the office and begin speaking without dialing. Such a man gets his tie right without benefit of a mirror, for all exteriors reflect him. A born instigator, he carries plot the way the rest of us carry bacteria.

Movies prepare us for movies.

❏ ❏ ❏

The Spartans landed among us in sixth grade as half of an object lesson. They were the antidote to the Athenians, who, for all their touted Periclean ambitions and the gleaming Apollonian marinade in which Mr. Lyman laid them lovingly down, seemed too pampered by half for adolescent boys. Athens was a classroom of teacher's pets, shrilly seeking approval in clothes their mothers set out for them. We preferred the severities of the Spartans, who represented muscularity and hunkered-down discipline of their own devising. One Batman trumped a dozen Medici, after all, and one Bogart a squad of plodding cops.

We were warded off the Spartans because they were the bullies, whose performances were coarse and ideas squat. They refuted school. No instruction could pierce or art insinuate past such cultural bluntness. They were also brave the way we hadn't the chance to be and would not be if we had.

Massed in battle gear and encircled against impossible odds for the Friday quiz, they retained their discreteness somehow, as their Athenian counterparts did not. Citizens of Athens were a burnished composite, but a band of Spartans were one and one and one and one and one. Thermopylae was a false density.

In the movie, a rain of arrows did them in.

◻ ◻ ◻

Soon will come the validations of occupancy. The Girl Scouts will find me out, surely, or kids from the elementary school descend from the bus to bear the latest racket to my door. Soon, I tell myself, I, too, will be buying up the peanut brittle, outfitting local campers, battling local cancer. Right now, my being here is barely sufficient to satisfy the neighbors who used to know me. I practice attitudes of groundedness and credibility before going out to claim the mail. Children stop pedaling as I near the street. Dogs stall. I tuck a notice about extended mall hours beneath my chin as though posing for a police photographer. I recall how amply the world once knew this house, how insistently it sought us out here. "You see? OR CURRENT RESIDENT, it says. That's me. See the resemblance?" I show my papers: they tell of white sales, starving Ethiopians, the Republican National Committee, lingerie. Mothers steer their charges around me, reel the dogs in tighter to their sides, and press cautiously by.

◻ ◻ ◻

In "I Look Out for Ed Wolfe," Stanley Elkin presents a man who commits himself to systematic depletion. Ed Wolfe siphons himself out; he drains his excesses as if his possessions were boils that needed lancing. Where he wrings himself he leaves a brief cash flow, then he ends up dry and anonymous in an alley. Poured out in words. Decultivated. Out of words.

❏ ❏ ❏

My journals used to germinate everywhere, my books bloom. I am down to eleven and eighty-three, respectively, not counting the nests I've scraped together in the office. Maybe instead of shelving these together I should seed the house with them to see what might prosper in this light.

❏ ❏ ❏

William Gass writes of "Simplicities" that they represent "a longing: for less-beset days, for clarity of contrast and against the fuddle of grays, for certainty and security, and the deeper appreciation of things made possible by the absence of distraction, confusion, anxiety, delay." They testify to "completeness and closure, the full circle, something we can swing a compass round—to hammer out the line—get really straight." I mull this over and the circle widens; with so few interrupting objects about, it spins out to vanishing. I should keep to unadorned, simple sentences, I think, the one-two-three-kick of subject-verb-object.

Gass spreads beyond the ordnance, of course, even as he estimates its appeal. I have been to his house. Tastefully appointed, is the conventional approval. His wife is an architect, I remember, or a designer. Richly upholstered. Snug as parentheses. Endowed. That professor could land a chair anywhere, I know. Any home would gladly have him.

❏ ❏ ❏

The human body is a dispensary. The annual output of sweat and urine would fill gallon jugs. Howard Hughes, miserly even at the level of his own waste, would know how many. We speak, spit, shed, shit incessantly, ousting ourselves from ourselves, skimming the cellular topsoil, showing our excrescences the door. Nature takes its tithe, its house percentage. We give off enough carbon dioxide to sustain a garden. Not to mention words, nails, regrets, and a laboratory's worth of stinks. Even dandruff comes from the day's steady sanding us down.

The valediction of the body is a daily performance. Everything physical is prone to centrifugal forces. We are nothing to hold on to.

❏ ❏ ❏

Here is a phrase from Emily Dickinson, who lived in her house like a sachet in a dresser drawer: "sumptuous Destitution." She bundled her poems in fascicles and kept them, well, like sachets in her dresser drawers to scent her solitude. How could her house help but be full of her, who found a thousand ways not to leave it? Here is another phrase: "Banquet of Abstemiousness." Dickinson even capitalized according to some secret caution.

❏ ❏ ❏

Park Superintendent Griffin is speaking on National Public Radio in the wake of the recent flooding at Yosemite. She says that the first job she faces once the park can be safely reentered is the restoration of the infrastructure. I am surprised by her application of "infrastructure" and pleased to hear that it extends beyond corporations. I like the word, which connotes something at once fundamental, organized, preexistent, inextinguishable. Auden once described the work of the poet as scraping away at a dusty

stone to see what the inscription is. I like that, too. The true sense
of things is already in place.

Surveying my carpeting, I realize that I could very well
abide by the impressions left by absent furniture and duplicate
that logic now. Certainly it would be reasonable to hang pictures
over the scars left on the walls by the removal of previous pictures. Even the most flagrant traumas caused by the last move—
the gouges where the bookcases were nailed in, the bleached
linoleum opened like a surgical field where the refrigerator had
stood—could be countered by savvy interior decorating.

The park superintendent is reminding the reporter that
Yosemite National Park was established to respect and preserve
natural phenomena. It might be argued that we should not
except floods, fires, foliage diseases, and the like from that pro-
tected status. From one point of view, she says, "natural disaster"
is a contradiction in terms, for it has only to do with human
inconvenience, not with what nature needs. She quickly admits
that this is only a philosophical premise and that it does not
affect her commitment to getting the park in shape for the influx
of tourists expected this coming spring.

◻ ◻ ◻

If we think on the scale of human history, the private domestic
retreat is a relatively recent concept. Among its fundamental
concerns is the nature of the furniture it will contain, in part, one
suspects, because that furniture is in some sense assigned the
task of containing us. Vitruvius listed the ancient standards of
furniture as "commodity, firmness, and delight," a trinity of
canonical virtues. Although it is not explicitly numbered among
them, "comfort" is surely suggested, as are "leisure," "security,"
and "intimacy." Nevertheless, one of the prerogatives of contemporary furniture design appears to be a subordination, if not
a wholesale repudiation, of bodily imperatives. The interior
designer seeks to create objects of attention whose presence

supersedes the function of accommodating the human forms slumped, squirming, or collapsed upon them. Instead of constituting a servile background to human drama, pieces of furniture bargain for prominence in the household they share with us.

One of the hallmarks of modern art is self-conscious unease, so we should hardly be surprised to learn that furniture artists can be just as presumptuous as painters, musicians, and poets about lacing their works with reflexivities. Witness the chair that does not invite us to sit but rather remarks upon the concept of seatedness. A couch becomes a context imbued with couch theory. A credenza is stocked with implied commentary. The deconstructive thesis of the modular sofa. Coffee table ironies. Contemporary decor is another embattled imaginative precinct. Collectibles nudge one another knowingly in a breakfront built to look like a breakfront. Nothing brooks innocence. Nothing we live with lets us relax.

◻ ◻ ◻

Suddenly it is important to find out why fish survive the winter in frozen ponds. It so happens that ponds freeze from the surface down. This makes sense and coincides with what I already know of ice in glasses, buckets, and puddles, but the discovery still packs force. Beneath that rigid ceiling, the fish move imperceptibly, but perhaps somewhat slower for the cold, in a secret cortege. Although it is difficult to detect, life keeps happening to them below.

◻ ◻ ◻

"Westerners are amazed at the simplicity of Japanese rooms," writes novelist Junichiro Tanizaki, "perceiving in them no more than ashen walls bereft of ornament. Their reaction is understandable, but it betrays a failure to comprehend the mystery of shadows." Westerners plump where Japanese purge. Cultural distinctions are captivities as well as subjects for discussion, so it remains debatable whether habitation is better achieved in alliance with light or shadow.

In his honor I listen as I drive a spoon down the black lacquer bowl through the pasty sludge of rice. The resistance is contemplative, intestinal. The tip of the spoon meets the bottom of the bowl with a pleasant "cluck," sufficient to center the evening's solitude.

⊐ ⊐ ⊐

As I climb the aluminum ladder, I can feel the gutter give in rhythm to my ascent. The rubber feet of the ladder are unequally steeped and unsteady in the pebbly muck. It is a self-conscious, tentative business, scaling the house.

There is no proper tool for ridding the gutters of debris. I have brought with me a garden trowel, a screwdriver, and a plastic drinking cup, having rejected the kitchen knife as too risky to clamber about with. Yet there is nothing delicate about the surgery, which consists of a lot of fumbling, scraping, and coaxing lodged matter to arm's length. It is hard on my hands, too, but it would not be possible to negotiate the metal narrows with gloves. I stop often to let the pain rinse out of my shoulder and wrist—there seems to be no way to make this a natural task, so I am constantly wrenching myself—and I scan the neighborhood through my trees. For some reason, this proves to be a noisy perch. The birds are louder up here, the branches chafe against the roof, and conversations in adjacent yards seem to rise to find me out.

I think of clichéd pirates lifting glittering slaws of treasure from stolen chests while I remove one organic glop after another. I let each one fall with a satisfied disgust. When the right bulge is loosened, water starts to gurgle through the clawed club oak leaves and the obscene ropes of blackened seeds. The sound this makes—snarled, sucking through—is the sound of craving.

❐ ❐ ❐

In *The Amityville Horror*, a young family purchases a haunted house. The curtains molest them; the windows shatter, flinging glass shards at their heads; the hallways moan at their approach; the walls pulse and bleed. Committed to their investment and to feature-length, they endure this for days before evacuating. There is a sequel to this movie, in which the house has been resold for $70,000 to another young family riding the crest of their own devotions. Assorted morals are available here, the most obvious of which relate to the seaminess of American popular culture, the predictability of consumer taste, and the lucrative possibilities of a career in real estate.

❐ ❐ ❐

This is poet Mark Strand commenting on a painting by Edward Hopper: "The house shines with finality. It is like a coffin. It is beyond us, and so absolute in its posture of denial that attempts—and there have been many—to associate it with loneliness only trivialize it." The painting is entitled *House by the Railroad*. "The house demands nothing from us, in fact, it seems to be turning away from wherever we are headed. It defines, with the simplest, most straightforward means, an attitude of resistance, of hierarchical disregard, and at the same time a dignified submission to the inevitable."

In Hopper's paintings, people cannot improvise. The rooms are immune to further narrative. People often seem to be waiting, yet there is the sense that their gears have locked before some vague confinement or unknown defeat. This may be a trick of the light.

Regarding another Hopper painting, *Hotel Room*, Strand recognizes the "cramped neatness of the room, the merciless white of the illuminated walls." The window reveals "nothing but a black square, an irreducible conclusion, a place for a vanishing point." This, too, exhibits the artist's manipulation of perspective.

❏ ❏ ❏

Missouri features regular outbreaks of ramshackle barns along its highways. They are the state's broken scabs cauterizing in the weather; you can drive through Missouri the way a dermatologist hunts across damaged skin. If the photo calendars are any indication, these barns are regarded as more picturesque than bleak or forbidding. So it might be appropriate to view them not as symbols of loss and the irretrievability of the past but as larval casings, as if things have gotten out and obtain elsewhere. Optimism is a choice we have to be alert to when the opportunity arises.

❏ ❏ ❏

I have turned up the volume on the telephone ringer so that it can find me anywhere. It goes off like a bomb now, leaving me too frazzled to deal with the cable television inquisitor on the other end. At the very least, she deserves coherence from me. I consider explaining why I sound so flustered when she asks about why I no longer subscribe, but I know that hers is a volume business and that she would treat anything other than a direct answer as abusive. I suppose I could muffle the telephone, but I might miss an important call or insult someone who knew I was there. It is a dilemma, but I keep it to myself and let her go on about how the cable company is concerned about my satisfaction. From where I am standing as I talk to her I can see the black cable cord, now unattached and extending like a tentacle from the baseboard, still groping blindly about after it has been severed from the beast.

❏ ❏ ❏

By way of clarification, Harold Pinter provided an insert to the program brochure for the Royal Court Theatre performance of *The Room* and *The Dumb Waiter* on 8 March 1960. He included the following warning:

A man in a room and no one entering lives in expectation of a visit. He will be illuminated or horrified by the absence of a visitor. But however much it is expected, the entrance, when it comes, is unexpected and almost always unwelcome.

Pinter then offered the following parenthetical comment, an insert to the insert:

(He himself, of course, might go out of the door, knock and come in and be his own visitor. It has happened before.)

How much help or encouragement these koans gave the audience is unknown. The playwright could conceivably have added a further insertion within that one, and so on, enfolding interiors ad infinitum, with each gloss increasing the density, compounding the darkness. Pinter has a knack for triggering susceptibility, so it is likely that people latched hopefully onto whatever direction was given them, however obscure.

◻ ◻ ◻

Living alone accelerates the progression of absent habit into studied ritual. For example, it may begin when you decide against spooning the beans onto the plate and opt for eating out of the pot directly. Soon enough you find yourself eating over the kitchen sink to catch the spills more efficiently. You define the elimination of social graces as efficiency. What keeps you from turning into the sort of person whom the neighbors say kept to himself and bothered no one when the police find his cache of plastic explosives or human teeth? Perhaps it is that you look out the window as you eat or that you remember to turn off the television when you leave a room. Habits can keep you afloat, too, keep you a member in good standing in the community in spite of your eccentricities.

◻ ◻ ◻

The opening lines of a poem by Donald Justice:

Men at forty
Learn to close softly
The doors to rooms they will not be
Coming back to.

I would call this style of writing winningly elegiac or craftily poignant. Whatever I would call it, it would certainly be deftly phrased as a contradiction in terms.

◻ ◻ ◻

Here is the dream: Two hoodlums break into the house. One restrains me from behind while the other demands some valuable of mine which he does not name. "Where is it?" he barks. "Where do you keep it?" I don't have a clue as to what he is talking about. I tell him that I am not hiding anything and even suggest that he go through the house if he wants. Once I am awake, of course, I realize the absurdity of granting him that privilege as though I could have denied him anything anyway at that point. I also realize that I have never seen him or his partner before. If either or both represent a symbolic composite or disguise or personified neurosis, it is lost on me. In other words, if there is a lesson that my subconscious is crafting for me, it is not coming through.

In any event, he starts savaging the place, which in the dream provides more to tear up than my waking state reveals. In fact, there seem to be infinite particulars for him to handle, rage at, and roughly disqualify. "Tell me where it is!" he roars. I am willing to comply, I think, or at least so it seems to me in the dream, but I haven't the means.

I tell him the joke about the man with the wheelbarrow who passes the consternated border officer each day. The officer is convinced that the man is smuggling something across the border, and each day he rummages through the straw in the wheelbarrow, inspects all around and beneath it, picks with a penknife at the wooden handles, and goes over the spokes of the wheel with a magnifying glass, but he comes up empty. Finally, overcome with despair, he decides to quit his post. He pleads with the man to tell him what he has been smuggling, for he knows that it must be some subterfuge that brings him there each day. "I give you my solemn oath that I will not turn you in, only you must tell me what it is you are smuggling." "Wheelbarrows," he replies. I tell the hoodlum this joke, which in the dream seems to me not only acutely relevant but richly insightful. Perhaps I think it is what he is looking for after all, although, either awake or asleep, I cannot be sure. Whatever the case, he thinks I am trying to get something past him. The dream ends with his moving menacingly upon me, ferociously unimpressed, although not necessarily unjustly so—an equanimical position I arrive at only well after I have been awake. Humor is a fragile, subjective enterprise, and the dream does not repeal that fact.

❐ ❐ ❐

"The Burrow" is Franz Kafka's paean to paranoia. "I have completed the construction of my burrow and it seems to be successful," it begins, as our unnamed narrator proceeds to congratulate himself on having battened down the hatches and restricted the risk in the vicinity. Obsession is his idiom in consciousness as it is in construction, so he goes on for forty pages, keeping watch. This is not to say that there is no self-satisfaction to be had in "The Burrow." We are advised that "the sheer pleasure of the mind in its own keenness is often the sole reason why one keeps it up." The "it" refers to the method of tunneling, which the narrator achieves by ramming his head against the walls. We need to be alert to the joke here. "Sometimes I lie down and roll about in the passage with pure joy," he confides.

Exhilaration is a rare commodity in Kafka. When a character does somehow accomplish it, it tends to be at unexpected, even inappropriate, moments; in view of the general tenor of his life, how could it be otherwise? He takes his incongruous pleasures when he can.

◻ ◻ ◻

You can make a distance out of almost anything. This is not news. Anger, laziness, stress. The talk shows constantly evidence this. Disappointment, preoccupation, indifference. A battery of bestselling books can be brought in to verify. Success, too, oddly enough, as well as money and lack of money, career advancement and stagnation. Distance is cutting edge, rivaling breakthroughs in dieting and foreplay for prominence in the marketplace. Distance covers familiar ground, but our appetite for distance shows no sign of slackening.

There was nothing ingenious about the distance we made. It fared better than the checking account or the houseplants, continuing to thrive even on days we were gone or distracted. Boredom, despair, betrayal. The tests coming back positive or the tests showing nothing at all. You nurture distance through concentration or neglect. It feeds on the atmosphere itself. The hard sciences have not yet weighed in conclusively on the matter, but preliminary indications are that distance contaminates everything in the area, disrupting structures, loosening bonds. Desire and resignation. You watch it wear away the fabric, craze the enamel, split the seams. You swallow it down and start to come apart.

❐ ❐ ❐

In the dream, or in what I make of the dream after its departure, the most significant distortion is the ferocious assault. What is really most ferocious, I have found, is composure.

I organize a card game, and all the glad chatter and the cadenced snap and soughing of the cards is drawn up on invisible strings into a delicate, tensile network above us, which we ignore. All of us make the same salary, more or less, and the game soon finds its proper level where there is just enough interest and no real damage possible. No one will make a killing or take a fatal hit. Under these rules of commerce, which we understand and know not to mention, we feel companionable, snug. Our words ascend and disappear into the insulation. I think I could risk a name I have not yet spoken aloud since returning to this house and wait for it to be gathered up.

I check the window to confirm the change in the weather. Robert Frost noted "the thin frost, almost in separate stars, / That gathers on the pane in empty rooms." Frost was never too somber to enjoy the pun that took his name in vain. If it weren't so cold out tonight, I might take time out for a look at the night. I admit to a taste for astrology, which turns the heavens into an interior, too. The sentient sky presiding, all inlaid with reference and cause. The woven stars presuming overhead.

The game needs me, so I stay where I am.

❐ ❐ ❐

Within this house there wait for you such gifts
From which I urge you help yourself, for this
Is hospitality's domestic law.
For homage is true enterprise of grace.
Let no one pass his grieving unassuaged
By fullest tribute, as befits his needs.
No lamentation here shall long ensue

Till it be salved by proper amplitude.
Although this hall is simple, it abides,
And all within may soon serenely dwell.
Let goblets swell and heaping bowls bestow
Such tidings as your hardships now require.
Let gentle welcome compensate and soothe
The stranger landed here, so softly bear
His murmuring descent from better days.
And so with blessings victuals be spread
And everywhere unmeasured portions set.
Crowd out the clinging absence that besets
Him so, nor let him make a harbor of regret.
For here provisions, honor, courtesy,
And all heroic custom shall obtain.
Remove your rags and coarsened attitude.
Remove the rotting mantle of your loss.
Within this house, permission and fair sleep
May freshen you and stave off vacancy.
There will be time enough to listen when you rouse
To tales of separation and dismay.
But now, most worn in thought and trial, partake
Of these my comforts and solicitude.
My lot is small, but offers well enough
To make a stay, then speed you on your way.

◻ ◻ ◻

"These fragments I have shored against my ruins," Eliot wrote.
The sea-blue volume is tightly fitted among the rest of my
books. Their spines protrude like the staves of the hull of a ship
that bears me, somehow, onward.

action figures

The guy, whose name is something like Herb or Bert, is from one of those quadrilateral states west of the Mississippi, one of those that need a couple of area codes at most to manage any call you might conceivably place there. It is one of those states that make the evening news only because some natural disaster has laid photogenic waste to it, or because police are tweezing the woods for an escaped convict, or because there has been an outbreak of quaintness or idiosyncrasy. This Mac or Ned is riding a bulldozer into the side of his own house. Somehow word had gotten out to the local news station—possibly Bob or Ed had called it in himself—and the crew rushed over to catch his act in time for the five o'clock report. Rosy and wry, the reporter on the scene explains that a divorce court has determined that this Roland's or Joey's ex-wife has been awarded the right to half of the house. We cut to his conversation with the reporter, which had been taped just moments earlier: "They might could give her half the house, but I still own my half, and I can do what I want with it." When we cut back again, the bulldozer is gnawing at the north corner of the house, going back and forth like a Rottweiler grinding at a knuckle of bone, growling like that, too. The camera pulls back to reveal the fresh debris, then to the gleeful Amy or Donna, who has to shout to send us back national.

The smiling anchor does not comment, but his countenance suggests that we are joining him at some higher altitude—a consensual judgment something on the order of "It takes all kinds to make a world." But what I believe Jack or Fred wants us to understand, apart from the integrity of his defiance, is that the proof that something is yours is that you can destroy it if you want to, and that when you do, the ruin belongs to you, too.

Now I do not belong to that category of men who know how and where to lay their hands on construction equipment on short notice. And yet, even behind the camouflage of privileged station and periodic sentences, I understand that the real distinction between us is that he is the sort of man who dares before the double dare is laid down. He is the sort who, when crossed, scale bulldozers; I am the sort who join the journalists, watching and commenting and hanging back with the crew. My breed is the domestic one, whose members smuggle their grudges beneath their coats. The pathetic syllables of our dissatisfaction—we are irked, we are vexed—creak like seesaws in a school playground. But watching this guy on the news bear down on his premises, I realize that he transcends irony, which is the real story, after all.

Actually, I can appreciate the bliss of demolition as well as anyone else. One night on *The Tonight Show* there was a man who came on stage in a tuxedo. The curtain parted to reveal a gleaming grand piano. The audience braced itself for the anticipated blow of culture. Then, from behind his back, the man produced an axe. The audience reacted, first with alarm, then with nervous excitement. He approached the piano, paused for effect, and then began the assault. With savage efficiency, he brought it to the ground, with every whack of the axe causing another roughened chord to rise as though the stricken instrument were an ox lowing beneath the slaughter. The din of approval grew louder, and within a single minute not a note of complaint came from the wreckage. The last hacks brought the audience to their feet, and in my bedroom I was standing with the rest.

From this same atavistic core comes the desire to believe that professional wrestling is real. It is the true motive behind our paying to swing a sledgehammer against the donated car to raise funds for the Campus Activities Board, as if the bashing were a means and not a splendid end in itself. It is why I'm nostalgic about the boy who would piss in the neighbors' bushes when the bathroom was too bothersome and too far, or hurled stones in the hope of smashing glass at a construction site. It isn't innocence I miss—vandals at heart, we kids were kept from consequence by our size, not our sensibilities—but the sensuality of damage, its sizzle through the viscera. Those of us who mince symbols may mock the obvious, but just try elevated banter on explosives and see how far you fly. It's no accident that the biggest blockbuster American movies bust the biggest blocks. The grander the Guignol, the better. The philistines get that much right: the art that counts is kinetic.

Jeremy is four, and he already knows this. He is drawing on butcher paper on the kitchen floor, and his latest Batman refuses to be born out of a blue slouch. Clumped and bulging, he is more of a custard than a crime fighter. His Robin is no consolation, either, if I am right in guessing that mass's hidden identity: he seems positively Cubist, cursed with twice the normal allotment of joints, and impaled by the skyscraper Jeremy has hastily sketched in to prevent his plummeting from the space at the top of the page where he had been conceived. There are other problems as well, impenetrable to my aesthetic but all too offensive to the little boy's. Versed in the standard sophistries— I read the experts before fathering and after—I tell him that some of the most honored works of art resulted from mistakes their makers treated as challenges. Be patient, I say, hoping to help him save face and paper. Errors can be opportunities. Do you think we can figure out what this picture really wants to be? I can't seem to remember whether it was Hopi or Navaho who deliberately left flaws in their weavings so as not to compete with their gods, but it's just as well, because Jeremy has aborted the misbegotten project. Four years old, and already he recognizes that revision is a piddler's game. I would muster sympathy if ripping up the picture didn't so clearly delight him. "I want to do another one," he announces. I am not sure which prospect, drawing a new picture or mangling another expensive sheet, is inspiring him at this point.

School will dilute his acids, of course. Most children taper as they age. They usually mature into the ability to lay low to get by. Parents, take heart: you learned the motto of redress for success, and your violent darlings will pick it up in time. Socialization will wear down their edges enough that they won't forever be barking their egos against the world. (That comfort comes from some childcare manual, too, in the chapter on tantrums.) They'll learn to breathe deeply instead of lash out from their longings. Most alpha males mollify down the alphabet a bit.

Still, watching Jeremy, I can imagine him revving a bulldozer in anger some day. Nothing precocious about it, really—how old do you have to be to be turned on by the magnificence of squander? A specialist in comic book superheroes, he is not impressed by the level head or the even keel. Bruce Banner is believable but a whiny bore; when is the Incredible Hulk going to burst out? Imagine the liberation when life's intricate give and take comes down to trading slugs in the belly. Then the trick is to take the brunt of it, shake off your handlers, and keep on sneering.

My own father, in fact, fed a private fire throughout his life. I don't think I ever saw him hesitate or disavow, cower or retract. As the elegantly bred would put it, he did not suffer fools easily, either. Going to restaurants with him was a particularly risky undertaking, given how many things—a misplaced reservation, an undercooked steak, cold coffee—could prove incendiary. When his food arrived, the family froze; Edison never prayed so hard over a test filament as we did over his filet mignon. If it was acceptable, he said nothing, but simply started in; his demand

for competence having been satisfied, he moved on to his other
appetite. However, if the meal fell short of the mark, he would
summon the waitress and ask, "Excuse me, sweetheart. What did
I order?"

"I'm sorry, sir. Is there something wrong with your dinner?"

"No, no. I'm asking you a question. What did I order?"

"Isn't this your order?"

"Are you saying that you don't *know* what I ordered? I am
interested in what you wrote down. You did write it down, did-
n't you?"

"Sir, if there's been some mistake, I'll send in another order
for you."

"That's not what I want, dear. What I want is for you to tell
me what you think I ordered. Is there a reason why you can't
answer that one question for me?"

It was like a Catskills skit, and we cringed against the vinyl
booth in vain as she went to get the manager to see what the
problem was. Dad could muster ruckus at a moment's notice. For
the suburban middle-class, what could be closer to kingship than
the ability—the will, really, yes, the will—to send it back? I
could see the talent in that, the election, the art; I could see that
his capacity for generating heat had its own compensations for
him, whatever discomfort it caused the rest of us. You might say
something snide about too much caffeine, but there was something more at stake here. Call it principled ire: it helped to make
up for the wrong vegetables or the missing bread. It also refuted
the fallacy of turning the other cheek, which in his estimation
merely provided a fresh surface for the second slap. Let that be
a lesson to his sons: the meek inherit the dirt they deserve.

For there is nothing so unprepossessing as civility. Common
courtesy keeps us common. How liberating to plunge ahead
before checking the odds, the reviews, or the weather! I remember Stanley Elkin's story "A Poetics for Bullies" and the first article of faith of its narrator, Push: "I will not be reconciled or halve
my hate. It's what I have, all I can keep." The blatant rule of

muscle and gut: what better antidote to all the hedging we learn to settle for as our portion? Truly, the day belongs to the vertebrates. In rage's nature, there are only straight lines. So Elkin's Push always comes to shove: *"I push through."*

As anyone knows who has spent the time and money on a self-defense course, you need to be assaulted to stay sharp and relevant. What I think of as my father's defining moment occurred at O'Hare Airport, where he was dropping me off for my flight back to college. To get to the terminals, you have to drive off the expressway onto one of five feeder ramps, each of which takes you past a bank of airline entrances and then rejoins the expressway. Parking is available, but it is expensive and far away. These ramps are exclusively reserved for the dropping off of passengers. Drivers must nose their cars to the curb like fish converging where the food clings to the side of the tank. Then they must pull out into the stream of traffic again. If anyone delays to embrace a departing lover or advise a son, honking and invective immediately shoot down the sentiment. (The City of Big Shoulders uses those shoulders for blocking.) On occasion, I've even seen a waiting car thump the bumper of the malingerer in front. "If I want to see a movie, I'll rent one! Let's go! While we're young, huh?" a driver once hollered from behind. You've got to admire the gumption.

Anyway, on this occasion my father simply parks—parks, mind you!—a good ten feet from the curb, pops his trunk, and, slowly extracting himself from the driver's side—he was a big man, and it was not in his makeup to hurry—proceeded to unload my suitcases. Already shaky from the drive—it was Dad's tendency to editorialize at length and loudly about the tentativeness of other drivers whenever congestion thickened—I broke for the bags, hoping to keep our misdemeanor brief. But as I say, Dad took his time and everyone else's.

When the cop drew near, he correctly figured me for a hostage to my father's resolve, and so he narrowed his focus onto Dad. While I shrank back and mimed apology—we were not so

distant from the Democratic National Convention and Mayor
Daley's sanctioned belligerence against ragged teenagers that I
could feign nonchalance in front of the police—my father,
ample and intent and supremely *present* in a way I had never been,
did not turn around.

"Sir, there's no parking here. You're going to have to move
this vehicle."

Dad just kept unloading. This was a man to whom repen-
tance was as pointless as a rearview mirror.

"Sir, I said you'll have to move."

Still unloading, still showing the law his backside. Yes, a
man to whom tact was as unnatural as napkins to Nietzsche.

"Move this vehicle now!"

And without turning around, without even straightening,
Dad replied, "You've got a gun. Use it."

Game, set, match. Stunningly compulsive, the man could not
be compelled. Who could match smolders with my father?
Whose throw weights could compare? It was a response adapted
from Humphrey Bogart in *Casablanca*, when he steps in closer to
Ingrid Bergman, who has a gun trained at his heart, and tells her
to go ahead, she'd be doing him a favor. That's the model: a jaw
like masonry, trench-coated, and drenched in noir. How much
longer would it take to shunt my father's bulky corpse to the curb,
not to mention endure the paperwork or the press? Yes, the press
relishes the sight of bureaucracy stymied and blind convention
balked. Can you imagine trying to budge a Bogart? Even a beat
cop could see that this guy was his own bulldozer. He left his gun
in its holster and headed off to round up the usual suspects.

So that was Dad—suave as a bomb. I'm not complaining. I
made my plane back to school in plenty of time.

At college I succumbed to another curriculum, one which
centered on culture and courtesy. And today I'm living in a town
whose entire population is less than the number of people you'll
see at O'Hare on any weekend. People idle in grocery lines to
talk about their kids. Rarely does anyone hammer the car horn

the moment the light turns green. On Tuesdays the local evening news features pets from the animal shelter they hope we'll call in to adopt. It's that kind of town.

When I do return to visit the city, I find myself gravitating toward delicatessens instead of museums. I find that I miss the sounds of urban Jews holding forth. I miss their raspy, competitive chatter, their bold and endless declaiming.

Once I came back to Chicago with a friend from college, who was kind enough to neglect his Fodor's Guide's advice for a day and accompany me to my favorite haunts. As a reward, I decided to treat us to a fancy dinner. (Who could have guessed I would grow to become a man with credit?) When we arrived at the restaurant, one of the city's most notable—my friend found it singled out for approval on page 62—they told us that our names were not on the list. We were welcome to wait at the bar if we wished for a table to open up or for a possible cancellation. My reaction was elaborate, rabid, and sustained; it was swift, absolute, and a surprise to everyone, myself included. I threatened. I crescendoed. I held out a business card like a stiletto and told them that they may have forgotten who we were earlier, but I would make certain they would remember it from now on. They offered the manager. Bring him on, I cried. They apologized. I told them we couldn't eat apology. It was your mistake, so it is your responsibility, I concluded, loud enough for the whole room to hear. Now what do you think you should *do* about it?

My friend told me over our complimentary appetizers that he had never seen anyone go off like that before—that is, not outside of a movie. I admitted that it had been a long time for me, too.

The meal, by the way, was as good as advertised. The next time you're in Chicago, you really ought to try that place. Mention my name.

from the letters to gamma man

Gamma Man can be reached c/o Astonish Comics Group, 211 Madison Avenue, New York, NY. All letters to Gamma Man become permanent property of Astonish Comics Group and the Bartlett Corporation.

Dear Gamma Man: Why are you powerless against ultraviolet rays? What else are you powerless against?
—Michael F., Emporia, KS

GM: As you will remember from *Gamma Man* #2, which I believe is still in print and available from Astonish Comics, my accidental transformation into Gamma Man after the explosion at Professor Kroton's laboratory irradiated and altered my genetic structure in ways I am still learning about. My vulnerability to ultraviolet rays might have been explained by Professor Kroton, but, as you know, he was killed by the same blast that created Gamma Man. Such are the vicissitudes of fate. I have since discovered that I am also powerless against a variety of metals and gases generally congregated on the right-hand side of a conventional chart of the periodic table of the elements. Yet I can fly faster than many small passenger planes and bring down solid walls by simply focusing my attention. It appears that superheroism is an elaborate system of sacrifices and compensations.

Dear Gamma Man: Why doesn't your costume get destroyed when you do a molecular shiver through fire or when you get bombed? Is it a gamma costume, too? Do you have lots of them, or what? I've been arguing about this with my two brothers, and we can't figure this out.

—Gina B., Tyler, TX

GM: Johnny Incaviglia, the Art Director for *Gamma Man* and Astonish Comics, advises me that the suit actually emerges as part of my gamma incarnation, which means that it shares the properties of my own radiant manifestation. We are what we pretend to be, you might say, but this is as much a philosophical issue as a subatomic physical one. On the other hand, please don't argue over hypernatural phenomena with family members. Like discussions about religion, sexual conduct, and the intrinsic value of public television, it can only lead to divisiveness and pain. Life, as poor Marilee Davis discovered when she unwittingly and with the best intentions opened the door to Magma's henchmen in *Gamma Man* #22, is too short, and happiness too fragile, to bear much insistence.

Dear Gamma Man: Chaotica has sworn eternal vengeance against you. What is her problem? Did you hurt her or kill somebody she knows?

—Jeremy D., Schenectady, NY

GM: Chaotica is a complex creature, to be sure. I honestly have no recollection of having done anything to offend her, yet she has sworn eternal vengeance against me, as you correctly recall from *Gamma Man* #14. Possibly she is delusional owing to her captivity in the Containment Center, or perhaps the strain of assimilating to earth's atmosphere and gravity has caused some psychic distortion. (I could sympathize if this were in fact the case, for I myself have not fully recovered from exposure to her

Terminal Wave in that very issue.) This is conjecture on my part, however, and quite possibly unfair to her. What is clear is that she blames me for some ambiguous trespass, and trying to reason with her (*Gamma Man #18*) only increases her wrath.

Dear Gamma Man: What is it like having to keep your identity secret? Don't you sometimes just feel like yelling, "Hey, I'm Gamma Man!"?

—Robert T., Lebanon, MO

GM: I suspect that the reaction would be skeptical at best, irritated or dismissive at worst. Just as it would be if you did it. Try it and see if I'm not right. The fact is that the world does not crave our exposures. Do you think it would be all that difficult for someone like Doctor Crypto to track me after some public and very exhausting exploit in order to discover my true—or should I say, additional—identity? For that matter, it wouldn't require extraordinary powers of ratiocination for my coworkers at the Plant to suspect me. With a simple check of my punchcard in *Gamma Man #3*, all would have been revealed. But people have their own agendas and day-planners to attend to. You will learn that surprise, like devotion and pity, is a finite commodity, and most people you know are already overcommitted. Still, in answer to your question, yes, I do.

Dear Gamma Man: My father is a biochemist, and he says that anyone who got bombarded by the kind of radiation you did would not get super powers. He says he would not even survive. He would be killed or just start dying, but no super powers. Can you explain this?

—Travis M., McMinville, OR

GM: I admit to being as much at a loss at your father, who is undoubtedly earnest in his work and devoted to your proper development. We need more fathers like yours. You might ask him whether or not *his* life has turned out the way he thought it would. I am certain that he is the sort of man who would be moved rather than vexed by his son's persistence and would treat it as your taking him seriously. He might even quote Thoreau to you: "The world is more wonderful than convenient." This is relevant, although it does not really answer your question. Or you could mention this quotation to your father. Biochemists could do worse than reference Thoreau.

Dear Gamma Man: I bought the telemeter gun advertised on the back page of Gamma Man Comics, the one you used in *Gamma Man #4* against the Kandros terrorists and in *Gamma Man #9* to help you outwit Infernus. The main imploder unit cracked the first time I used it. Also, the reactor sheen does not fan out the way it's supposed to. It just kind of spurts out, and it leaks onto your hand. I spent my own money on this.

—Stuart O., Flagstaff, AZ

GM: You probably don't need me to tell you that this is a toy replica of the telemeter I devised and use in my adventures. A real telemeter oriented to gamma chemistry would be lethal to anyone else who tried to operate it—you'll remember how Infernus himself learned that lesson the hard way—much less in the hands of a child (no offense intended). To be honest, the U.S. Post Office is too responsible to allow such a device to be sent through the mail. Along with the interstate highway system and the Coast Guard, the postal service, for all of its well-publicized faults, shows that the government is not entirely irresponsible. Because it is a toy, your telemeter requires and rewards a working imagination on the part of its operator. You must actively contribute to its effectiveness, which is what makes it different than your television set and your computer terminal, both of which you undoubtedly own, too, although they were not paid for, I suspect, with your own money. As for the leaking, a pair of neutralizing gloves like those you see me wearing on page 9 of *Gamma Man* #4, and which are also advertised on the back page of this very issue, would solve that problem.

Dear Gamma Man: Why did you quit the Intergalactic Alliance?

—April T., Modesto, TX

GM: In fact, I did not quit the Intergalactic Alliance. It was a noble experiment doomed by the false hope that allegiance to principles of justice could overcome the inherent volatility of its membership. Just consider the tormented, unholy blend that was Janus, whose entrenched resident personalities led to his / their splintering into separate life forms. For that matter, how many of us were actually "evil" characters at one time or another, or at least perceived as evil? As you know, I myself have not enjoyed uninterrupted trust among earth authorities, who are wary of my powers and the underground nature of my activities. The point is that good and evil represent a false dichotomy. Like fantasy and reality, mutational free play and elemental limitation, figure and ground, there is a lot of ambiguity, unpredictability, and overlap to contend with. Also between prodigious powers and a fundamental helplessness. There are no separate camps, just a growing, foggy betweenness.

Dear Gamma Man: Metaphysto had you beat in *Gamma Man* #19. The way I figure it, you only defeated him because he got careless when he thought he had you trapped in that denaturizing unit of his. My question is, could you beat Metaphysto now in a fair fight?

—Timothy R., Racine, WI

GM: What would constitute a fair fight? The Declaration of Independence notwithstanding, we are not all created equal, as even the briefest glance at Metaphysto's cell structure would prove. All of us are differently endowed and use what we have as best we can. In fact, I do not think that Metaphysto could beat me or vice versa, not in the sports contest sense of one beating the other. Anyway, annihilation is no victory, just an elimination of potential. I told the Intergalactic Alliance (*Gamma Man* #8) that the superhero congress which governs best governs least, implying among many other things that we may work to rehabilitate rogue inhabitants of all sectors but must remain open to such variables as the fluxional quality of the incentives and physical attributes of creatures like Metaphysto. Survival with dignity, negative capability, the preference for elegance over crudity—these are more reliable and more relevant tenets. Anyway, Metaphysto's weakness was his ego, which was also what made him so formidable an opponent and so great a threat to the human race. The growth of ambiguity goes on regardless of the outcome of my battles past and future with Metaphysto. In that sense, I guess, you could say that we have both won and lost in advance. It is not just semantics which renders the comment by one of the poor cops at the conclusion of *Gamma Man* #19 that "Metaphysto is now in custody" a contradiction in terms. Everything is elusive, and Metaphysto is no different in that essential regard. I think you can bet on running into him again in the September or October issue.

Dear Gamma Man: Are you happy?

—Joe K., Portland, OR

GM: Portland is supposed to be a beautiful city, Joe, a perpetual darling of the *Places Rated Almanac*. The ocean is a constant source of serenity. The economic base of the city is reported to be quite sound. The people are congenial when the traffic lets them be, and it does not rain nearly so often as it does in Seattle, which mitigates that city's trendiness, doesn't it? Think of "happy" as a verb, Joe. It is a process more than a destination. I am still evolving, as you are, and in spite of the unprecedented quality of my body chemistry, I suspect that my fate is no less predictable than yours. So why complain? As Thoreau wrote, "We need to witness our own limits transgressed." The laboratory accident that recreated me as Gamma Man apparently guaranteed that this transgression will be ongoing in my case. I am always already inchoate, kid. And so are you. Your own uncontaminated body completes a comprehensive sloughing and replacement of its own cells every seven years or so. (I am quite certain that Travis M.'s father could verify this fact for you.) The possibility of my wholesale deincarnation—a very real possibility given the instabilities my gamma-radiated body hosts—by no means disqualifies that. If you listen to the viscid rush of my heart, it sounds like either distant cheering or diligent sobbing. That is how it persists. Like yours.

objects and empathy

Keep your places, objects than which none else is more lasting.
You have waited, you always wait, you dumb, beautiful ministers,
We receive you with free sense at last, and are insatiate henceforward,
Not you any more shall be able to foil us, or withhold yourselves from us,
We use you, and do not cast you aside—we plant you permanently within us,
We fathom you not—we love you....
                    —Walt Whitman, "Crossing Brooklyn Ferry"

Go through my desk and you will find, amid the shrunken
thumbs of eraser, the brisk geometries of shaved pencil, and the
tidy shrapnel of paper clips, my feeling stone. Touchstone, some
would call it, "feelie" for short or slang; a beveled lens or tun-
neled chunk of wood probably performs the same unsung function in other hands. I am convinced that there is some unpubli-
cized, unInternetted fellowship of the rings, keys, pennies, and
other compliant, smoothable solids that regularly defer to our
stresses and pressures. They are unassuming fetishes, these bits
of orphaned manufacture, to which no prior sentiment attaches.
They are not trophies or souvenirs. The coins commemorate
nothing but the clatter they made when they dropped to the
floor; the popped shirt button, trailing its pennant of thread, has
no story other than entropy to cozy up to. They are odds

without ends. We rub them not to spring jinn from within but
for the pleasures of the texture, the satisfactions of the grooved
slots and lacquered surfaces themselves.

Extracting my stone, a cool kidney of lapis blue, I think how
randomness and obsession must both have been unconscious
components of my selection process. Feeling stones are happened upon—their feeling is centrifugal, radiating toward
prospective adoption—but they must be checked for size,
shape, and a dozen other demands of instinctive quality control.
My father, himself a proud owner of a shallowly porous lozenge
of limestone, once spoke of the many rejections that preceded
his discovery of the right accessory for his suit pocket. The story
reminds me of nothing so much as his recounting the time he
first realized that he was going to marry my mother.

It is the foundation of Romantic myth, the principal suspi-
cion of Transcendentalism, the enabling faith of poetry that the
physical universe returns our observance. Phenomena favor us
when they appear with their endowment of words. Where better to worship than in the midst of an articulate environment
composed of resonant, answering matter, in which the furthest
structures are purged of alienation by the proof that they are distant syllables aimed at our compensation? Under these auspices,
the vault of heaven is an echo chamber, only the outermost layer
of mind, while our possessions are witness condensed: neighborhood citizens of humble station, they dutifully brood about
our needs and griefs.

My stone warms in my hand, warming my hand—"Touching
topaz, / one is touched by the topaz," Pablo Neruda writes—and
I learn that the talent is not restricted to precious gems. Perhaps
the humblest objects reward our fidelity best because they
require us most. Animation need not be a prerequisite for intimacy; not only streams and trees receive us. Consider the
wraithlike population of Samuel Beckett's trilogy, all of them
promptly reduced to their descriptive capacities. Molloy's greatest ingenuity is spent on the problem of how to offer equal,

successive nurture to the sixteen sucking stones he deploys about his body as a kind of ethical ballast. Molloy is as adoring as any parent, ever-alert to his jealous, competitive children. A ramshackle bicycle, an umbrella with spokes exposed like bones gleaming on the beach, a bit of rope, a decent stick: each fragment stored against the ruins, against the dissipation of mystery beneath an unremembering sky, is, like the narrative itself, assiduously scrupled over. For all of his paeans to absence, negation, respite, and the final silence of the stammering heart, despite his dismissal of his every passion in favor of a righteous zero blacked in to its borders, Beckett waits on *things,* and in his penury feasts on the scrabble of tragic details.

Speaking of his Sunday dress, Moran complains, "This gross external observance, while the soul exults in its rags, has always appeared to me an abomination," but even the ragged soul may be granted grace when observance is keen. We persevere by expanding upon the nearest nouns. So Malone dies down among the subtle company of worn pencils, a needle housed in cork, a broken pipe, about whose useless bowl he conjectures at lengths one would expect to be reserved for an old lover:

Perhaps I thought it pretty, or felt for it that foul feeling of pity I have so often felt in the presence of things, especially little portable things in wood and stone, and which made me wish to have them about me and keep them always, so that I stooped and picked them up and put them in my pocket, often with tears, for I wept up to a great age, never having really evolved in the field of affection and passion, in spite of my experiences. And but for the company of these little objects which I picked up here and there, when out walking, and which sometimes gave me the impression that they too needed me, I might have been reduced to the society of nice people or to the consolations of some religion or other, but I think not. And I loved ... to finger and caress the hard shapely objects that were there in my deep pockets, it was my way of talking to them and reassuring them. And I loved to fall asleep holding in my hand a stone, a horse chestnut or a cone, and I would be still holding it when I woke,

my fingers closed over it, in spite of sleep which makes a rag of the
body, so that it may rest.

Shall we in our sophistication forego the scant enchantments of
the proximate? This modest yet insistent litter—these infinitely
gentle, infinitely suffering *things*—still warrant and reward our
compassion.

I, too, suspect that a subtle, symbiotic connection may exist
between the imagination and even the shabbiest things. Perhaps
a sentient, unifying something conducts all Creation. I may have
first encountered this presumption in the gloom of horror stories
that used to send me shuddering to bed. (You could not tuck me
in or tucker me out with wholesome tales in those days.) Girding
the hero's dreadful ecstasies was an obsessive registration of
details that seem to sense the intruder. Perspective was ever on
the boil, as he was painstakingly escorted through one agitated
space after another: masonry trembled, panes perspired, linens
bled, shapes blistered and frothed. Gruesomeness exuded from
every dank corner, and I balled beneath my blanket against the
stuff that conspired against me from atop my dresser. Especially
at night, everything was on notice.

But it is not just in a child's overheated imagination where
objects plot and churn. Contemporary physics confirms inconti-
nence at the molecular level. Every object is on the move—the
site of invisible riots. We have to revise the simplest definitions: a
block is really a blur, temporarily beheld. One physicist, D'Arcy
Thompson, determines that an object is really a "diagram of
forces"; a second physicist, Richard Feynman, asks us to consider:

What is an object? Philosophers are always saying, "Well, just take a
chair, for example." The moment they say that, you know that they
do not know what they are talking about any more. What is a chair?
Well, a chair is a certain thing over there ... certain?, how certain?
The atoms are evaporating from it from time to time—not many
atoms, but a few—dirt falls on it and gets dissolved in the paint; so to

define a chair precisely, to say exactly which atoms are chair and which atoms are air, or which atoms are dirt, or which atoms are paint that belong to the chair, is impossible.

The physical reality is that atomic interaction is implication. When he steps up to the plate, not only is Casey at the bat, but the bat is at Casey, too. And so, a "certain thing" is the stuff of sentiment. Watch Roald Hoffman worship the startling digressions of glass in "Deceptively Like a Solid":

Atoms wander
from their places, bonds break,
tetrahedra

in a tizzy, juxtapose, chains tilt,
bump and stretch—Jaggerwalky.
The restive structures

in microscopic turmoil
meld to gross flow, bubbling
eddies of the melt.

Feynman urged his students to explore "the vast frontier of small things," and the call clearly crossed disciplines. Physicists and poets alike consent to secret seductions at the subatomic heart of things, for the world's homeliest particulars are somehow flowing, reflective, conversing with and full of us.

Versed in the latest sciences, many recent poets depict an environment ignited by human attention. For instance, Alice Fulton finds in fractals and lightning strikes accommodations for human moods. When she examines in "Cascade Experiment" how electrons shiver in and out of adjacent forms, I consider whether my stone and I commiserate more intimately beneath higher powers of focus, exchanging subtle gravities. John Allman demonstrates in "Chemistry" how the material world inhabits us as we reside in it, locating our emotions and gestures in isotopes, prisms, heat exchanges, floating oxides, and hydro-gen bonds. The "semicolloids of his perception" are as invested in the laboratory as they are in ordinary life, and his wistfulness is as likely to be stirred by a telluric helix or bars of sodium as by lazy evenings or letters home. And Albert Goldbarth, contem-porary poetry's high priest of kitsch-and-tell and a long-standing advocate of thingified pleasures—"I'm weary of every gasleak / of abstraction," he snarls in "Some Things," so "for now give me things"—suggests that molecules are somehow thoughtful enti-ties. Is it too great a leap to imagine them as being mindful of us?

Pattiann Rogers comparably contemplates herself in mirrors of mildew and mulch, in toad spine and shark sperm, in a shard of coral, vein of sycamore, curve of egg. She likewise recognizes the turbulence lurking in seemingly stable compositions, as she uncovers, in "The Image in a World of Flux," "rocked" cores, unstilled "rackets" and "exploding equations" inside spellbound, serene details. Meanwhile, Diane Ackerman channels for cosmic bodies and slices Pi, but she also stoops to admire viruses and translate fossils. "Still, the bone tumblers / ogle my chalky remains," a trilobite boasts to her, "this herringbone shell / — wonderwork / risen out of panic."

With all this wrestling going on, can any matter truly be set-tled? I wonder what wanton energies stir in the polished dark of my own desk. So much clutter caught in the act! The main drawer seems to me more of an unregulated port than a formal assembly, no orthodox temple but an Ellis Island of refugee wrappers, caps, and screws milling disjointedly about. But the commissioner in us cannot stand too much chaos in the coop and bends to his knit-ting. "Somewhere in the city of New York there are four or five still-unknown objects that belong together. Once together they'll make a work of art," speculates Charles Simic in the presence of Joseph Cornell's boxed collages. Our interest is peaked by arriv-ing on the verge of the significant image, by the promise of coherence under construction. Might an inventory of some of the contents of Cornell's Cléo de Mérode disclose aesthetic method?

Doll's forearm, loose red sand, wood ball, German coin, several glass
and mirror fragments, 12 corkstopped bottles, cutout sphinx head,
yellow filaments, 2 intertwined paper spirals, cut-out of Cléo de
Mérode's head, cutout of camels and men, loose yellow sand, 6 pearl
beads, glass tube with residue of dried green liquid, crumpled tulle,
rhinestones, pearl beads, sequins, metal chain, metal and glass fragments, threaded needle, red wood disc, bone and frosted glass fragments, blue celluloid, clear glass crystals, rock specimen, 7 balls,
plastic rose petals, three miniature tin spoons for a doll house

Plots abide in this blasted residence, though the crippled orna-
ments will never deck a darling out again. The glass and paper
fragments will not restore the scene they scattered from, nor will
the petals recover their stem, yet the salvage speaks as much of
redemption as of loss. Though the slivered toys will never again
submit to play, the doll resume the first narrative she figured in,
or the jettisoned penny spend, the forage is discriminatory, and
that forage implies constancy and underwrites belief.

   The self-sufficient charms of accrual and display inspire some
to load cupboards and drawers, others to stock paragraphs and
stanzas. Following this logic, list makers may be seen as the
purest literary equivalent of conservationists. List makers are ran-
sackers with poetic consciences. They temper immersion with
scrutiny. Moreover, they exalt the obduracy of stone, which is
one of its most agreeable characteristics, because they seek "triumph over time." Robert Harbison explains in *Eccentric Space* that

Each item of a list is repetition and novelty at once, conflates the past
and the future, makes things co-present. Listers and cataloguers often
seem to have left their material in too rough a form; it is only the raw
matter of learning and needs transforming by digression. But burying
their conclusions as well as concealing their maker, catalogues aim to
be incontestable, by being a selfless to become a virtuous form.

We recognize these indoor activists as bibliographers, statisti-
cians, and all inveterate barnaclers; surfers of surfeit and lovers

of catalogs that thicken like stews; rhapsodists of garage sales, who cannot pass a flea market without flinching; Thanksgiving guests who recklessly plunge their hands into the turkey to get at the oily swags of stuffing, richly glinting and cloaked in steam. As authors, they assiduously cull in the service of secret harmonies. (Let us not neglect their readers either, who, Harbison notes, "have unfailing appetite for information about things that repel them in reality when it grants them intimacy all at once.") Curators of words, they shamelessly savor and accessorize, for they believe that *more* is more. So Steven Millhauser demonstrates in "The Sepia Postcard":

I saw at once that there were other rooms: PLUMSHAW'S RARE BOOKS was a warren of small rooms connected by short dark passages lined with books. The invasion of alien objects was more noticeable as I moved deeper into the back, where entire shelves had been cleared to make way for stacks of maroon record albums containing heavy, brittle 78's as thick as roof slates, boxes of old postcards, empty cardboard cylinders the size of soup cans each bearing the words EDISON GOLD MOULDED RECORD and an oval of Thomas A. Edison, daguerreotypes, tintypes, stacks of pen-and-ink illustrations torn from old books, a moldering gray Remington typewriter with dark green keys, a faded wooden horse with red wheels, little porcelain cats, a riding crop, old photograph albums containing labeled black-and-white photographs (Green Point, 1926) with upcurled corners showing traces of rubber cement, a cribbage board with ivory pegs, a pair of high cracked black lace-up shoes. Here and there I saw brass standing lamps with cloth shades and yellowed ivory finials, and armchairs with faded doilies; I wondered whether they were for sale.

Held together by rhythm, alliteration, and desire, items in lists stand for articles of faith. They whisper their little essences at us; they tug at our cuffs. Here we see the generosity of nouns patient before the slow work of vision. Would that every honored shred, every errant speck and lowly stone, prove so touching in the eyes of God!

Oh, but when the objects by which we would hold ourselves accountable refuse us, there is no betrayal so acute. Accordingly, Elizabeth Bishop's Crusoe, rueful and obsolete in England, finds his current isolation defined by inhuman rejection:

The knife there on the shelf—
it reeked of meaning, like a crucifix.
It lived. How many years did I
beg it, implore it, not to break?
I knew each knick and scratch by heart,
the bluish blade, the broken tip,
the lines of wood-grain on the handle ...
Now it won't look at me at all.
The living soul has dribbled away.
My eyes rest on it and pass on.

Crusoe endures an exile so severe that even the surviving relic of his earlier island rejects his witness. (Or perhaps "surviving" is still too optimistic a reading: the brute blade has been strangled and will not rouse.) The nimbus of familiarity having dissolved, Crusoe's knife now nests in its uninvadable state like ... like nothing else, for connection fails. Nostalgia is a pointless courtship, and metaphor cannot coax a kinship or grab a handle. The knife will not be dear.

Then there is "The Pebble" that headlines Zbigniew Herbert's poem, "filled exactly / with a pebbly meaning" and, unlike my own feeling stone, which invariably seems to soften beneath my appeals, flouts all such arrogance and tightens its atoms against the speaker's hold. Self-contained, austere, knuckle-blunt, "with a scent which does not remind one of anything / does not frighten away does not arouse desire," the pebble turns from the speaker to recover decorum. The poem ends in remorse, apologizing for its trespass against the stone's cold conditions:

Pebbles cannot be tamed
to the end they will look at us
with a calm and very clear eye.

People will leave pebbles on tombstones as calling cards to mark
departures, as talismans of regard; but Herbert's pebbles are
more akin to a dose of sedatives or the barest line of prose than
to some vaunted spiritual contact. "Speak Plainly of Stone,"
Neruda warns in the title of one poem, and in "Silence Packs
Itself" endorses the way each stone represents

the mute word of earth:
it inherits primordial silence, the sea's immobility,
the void of creation, and has nothing to say.

From this viewpoint, when we call this one's demeanor "wood-
en," that one's glare "steely," and another's aspect "plastic," we
inevitably flatter ourselves. I say "my feeling stone" and await
indictment.

The proper acknowledgment of objects: it is the struggle that
governs things so small. Married couples in cold war will spurn
one another yet fret over chips in crystal paperweights. Jerry, in
Edward Albee's *Zoo Story*, prefers relationships with undemanding
goods over the strenuous complexities of dealing with people:

A person has to have some way of dealing with SOMETHING. If not
with people ... if not with people ... SOMETHING. With a bed, with a
cockroach, with a mirror ... no, that's too hard, that's one of the last
steps. With a cockroach, with a ... with a carpet, a roll of toilet paper
... no, not that either ... that's a mirror, too; always check bleeding.
You see how hard it is to find things?

We pray for things to watch over us. May nothing shrill or judg-
mental issue from their stoic, soundless cores, but may they
return our longings, admit our petitions and our praise.

For even when objects seem closed to omens, the composure of a cup or the benign indifference of an aspirin bottle can
draw us out. "Stanza my stone," cries Wallace Stevens's "Man on
the Dump," imposing poetry in an attempt to make his support
more supple. Buttons may suffer our fondlings, and, still inexpli-

cable, become tender, or so Gertrude Stein seems to say (for all
of her saying seems a seeming to say, it seems):

A CARAFE, THAT IS A BLIND GLASS
A kind in glass and a cousin, a spectacle and nothing strange a
single hurt color and an arrangement in a system to pointing.
All this and not ordinary, not unordered in not resembling.
The difference is spreading.

To be is ever to provoke, as she approves in "SHOES": "It shows
shine."

Stein is playing with sounds and etymologies the way a
painter mixes pigments or a child reviews his stash of marbles or
bottle caps. I am sure that that child would benefit from peering
into my drawer's maw, the desk's orlop, whose septic center is as
full of potential as the innards of the captured shark in *Jaws*. For
my part, I enjoy the way the feeling stone contradicts the
smooth utility of the desk. "In the midst of appurtenances char-
acterized by total consonance of design and purpose," writes
Daniel Harris in "What Do Office Workers Place on Their
Desks?", the incursion of personal objects "reads like bad syntax,
a playful suspension of practicability, a whimsical moment of
visual incoherence." Harris concentrates on the baited breadth
of the desk, so my *mining* the desk with a feeling stone may be
even a tad more subversive.

Stein's game also has a lot to do with foregrounding the fact
that words are things, too, if not specifically the things they
name. When earlier this century semiotics unknotted words and
things, we were left with these hard deposits aligning the page,
weighing it down. But remove the mantle of signification from
words, strip away the pedigree of conventional association, and
the succulent remains rival Estragon's chicken bones. And so I let
the sediment of reference collect for the pleasure of the
company alone. I defend my bootless booty, my bit of grit in the
throat of legitimate industry, for its own stony sake.

In a way, this is the wish of every writer: to make his concerns substantial. He would have each word he mounts become a stone, "more of an object than any object," as Marina Tsvetayeva said. He would gather his words into kiva circles and pay homage there. Don DeLillo notoriously suggests in *White Noise* that things forever threaten to possess their possessors or to crush them under their sorrowful weight; however, he also infers a visionary gleam that occasionally rises from ordinary forms: "Every word and thing a beadwork of bright creation." Thus our goods and their descriptions are sometimes symptoms of oblivion, sometimes "A cosmology against the void." Albert Goldbarth reminds us, in "A Tale," how God rained words upon the earth for ancient tribes to catch in baskets to constitute the multitude of languages we have inherited. We imagine along with him the strain of accumulating fluency, the heft of collected expression. And Pattiann Rogers weighs in again as well, refusing to neglect "All the Elements of the Scene": "The act / Of each thing being identified being linked to its name / Becomes an object itself here." Aficionados of sentences and of stones all hail the direct object.

In "The Beautiful Changes," Richard Wilbur congratulates his beloved for how her "hands hold roses always in a way that says / They are not only yours." He knows that hubris lurks close by possessiveness. William Carlos Williams describes his unique covenant with the literal, with things lying "close to the nose," in related terms. A plum, a green bit of broken glass, a rumpled sheet of brown paper—out of this elemental gist comes "the poet's business," as Williams defines it in his *Autobiography*. He claims redemption of, and through, the trivial: "Not to talk in vague categories but to write particularly, as a physician works, upon a patient, upon the thing before him, in the particular to discover the universal." How unseemly to have things bask in a Florida of adjectives when their "isolate flecks" fire so brilliantly against a clean background! You have to grant the very grains their dignity.

W. S. Merwin realizes in "Trees" that one of their most noble qualities is the fact that "their names have never touched them," and that depth beyond approximation, beyond commerce or allusion, is what survives the siege of language even as it inspires that siege. Nevertheless, it is difficult to give up the custom of dressing objects up and dressing them down, so as "not to see roses and other promising Things / in terms of a human future," as Rainer Maria Rilke explains in his First Duino Elegy. Maybe the poet's role is not to gloss, grasp, or ingratiate himself but simply to bless. He elaborates in his Ninth Duino Elegy:

Perhaps we are *here* in order to say: house
bridge, fountain, gate, pitcher, fruit-tree, window—
at most: column, tower.... But to say them, you must understand
oh to say them *more* intensely than the Things themselves
ever dreamed of existing.

And when our touch does not assume, when it caresses without clutching at or after, we may learn that these things are there to employ us. It is when we yield to the unsayability of things that they beckon and bid us speak:

And these Things,
which live by perishing, know you are praising them; transient,
they look to us for deliverance: us, the most transient of all.
They want us to change them, utterly, in our invisible heart,
within—oh endlessly—within us! Whoever we may be at last.

We live by things that live by perishing. What deliverance worth having would fail to include them? I take the census of my desk, parse each part and particle, elaborate and lay on hands. And as I pick through the spillway (I am something between the scientist imbued with clinical piety and the gull hovering over ripe garbage, I guess), I blunder upon one final irony: out of their ragged silence, objects do reveal a connate psychology of sorts. Best observed in solitude, they leave us somehow loved and less alone.

how to play

SORRY

Invented by Parker Brothers in 1934, Sorry has kept its tenure because it speaks to something fundamental in modern consciousness. Because of the several treacheries and disappointments we suffer during adulthood—indeed, because adulthood is itself a treachery and a disappointment—we feel that some compensation is due us. No compensation arrives, though we keep the phone clear and check the mail daily, so we decide to settle for an explanation. No explanation is forthcoming, though we keep strict accounts and submit to physical exams, so we hold out for an apology. It is our line in the sand, which we constantly patrol. Behind our sundry, sundered psychic parapets, we scan the city's sad expanses, the office horizon, and the weathered driveway for signs of its approach. For life owes us that much, of that much we are certain at least, at the very least, our ration of regret. Our Sorry.

Try it out on your spouse some day. Statistics dictate that, greeted first thing in the morning by an apology, most people will respond with "That's okay" or "Forget it" or "Just don't let it happen again." Even if you have no idea what wrong you're lamenting, more likely than not, your significant other has been waiting to have *something* righted. Some hide their gripes better than others, but you'd be hard-pressed to find someone who isn't steaming over *some* slight or another. If you listen closely in the middle of the night, if you pry beneath your wife's sighs or your husband's snores, you will hear a faint sound as if an aerosol can were leaking beneath the sheets. Deep within, we are all bottled hiss. Yeats famously bemoaned that the ceremony of innocence is lost in this decadent century, but do not underestimate the importance of the ceremony of *guilt* for getting a loving couple through the day. The ad line for *Love Story*—"Love means never having to say you're sorry"—does not hold up under duress. On the contrary, love requires that we swaddle one another in apologies, not necessarily because we did the bruising, but because we know how much it hurts.

The rules of Sorry are clearer to someone who has been weaned on the competition from Milton Bradley, Chutes and Ladders, a game which demands no capacity whatsoever from its players apart from a passing familiarity with counting to six. ("An exciting game of ups and downs for little people," Chutes and Ladders gently grazes the gross realities of Sorry, but it is no more edifying than when elementary school kids, visiting their fathers at work, are shunted off to the outer office to play with the adding machine while the dads deal behind closed doors.) From another perspective, because strategy is positively irrelevant to Chutes and Ladders—a plastic spinner, when it does not stick, is the sole arbiter of Fate—it is perhaps a less purely existential experience than Sorry, which by virtue of its more complicated set of choices and forking paths better sustains the illusion that one participates in the formation of his destiny.

In Sorry, each player is parsed into four pawns, whose goal, like the climax of a Thanksgiving television special, is to reassemble at Home. (This is a subtle but welcome dose of wholesomeness for kids who, all too often these days when both parents tend to hold jobs, must fend for themselves when they return from school.) The pawns are launched upon the board's squared streets, a marvel of exacting regulation and civil engineering. A pawn may clamber over an opponent on its way to finishing its turn; if the number of spaces prescribed by the turn of the card lands the pawn on an opponent's square, the opponent must return to Start. How many corporate advancements and misfortunes afford such equilibrium and statistical sanity? A given business may grow lousy with vice presidents, but in Sorry no gain is achieved without a countervailing loss, and any promotion directed by the board necessitates a demotion somewhere else along the line. When a player is bumped, the bumper offers his "Sorry." Indeed, when a run of contrapuntal "sorrys" occurs, the game takes on the atmosphere of a vaudeville routine or rush hour on the subway, where, more reflexive than sincere, the "sorrys" likewise compound.

The bumper may choose among several tones of delivery to alert and assuage the bumped. Chief among these: the sheepish, the teasing, the confidential, the ironic, the humiliating, the vindicated. Players should also be alert to the Sorry Cards that turn up during the course of play. These are the most flagrant, and thus the most delicious, of trumps because they allow the fortunate recipient to select any one of his pawns that still nest in the Start Circle to take the place of any enemy pawn at whatever stage of its career, thereby returning the supplanted pawn to its own point of origin. The tactic recalls how the brash and unforgivably young executive whose ascent threatens the summit is exiled to the branch office in Terre Haute or how a screw-up son-in-law is sent back down to Sales. Only one brand of "Sorry" will suffice in this case: it should be brayed just inches behind the ear and rolled down its octave like Sisyphus's rock to drive home for the opponent his plummet. Oh, possibly he had navigated the subterranean Slide spaces and patiently, uncomplainingly abided by the game's geometry until his reward was but a brief corner away. Now, discharged to his humble beginnings, he must slink to the circle's edge, trying to avoid attention at the reunion, which unavoidably falls at the time he falls, and in sober isolation relive his moves and imagine no alternative at all.

The logic of Sorry is sudden and ruthless. It is a game of primary colors and first principles, in which successes and reversals strike like hawks. Paradoxically, then, the winner will be the player who has been most obsessively apologetic, for, like Shakespeare's Claudius, he agonizes over dozens of distressed lines, but he never relinquishes his hoard. The throne is its own justification, and he whose offense is rank may equivocate, disclaim, or confess, but he does not atone or relax his grip.

MONOPOLY

The choice of playing piece is crucial. The cannon and the race car are the most desirable of the motley options, and the makers recommend calling dibs the moment you agree to play. The cannon's fortitude (thin-barreled but undeniably phallic) and the race car's brisk resolve are clearly in keeping with the pursuit of capital. If those pieces have already been wrested, consider the ship or the cowboy on horseback. The ship's insinuations of opulence and class distinction are impressive enough to make up for its connotation of indolence, a trait against which the true monopolist must forever guard. The anachronistic cowboy is woefully out of his depths in the burgeoning metropolis, as his horse, stymied by modern traffic, bucks amongst the gleaming utilities and bunched hotels; however, as a long-standing embodiment of the American myth of intrepidness and self-reliance, the cowboy retains sufficient, viable charm. (The fact is not lost on the many corporations that employ cowboys in their advertising.) But it would be better to surrender the chance to be the Banker than have to identify oneself as a thimble when trying to collect rent. The thimble, the boot, the hat, the wheelbarrow, and the iron are all such humble commodities—made things, not their makers—and their objectification of subservience, their representation of the lower end of labor, indicates that the struggle has already been lost. As for the Scottie, its cuteness may enchant the youngest players, but it is hardly built for the dagger-and-claw rise to prominence. Perhaps a

Horatio Alger could climb the ladder of success without putting
down his dog, but for serious getting and spending, you will
need undivided interests and both hands free.

One advantage of the disparate and seemingly unprincipled
nature of the playing pieces is that as they are lost over time,
markers from other games or, for that matter, any nearby bits of
household jetsam may replace them without disturbing the contest. Should the cat abscond with the race car or baby brother
gulp the boot, a rook may be recruited from a chess game or a
piece of evidence from Clue—the stamped plastic coil of rope;
the revolver, surprisingly substantial, like an ingot rolled
between the fingers; the seductively supple lead pipe—and the
game can continue without interruption. In contrast, come up a
checker short, and whatever scab you attempt to press into service, be it a borrowed quarter, a slick backgammon disk, or an
antacid tablet, will throw off the balanced arrays of red platoons
versus black, scuttling your plans; similarly, once army soldiers
are called in to cover for missing Uncle Wigglies or to shore up
devastated forces in chess, you might as well junk the remains
altogether. But Monopoly cannot be compromised; it can survive any work stoppage, epidemic, or on-site disaster.

The sole authenticating law of Monopoly is acquisition. If
the Zen Buddhist, believing that everything is God, becomes
more endowed by divinity with every molecule he absorbs,
experiences, and consumes, the savvy Monopolist takes on the
properties of the properties he obtains: weight, stature, prominence, the smug gravity of a Sidney Greenstreet. The secret of
greed is that you amass to master. Practice buying farther, buying faster. Neither the regimental Euclidean traffic of play nor
the enforced courtesy of waiting one's turn should distract the
player from the only real goal of the game.

Nevertheless, you will encounter players who take other
approaches to Monopoly, who abide by different rationales. A
given player may cling to designs impenetrable to the rest. For
instance, one may forsake all enterprises other than the

railroads. He may fall desperately in love with Boardwalk and
Park Place, to the extent that he makes ill-advised, even outra-
geous offers to add that pretentious pair to his portfolio. He may
crave a satisfying color scheme at the expense of sound business
dealings. In the rebellious spirit of the OuLiPo Group, he may
sell off any avenue containing the letter "e." But such eccentric
motives need not be understood to be defeated. In Monopoly,
aesthetics cannot save you. While the superstitious player
dithers and the sentimentalist strums guitar, to the ransacker go
the spoils.

Although the conclusion of Monopoly is rather quickly
determined—as in Restoration comedy, true quality quickly
emerges in Monopoly; as in Restoration comedy, it is rewarded
with purchasing power—the game may go on indefinitely,
inevitable ends teased out to epic duration by the eventual winner. He may, like the purring villain of melodrama, toy with his
prey, offering to take a few mortgaged properties off his hands
or to loan a few stray bills to encourage him not to resign.
Wealth can go stale apart from the manipulations that earned it,
so, in the manner of grinning Errol Flynn flipping the dropped
foil back to Basil Rathbone, one may urge a destitute opponent
into persevering until he has spent himself entirely. In this way,
one can be both the predator and the scavenger after the
bleached remains, the gourmet who claims the virgin taste and
the kid in the kitchen who steals back later to lick the bowl. The
very imagination that established an empire is capable of figur-
ing and financing entertainments that those hopelessly piling up
debts to him may never appreciate.

Note: It is theoretically possible to cling to the bars of the
prison that Milton Bradley based at the end of the lower-rent dis-
trict. Rolling doubles will get a player out, of course, but the
vicissitudes of the dice may never grant him a reprieve. Worse,
after several turns of denied parole, he may come to depend on
that cramped space for definition, and indeed, fear that he will no
longer be able to recognize himself out on the streets. Such a

player may disdain the offer of a GET OUT OF JAIL FREE card no matter how meager the price. It is an object lesson against hubris: even the budding entrepreneur may be stalemated by a Bartleby. Rockefeller may be the guiding spirit of the game, but the potential for a parable from Kafka looms only a block beyond the cheerful blue sky above Connecticut Avenue, where loiterers may lose the thread of purpose and waste away, unredeemed.

CAREERS

Your first task is the most important one; in truth, it is the essential burden of the game. You must propose and chart your fate. It is like buying off the astrologer or transacting with a genie. You register for outcomes like a still unravish'd bride for china patterns. You parcel out your potential in stars, hearts, and dollar signs.

It is a complicated business, authoring your prospects before they bud. For example, you can plot to become rich, famous, and happy in equal measures. You can contract to be happier than you are rich and remain utterly anonymous in the bargain. You can stipulate your wish to be showered with renown and barely pay the bills. You can be completely yet unaccountably content. Thus Careers provides not only an introduction to the uncertainties of the job market but also a philosophical debate. Just how rigid are the divisions between wealth and fame? Can you realistically live on romance apart from financial support? Is pure happiness possible? Novices tend to shy away from this sort of rigorous self-evaluation and more or less equitably distribute their desires. The experienced player, however, recognizes that there are more opportunities to earn happiness points on the board and in the cards, whereas fame is fleeting and money is tight; so he optimistically relies on a steady stream of hearts and wagers on euphoria to come.

The number of available career tracks is necessarily limited, but they have been cunningly devised to furnish players as much variety, personal fulfillment, and upward mobility as might reasonably be expected. Certainly, the breadth of opportunity on display at least matches, if it does not actually exceed, what awaits the players beyond the boundaries of the board in postindustrial America. One may quibble about the absence of one or more careers that currently dominate the classifieds, such as computer programming, hotel and restaurant management, crime prevention, trucking, telephone sales, or inner-city social work; however, second guessing so fluid and unpredictable an economy as faces us today would force the manufacturers to produce a new version of the game every five years or so, and the extra expense would undoubtedly descend upon the consumer. To the game's credit, Careers emphasizes prudent investment and obliges every player to go through College, for a degree is a prerequisite for accomplishment in all of the job tracks on the board save Sports and Hollywood. Admittedly, this sometimes encourages impatient, starry-eyed players to bypass College and go directly after these chancier disciplines. (Still, Careers is infinitely more responsible to young players than Life, in which the whole point is to marry as quickly as possible, then to propagate until the car is full. Indeed, Life bestows cars upon its participants at the outset, so they never learn what it takes to earn them, much less to pay for insurance. Parents should be cautioned that their children should engage in Life only under their supervision, if at all.)

Depending on how you have defined your dreams, you may circulate endlessly within a given career, dutifully accumulating dividends—a dependable, if rather tedious, method—or, like a rich dilettante or a Kerouac devotee, you may see what doors the dice deliver you to, emboldened by the belief put forth by novelist John Barth that roads should be laid where people walk.

The game ends when one player achieves the aspirations he outlined for himself. One admonition: Careers is an exceptionally long game. Typically it is reserved for rainy Sundays when there is nothing but televised golf to compete with it. Nowadays, it is usually the youngest child who, denied access to the Internet, campaigns for Careers as a way of extending the length of time his siblings will have to tolerate him. So although it is possible in theory for the remaining players to continue to play, in practice they will not persist after the inferiority of their futures has been assured. In Edwin Arlington Robinson's poem "Richard Cory," the poor masses strove and sacrificed in the hope of someday imitating his excellence—"So on we worked, and waited for the light, / And went without the meat, and cursed the bread"—but the poem ends abruptly once news of Cory's suicide spreads. It can only be assumed that they have no reason and no way to go on. One can only speculate as to what acids burned beneath Richard Cory's elegant tailoring or upon what awful precipice success abandoned him. Was he never able to fill his heart flush? Or was he destroyed by a fatal allotment of stars?

SCRABBLE

It is merciless. It reveals too much. No other game is so charged with implication and prospects for shame. If your errant thumb topples the Jenga tower or fuddles the clump of Pick Up Sticks, nothing other than your dexterity is doubted; if you cannot make your Rube Goldberg variation operate in Mousetrap or maintain your fleet in Battleship, no negative resonance or scent of failure follows you. But Scrabble always indicts someone in the room. It masquerades as play, but don't be fooled: it is another test.

Let's say that rain washes out the concert in the park, or you forgot to reserve the theater tickets, or the one sensitive film showing at the local cineplex has suddenly been shown the gate. Consider miniature golf to salvage the date. There, all you need do is demonstrate that you recognize the irrelevance of the score to prove your maturity, which, in the effort to impress a partner, is an underrated trait. Beware of announcing strokes as they're taken, resist becoming arthritic about the rules, and grant mulligans with casual largesse. (You may have seen doomed couples wrangle at the water hazard or, worse, a woman deliberately duff her putt on the seventeenth, throwing the match to soothe her man's ego, which it took him six errant jabs to extract from the alligator's jaws on fifteen. Take heed.) But do not try to placate your date with a round of Scrabble. Imagine her enjoying a regular diet of natural morphemes and ready blends, snaring the *x* early and pinching *q* and *u* at once, while you get stuck with a line of uninterrupted, nearly pointless vowels, which reads like the howl of a comic book character. No attachment can prosper in the wake of a double-digit trouncing. Better to go childless, she'll realize, than connect with someone who answers her formidable *quake* with a pipsqueak *tin;* who responds to her exotic *exotic* with stuttered *its* and stubbed *toes;* or who, after she plays *banjo* with flair, can only pick *nits.* She lays her tiles intricately, articulately down like a Byzantine mosaicist, while you can't even make a *name* for yourself. Any complaint about bad luck will sound like a whine. And it goes without saying that the belle lettered competitor will not endear herself either. Vanquishment never did lead to healthy, mutually sustaining passions.

For those who brave the game nonetheless, there is another issue to be faced. If victory is what you're after, the most effective strategy is to play defensively. If you've earned any lead at all, you must try to block up the board, providing no outlet whatsoever for your opponent's tiles. Crush any possible linkage like a cigarette on the sidewalk. Make the other player swallow his consonants. Practice the gag rule, and shove the utterances back down his throat. If you know he holds a *u*-less *q,* tuck away any *u* you have or jam it into a useless corner of the board so no *q* can queue up behind it. Force him like a bee trapped in a jar to buzz over his fruitless *z.* After a painfully protracted game—in this predicament, your opponent will pore over the dictionary like a Dominican prowling for grace in the hope of finding some archaism or slang to release him—it's a good idea to have something to occupy you in the widening intervals between your turns. Looming or scowling only makes the game go on forever, and you might be moved to surrender despite your insurmountable lead just to bring these stalled revels to an end. Instead, you might trim the nails you never get to or reconcile your checkbook.

There is an alternative approach worth considering. It is collaborative. As a team you can try to build as monumental a score as possible. Agree to be Beaumont to his Fletcher, Watson to his Crick. Agree to share the glory whose glow you nurse together. Build each word so it trails as invitingly as a stripper's boa. Mount rich upon richer syllable like some extravagant dessert. Open up double- and triple-word spaces like mini-Bastilles for one another's joyful assault. There are more ways to win than to win, you know? This life is too short to be cramped and miserable. And too long.

offerings

The birthdays of parents present special challenges to their children. Kids, of course, have more pockets than dollars to stuff in them, so the birthdays of those who bore and bear them daily become all the more imposing as they draw near. Kids begin with what they have, thinking to throw themselves and their slight accomplishments and possessions on the mercy of adults. (Watch a child let all of his coins fall from a humid little fist on the glass counter at the convenience store. Before he can figure cost or fathom tax, he shows the man all he is worth.) The smallest sibling is sent by his brothers and sisters into the glittery sump of the toy chest to come up with a suitable treasure, but they soon realize that nothing they have to give is of any use. Pointless the sacrifice of a hecatomb of plastic army soldiers. As to the glazed, arthritic pit of Barbies left months ago to their tangled motives, they do not do, they do not do.

So your kids swipe your watches, combs, and rings. They tape them into wads of *Sun-Times* or twist them into cocoons of aluminum foil. The birthdays arrive, and how agreeably you come upon these prodigal bits of yourself in homely packages. (Your kids have been fizzing all morning with the prospect of giving, like candidates for a Rockwell painting or a cereal commercial.) It is one of the sincerest pleasures people have, to turn around and find themselves again before they sense the loss. "Do you really like it?" your children ask, eager because they know you do, you always do. "Are you surprised?" Even without gifts of their own, children have that to offer: a way back to yourself.

At the same time, a darkness moves in. With their loving bluster, in their manic, candied assault, they make you think of your own death. It is cruel and selfish and tragic and crazy, but by the end of the day they make you think of your own death, and of their deaths, too. Your sprawling, wretched death and their tiny demises. What is wrong with you that a simple birthday cannot account for or cure? But there it is: you think of your own undeviating doom, and you turn away from the children. It is your birthday, and you do not want to share.

Before you had kids, back when dying was more or less a matter of late-night metaphysics, your best heaven was something like a bright room continuously replenished with pricey dessert wines and featuring an eternal poker game punctuated by bracing discussions of nineteenth-century novels. But that was back in graduate school, and death was conversational, instead of the gutless abandonment it becomes for a man with a family. Today your dying would be like gobbling the last of the cake and leaving no one else a bite. For their sake you imagine a pre-postmodern deity, a thoroughly unironic God Who plucks souls like ripe berries to drop one by one down His bucket.

These days, when you pray, it is no longer for God, like a patient professor, to clarify His assignment. Where once you asked God to show His hand, now you ask Him to stay it. You want Him to love you beyond what you deserve. For that is the point of love, finally: you need Him not only to love you, but to love you anyway.

◻ ◻ ◻

Last week I hit another squirrel with the Chevy. My third. I have also nailed two dogs, bounced at least two errant sparrows off the driver's side, and found feathers in the grill one evening that indicated other random subtractions from the local fauna. Once, too, I clobbered a raccoon on US 71, which reared up to meet my challenge, his eyes bright with resolve, facing my oncoming lights like a climaxing Lear or some raving general meaning to go down grandly. Two years later there was a coyote on that same highway which actually cost me a headlight. When I confessed that accident at a gas station a few miles further on, two men told me there was a bounty on coyotes and asked if I would mind if they went back to claim the prize. "It's all yours," I told them, but I did not wait around to learn what came of it.

There was a time when I might have gone with them in their truck. As a child, certainly, I would not have passed up anything remotely gothic in the vicinity. I was the ruthless sort—all of us were—who would go out after a heavy rain to goosh through a ravel of worms at the curb. In the glorious truancy of summer, I would take pains to behead the wildflowers, stomp the anthills, lay meticulous waste. Nature takes note and trembles before the rage of the eight-year-old. But as an adult, I had appointments, and I could not bother to join the posse.

Perhaps it is only my attempt to relieve myself of guilt or to keep from questioning my driving ability, of which I am rather proud, but I refuse to think of these animals as emissaries of some inscrutable design. All the nailed, stunned, and squashed scavenge seem to me debris, nothing more. I have read Robinson Jeffers, that tireless and surly attorney for the birds. I have consulted dozens of poets for lessons in the dignity of animals, including Richard Wilbur's toad, Richard Eberhart's groundhog, Denise Levertov's possum, and all of Mary Oliver's decaying carcasses dissolving to "holy protein." They tell me that even in their decrepitude animals disregard and beggar me. They pressure me to invent some ceremony of attention for every dimwit jay that finds my fender. Am I supposed to render an elegy for every one of the butterflies that regularly splash against the windshield? The poets would have me believe that the accidental crackle of a single beetle under a careless boot starts a slow leak in the massive gasworks of all Creation, but I'm not buying. The shoulder of the highway is like a triage site: a turtle with its back snapped, a dog of indiscernible breed in a heap, an armadillo overturned like a catcher's mitt on a closet floor. Countless anonymous insects unknit beneath my tires. Their end is as bewilderingly violent as their original birth bashings against their gluey shells. What do they want from me?

This latest squirrel struck me as particularly intent on his death because he actually tacked into my swerve to avoid him. I cannot guess what recklessness possessed him, what misbegotten sense of sacrifice. In the rearview mirror I saw him do a slow-motion sprawl over backwards—a real swoon, it seemed, a prima donna's dying. I have a version of this event which includes my going back to minister to him or at least bear a bit of witness. In this version, I follow a tiny light as it slides off his eye. Then I edge him off the road. I scrape out enough of a furrow in the dirt to fill with him, then sweep a few leaves and twigs over the grave. Now when winter locks down, it will keep him in place. But of course, this never happened. I never went back to browse, not even days later. I did not try to solve the broken puzzle of him, muttered nothing nearby, dropped no sentiment next to the body. In fact, it was more than a week before I happened to drive down that same street again. By that time, he had already disappeared. Possibly someone dropped him in the garbage or called the authorities to remove him. The city is pretty good about that.

❏ ❏ ❏

Writers make a habit of playing favorites. My favorite word is *shape.* I like its insistence and its delicacy. I like its connotations of creative activity and the modesty it brings to the task. I like its opening hush, keeping the maker humble, and the little kiss as it departs the mouth, like a benediction or a lover's departure.

I have witnessed *vivid* and gladly hosted *supple*. I have tasted the gentle carbonation of *infinitesimal*. I have come with a kind of awe before the prestigious firm of *igneous, sedimentary,* and *metamorphic*. But among all the words I maintain a special fondness for, I positively dote on *shape*.

Meanwhile, I pity the spiky trolls of the language. *Cacophonous* is so, well, cacophonous, a real train wreck of a word. *Lugubrious* trundles clumsily past like the old janitor in ill-fitting clothes. *Arachnid* goes cold behind chain mail. Cursed with flatulence and grime, *carp* can't even get close enough to beg a handout. The vile sugars of *carnal* do secret damage behind the teeth. No love grows near *dung*.

In fact, however, I find myself more drawn to these words despite the stench of homelessness they convey than I am toward more predictable pleasures. *Mellifluous*, for instance, suggests the streetwalker's obviousness and rumors of easy use. In surveys of favored English words, *mellifluous* typically ranks near the top, and I admit that I, too, used to succumb to its flutter and enjoyed its expensive, mentholated charms. Whispering it—it is an intrinsically unshoutable word—I appreciated the furtive appearances of the tongue like a child peeking out from the top of the staircase during the cocktail party. But I have learned to distrust its seductions. I think of those buttery labials, and I wonder: How many have known those lips already? *Mellifluous* is paid to sit in your lap, and while I do not deny its enticements, I keep my hand on my wallet, I count the silverware after *mellifluous* leaves the room. *Quintessence, gossamer, wisteria, lullaby*—their beauties are all frippery, the pushy gaud of flappers. Surely, *savor* has more savor. Or give me the frankness of *conjunction*, a word to do business with. Trust instead the honest clamor of *jukebox*. *Book, loom, knife, water, slump, sleep*—these responsible syllables do not beat around the bush (neither does *beat*, neither does *bush*). They vote regularly and put food on the table.

To my father, making a career out of literature was comparable to making a working motor out of sticks and rubber bands, but I owe him for putting up with my private (and from his perspective, highly questionable) passions. Certainly I had classmates whose tuitions were conditional upon their choosing a viable major. Student deferments had recently been eliminated, so college was no longer a refuge from Vietnam. Most of my friends now had to prove that college would lead to some specific white-collar consequence if they expected to receive financial support from home. My father was a lawyer, and he loved the law for its reasonableness and its practicality. "The law makes sense," he would say, on one of those special occasions when he would unpack himself. Beauty is beautiful when it is accountable. The man had seldom shown interest in words for their own sake. For him, words were for pinning down decisions in heavy dockets. Saussure had never visited City Hall. When it came to contract law, there was no crisis of signification. Words had a firm grasp on Things, thank you very much. If words got skittish like kids in the back seat with Disneyland still hours off, well, then, we can just turn the car around RIGHT NOW, I'M NOT KIDDING. Yes, Dad was a bear for correspondence.

And yet, he once confided in me his affection for *behoove*. "Judges love *behoove*," he said. "They appreciate *behoove*. They really perk up when they hear it. When I suggest that something behooves these proceedings, the court comes around to my way of thinking. Make no mistake, if you invite the court to be behooved, you have them." This came up during a drive back to Chicago from college. Ten quiet miles intervened before he took up the subject again. "*Sabotage* is a good word, too. It sounds subversive. A good, cagey word to use. Have you tried *sabotage?*" he asked, the way one might ask his teenager if he had dabbled in marijuana or socialism. He was smiling, having fun with his first son, but he never took his eyes off the road.

In that same freshman year, I read Flannery O'Connor's "Good Country People." I remember especially how Joy Hopewell commemorated—consecrated, really—her departure from the family that spawned so gruesome an intelligence as hers by changing her name to Hulga. I recall wondering why someone so devoted to renunciation of her origins would return home in the first place. After all, she had a Ph.D. in philosophy from the University of Chicago, sufficient imprimatur, surely, to earn her distance from the stupidity and treacle of girls like Glynese and Carramae (privately called "Glycerin" and "Caramel" by our Joy). "When Mrs. Hopewell thought the name, Hulga, she thought of the broad side of a battleship." It was like the deliberate stomping of the girl's wooden leg. But Hulga is irritated when Mrs. Freeman so relentlessly delights in raising the name like a blunt object against her. Worse, when after snatching her leg Manley Pointer lets her know that she is not so smart after all, "Hulga" drops like bad meat from his mouth. And now the question of how she could have gone home (but she did) became the question of how she could stay after her humiliation (but she would).

And so, as he drove me home for my first vacation, I sensed that my father was indulging me, the way he used to years earlier when he laid spinless pitches in for my batting practice, encouraging even my most pitiful foul tips, in my flailings still finding some promise. I grew pensive over the stubbled monotony of central Illinois, where words drain soundlessly away. As I watched my father brood over the stolid, changeless plain, I realized that he had nothing to do with the snide Mrs. Freeman, whose expressions were limited to the most rudimentary gears: forward, neutral, and reverse. As for Manley Pointer, Dad would have shown that fraud the door. (It would not have taken Freud to figure out the vulgar display in that name and stand between a Manley Pointer and a daughter, even a daughter emboldened by a college education.) No, he had not been mocking me. He just wanted me to take my stance, show him my cut.

Now that I have a child of my own, I understand that there had been something more to that discussion in the car. By talking to me about words, he was implying that my interests had merit. He could not appreciate where my penchants were taking me—in downtown Chicago, that inveterately serious city, you could not say "English major" above the fortieth floor. (Mrs. Hopewell shuddered at the prospect of telling friends that her daughter was a "philosopher." "That was something that had ended with the Greeks and Romans.") What Dad could do was offer me the freedom to pursue what mattered to me.

Mattering was something he could understand, approve of, and defend to friends. "A man has to do the right work for him to be happy," he once said. At the time he had taken me aside to explain why he was leaving his job with Milton Glasner to fend for himself. (*Milton Glasner*—what a wad of stale licorice to gnaw through!) He had worked for Glasner for years and dreaded it daily. Now he was making me a gift of his misgivings. "A man has to do the right work," he repeated. At the time I thought he was talking about himself.

This is what it meant to have an allowance at eighteen. He was letting me go where I was learning I had to go, which is another reason to let your child attend college, after all. As I say, I know better now that I have my own child, who will soon enough insist that I drop her at the corner so as not to have to explain me to the other kids. I have a better sense of what it must have been like for my father eventually to find his pitches batted past him faster than he had sent them toward me. Satisfying and sad. A glimpse of mortality whistling past his ear ... but only for a moment because his boy is on fire with it. "How did you like that one, Dad?" I cried, banging the plate, eager to lay into another, to sabotage the next strike. *Sabotage.* Right. A rich and lovely word.

"What do you read, my lord?" "Words, words, words." "What is the matter, my lord?" Little did he realize that the distracted young man was consumed by an oath he had sworn before the ghost of his father.

In talking to me about words, my father also had been trying to get a glove on my drives. We were nearing the day when he could not honestly put anything past me. Perhaps that was on his mind afterwards as we rode together in silence. After a while, to fill the space that opened before us, I tried to find a game on the radio. Dad tried to see how many cars he could pass before I-57 disappeared into the Kennedy.

◻ ◻ ◻

My father died last Memorial Day, fittingly, I guess, for most of what I knew of him had to do with soldiering. Going to work and back, going for treatment and back—he was on constant reconnaissance (truly a word to reckon with). Over his grave we lingered to recall his jokes and his gestures, his moods and his words. Now I give his words back to him. Here is the *right work* you prized. Do you recognize it? It is yours. Take back *behoove*, which you once told me you won with. I am returning the *law*, with its grace and good sense. I lay *sabotage* beside you. Know that I labor in your name. Accept my best, my loving words.

call it in the air

It takes a crowd to dissipate the shame of a dateless Friday night. Hiding out in a library carrel, renting out an isolated table at the pool hall, or simply taking his disillusionment at ten o'clock to bed is no consolation to the solitary undergraduate, as useless as trying to duck his own stink. That is why so many of us at college collected at the Auditorium for the weekly midnight movie, to justify our splintered disappointments and anonymous stresses by gathering and binding them together into a guided mass. It had nothing to do with the movie, which, whether hackneyed or whoring, was always low-budget and clumsy and begging for sarcasm. It had everything to do with being counted among the meld. It had to do with gathered heat. The forgettable film was never the issue, anyway. While it was featured in order to be forgotten—a laxative to speed the passage of another sluggish Friday night—we were the show.

And as the show, we had more responsibility than "audience" implied. We participated. We performed. We filled in the gaps with comments, applying caustics to widen the wounds to sensibility the movie gushed from. As it gassed haplessly along, with knightly Hudson predictably lumbering toward jocund Day or a single reefer transforming teenaged Jekylls into manic Hydes, we urged ourselves on. We preened at the screening of our estimable, clever, relentless selves.

But the zenith of our achievement preceded the film altogether. Every week, beginning a good twenty minutes before the showing, there was a paper airplane competition. The indeterminate signal was given, and out of the upper balcony the staggered sorties commenced. The discipline admitted all manner of mutation and infinite variety. Some were honed and some haphazard; some were groomed and some ungainly. Full-grown flyers strove against fledglings, and the richly garnished knocked hulls with the spare. That the technology was disposable did not detract from the exhibition; on the contrary, because the building of paper aircraft carried no ulterior motives—weekends were by definition gradeless—it was one of the purer labors conducted on campus. The competition earned no prize, no purse, and no renown—no one could follow the most successful flights reliably back to the hands that launched them—so it was rendered all the loftier for its nonutilitarian commitment. In short, it was art.

From below the domed ceiling of the auditorium, we could imagine that the atmosphere was being scored by dozens of invisible glide paths. We were like children rapt beneath the bright distensions of immense cartoon characters bellying over them at the Macy's Thanksgiving Day Parade, or like tourists drawn up before the vaulted Genesis at the Sistine Chapel. True, many of the planes sank before they ever soared. Some torqued in upon themselves, wrenched backward, or simply wilted; some suddenly seized up mid-excursion and dropped the way Wile E. Coyote would whenever he realized he'd dashed past the edge of the cliff and was running on the void; some darted down, spun down, plunged down as though struck with afterthoughts or pangs of regret, and these were booed with vigor, as though we'd risked tuition on them. If the goal was to strike the screen, many, like star-struck high schoolers hoping to make it in Hollywood, were turned away after only the briefest glance at their capacities. Only rarely is the dream of altitude answered, and we were always a tough audience.

But once the pretenders had sputtered, the architecture and engineering students took up their positions. Now we readied ourselves for the real spectacle, the main event. One by one, like supermodels flourishing solo down the runway, the pride of the air force coursed over us.

The best were unrecognizable as planes per se. They were projectiles, teasing and tumbling in currents we could only assume but that their makers accounted for with certainty. The fastest would bite and dive like seabirds, or like Howard Nemerov's blue swallows—those ambiguous incisors, those ghostwriters that carved mysterious calligraphies, evanescent and undivinable—autograph the sky. But our greatest fascination rose for the slowest, for slowness gave us the chance to contemplate and admire. (We may be impressed at a moment's notice— the radiant lash of the falling star—but holiness grows in the spaces we have time to cultivate.) The slow ones abided by a different aerodynamic: they were measured ventures, manifestations of poise, hovercrafts, luxury cruisers. One by one, dreamy cylinders, rhomboids, and cones stole past in a steady, speculative drift—God's own geometry, or perfect polygons wafting directly out of Platonic theory. Tacking and dodging drafts, they rode the complicated thermals ascending from our eagerness and wonder below. Like Shakespeare's Cleopatra, regal in her element and barging opulently through the second act, they took their time, taking time by prerogative. Like Jorie Graham's paper bag in "So Sure of Nowhere Buying Times Magically to Come," magically borne up and along by freeway fumes, "quarrying the emptiness for furling laws," they suggested songs or what we could presume for souls. They led charmed lives, and we could suppose some vague, saintly assurance guided them— yes, the sort of faith that lifted saints out of physics—so serenely they proceeded over nothingness. And so, somehow inspired in that blank surround, adhering to some unknown syntactic resolve, they took every subtle implication of the air and eased, without flinch or shudder, toward the screen, until finally, in a series of noiseless, almost tender concussions, they began to collide with it. Then they started swooning like a squad of divas to the stage floor, and we stood and cheered the way NASA personnel did, amazed at the touchdown they themselves had plotted against the night. The way I remember it, the projectionist was savvy enough to wait until the show was over and all the elegant litter had come to rest before he started that other feature we had come to see.

I have since learned that dancers have a term for what we were marveling at: *ballon*. It means protracted elevation, or nearly means that, because nuance lifts it just out of reach of translation. You see it in the ballet dancer's disdain for the gravity that keeps the patrons in their seats. It is in the leap that seems to leap again, as if, grazing heaven, the spirit were making a last plea against the earth's judgment. Call it ecstasy, for the body is a walled city to be scaled, with every station of flesh and bone a bureaucracy that holds us up and holds us down. Because it promises, if only for a moment, to transcend the creaky machinery of being, to relinquish the sullen self—in Richard Wilbur's phrase, "to win for once over the world's weight"—*ballon* is a quality of unselfconsciousness. I once saw Michael Jordan submit to a sitting on *60 Minutes* as a scientist, referring to a battery of graphs and stop-action videotapes, dissected the secret of His Airness's ability to stay in the air so long on his way to the slam. As the scientist went blandly on like a skeptic inverting a magician's sleeves, Jordan looked embarrassed and, worse, disturbed. He could barely bring himself to watch.

I have never experienced any athletic version of *ballon*, although I've often fantasized about swinging a deal for any number of sentences I may have risen to, but I have a theory about airplanes that I think glosses Jordan's response. Basically, I believe that heavier-than-air flight is impossible. What is more, I am convinced that other people—most other people, actually, in fact, most *passengers*—believe that it is impossible, too. So when we do get ready for takeoff, the first thing that must be suspended is our shared disbelief. As long as we don't give each other that knowing look—that look of intelligent panic that says, This isn't happening! There's no way to keep tons of us up here!—we'll straighten up and fly right. On the other hand, if we all suddenly confront what must be true, and an epidemic of doubt spreads through the cabin, we will drop like, well, like something that weighs as much as we do must, and whistle Wile E. Coyote-fashion down to the same puff of dust he does, ending up flat as cartoons. But we don't, and we don't, and whatever sanction let us rise keeps us sliding along this solid, hypothetical length, and we sit back, barely aware of the splendid tension that makes it happen, much as Jordan doesn't dwell upon his distance since last touching the gym floor.

It must be faith that rallies our physics, that keeps our spirits up after all.

In John Updike's *Rabbit, Run*, Harry Angstrom, whose best basketball was left on the court a decade earlier, who often finds himself winded and baffled and betrayed by the world's weight and his own, is surprised to discover *ballon* on the golf course. After numerous indignant, unnatural hacks, he suddenly, unaccountably strikes grace:

[H]e looks at the ball, which sits high on the tee and already seems free of the ground. Very simply he brings the clubhead around his shoulder into it. The sound has a hollowness, a singleness he hasn't heard before. His arms force his head up and his ball is hung way out, lunarly pale against the beautiful black blue of storm clouds, his grandfather's color stretched dense across the east. It recedes along a line straight as a ruler-edge. Stricken: sphere, star, speck. It hesitates, and Rabbit thinks it will die, but he's fooled, for the ball makes his hesitation the ground of a final leap: with a kind of visible sob takes a last bite of space before vanishing in falling.

Simple, mysterious, unitary, definite, complete. The ball's *ballon* confirms the firmament and bubbles the blood, marks

divinity and mocks death. If it must dwindle ultimately, it does
so toward heaven, rejecting the premises of the terrestrial. In this
passage, the ground is not the destination but the foundation of
a final leap; so that like the sentence that describes it, the ball
denies closure, springing into higher and higher valences, refut-
ing embodiment, free. For a time.

"Happiness is ... equilibrium. Shift your weight." The line
belongs to Henry, from Tom Stoppard's *The Real Thing*. Henry is
a playwright who argues that ideas will not take off without
well-written words to drive them, the way a good cricket bat,
"cunningly put together in a certain way so that the whole thing
is sprung, like a dance floor," can make the ball sail. Happiness
is riding on that airy cushion, treading deftly over the ellipsis—
ballon sprung from punctuation—so as not to break the spell.

For *ballon* is buoyancy, and buoyancy is happiness. Watch a
seal cleave the sea and seem to peel out of its bulk. Watch
Stanley Elkin ramify a paragraph, nurse it lovingly toward what
must be its last moments, then resuscitate it with the shock of
metaphor, in the return to cadence rediscover a pulse, or stave
off rictus with another alliterative lift. "Listen, disdain's easy, a
mug's game," he writes in *The Making of Ashenden*, "but look close
at anything and you'll break your heart." Elkin feasts and fattens
on anything he happens upon, and like a dog excited by the out-
doors, he can barely go a block without getting distracted, shov-
ing his muzzle in, and coming up with something unexpected,
organic, and impossible to part with. Here, from *The
Bailbondsman*, is one of hundreds of Elkin set-pieces worth mount-
ing on their own:

The street had changed. Not so much money here, not as much taste,
but even more style. The shops burst with an egoism of the present
tense, the bright letters of the bright wood signs molded in a sausage
calligraphy like those quick, clever strokes that leg and backbone animals in balloon-blowing acts. Or black, no capitals, a svelte, spare
geometry of case. He remembers these shops, could tell you stories,

recalls like a perfect witness their former, failed incarnations. The woman's shoe store, Bootique, was once Kefauver's campaign head-quarters, then a bookie joint with empty cigar boxes and tire irons half-heartedly showing form's flag in a casual lip-service hypocrisy in the front window. After that nothing at all for a time—though once, initially, Tyson's Liquors, as he still thinks of it, really. Most of the shops won't last the year. But never till now, the witness thinks, so uniform, locked into style's faddish contagion, a terminal domino theory. What discrepancies he perceives between will and doom, these tenants' signs like life's campaign buttons. He looks for reasons but sees only the irrational, a self-conscious hedonism. The signs, these shops, this business and that enterprise, this landscape, seasonal as the pictures on one of his calendars, are all jokes. The toy shop, with its expensive Creative Playthings and Chinese boxes and big stuffed animals and folk dolls and folk tops and folk sticks and folk hoops and folk balls and miniature green and black boilers of real steam engines for curator kids who never existed, is called—in rainbow letters, yes, it is the rainbow sequence: yellow catching green, green blue and so on, on the glass—"Kinder Garden." And the butcher shop, sawdust on the floor like cereal and the butchers in boaters, and skinned, unrefrigerated rabbits, plucked chickens and carcasses upside down on hooks that could hold coats, is "The Meating House."

I pause here, although Elkin does not—he perseveres through *fifteen more* examples because every bad pun is too good to lose—to savor the carbonation he generates. I'd like briefly to anatomize his method, at the risk of having the author posthumously cringe before literary criticism the way Jordan did before kinesiology. "The street has changed" in another conversation would be so casual and pedestrian an observation that the casual pedestrian would just keep walking. But with the mention of "style," Elkin is off. In the next sentence, he sets off bursts of *b*'s and verbs "leg" and "backbone" in the service of associative novelty. He notes "style's faddish contagion" on a street surrendered to kitsch, and in noting it at such length he sponsors his own stylized contagion, one that navigates the middle course "between will and doom" more artfully than the bewitchingly awful advertisements can. The blare of "self-conscious hedonism" has nothing on the sort the author practices in declaiming it, which turns out to be the healthiest enterprise, the most going of the going businesses on the page.

That anyone in an Elkin fiction would characterize the landscape as "all jokes" is at the very least ironic, given how irrepressible a comedian is in charge. Elkin is a comic who never resists an encore, who forever demonstrates that any bit worth doing bears overdoing, who contends that funniness does not respond to "Cut!" He has the gift of making us forget that there is some plotworthy something other than his obsession to pursue. Who could help but linger with him? Who would be so crass as to admonish such democratic love of stuff, such yeasty linguistics, such richly marbled wry?

As for *ballon*, try hitching a ride on either of the last two sentences I've quoted. The prepositional phrase does not modify so much as bury "the toy shop" in inventory, whose stash includes "folk dolls and folk tops and folk sticks and folk hoops and folk balls"—as individuated a census as one might reasonably require, with all the "folk" variations linked by "ands" like a family grasping hands at Thanksgiving. Sixty-two syllables are sustained before Elkin pauses for a comma, and then he rejoins the itemization in progress, skewering another squiggling set of descriptors between dashes like a hot cob between cornholders—and even this interpolation is pestered by qualification ("yes, it *is* the rainbow sequence"), as from an interior colon sprouts another tributary that does not end but continues out of sight into the undergrowth of "and so on." The toy shop is called "Kinder Garden," but the sentence's coming attractions—its extended preview and acrobatic opening act—let us rove and play in the store before the purchase is made and well past closing. In the next sentence, the butcher shop, too, packs the same baggage for takeoff and likewise hovers for several breathless, alliterative details before coming in for a tight landing on its tiny predicate.

Ballon keeps Robert Frost intact while climbing birches "Up to the brim, and even above the brim," and from that wistful, iffy perch he gets a glimpse of heaven, before earthly love threatens to snatch him back. It encourages John Keats to float "on the viewless wings of Poesy" after an unsuspecting nightingale, trusting the trajectory of his craving to direct him and the crafted ode to carry him "away into the forest dim." His reverie keeps him aloft for half a dozen stanzas until the fancy shatters, and he must clamber back before pitching irrevocably over the edge of reality. Sublime cadences would cushion those falls, else the poets would plummet through torn haloes like the one that sometimes traces the wake of the tragicomic coyote. In every episode he drops down the same invisible chute, holding up a YIKES! sign and leaving an instant's silhouette of dismay. In every episode he is amazed by the crush of self.

There is a level at which the exploits of springy athletes and the sprung rhythms of elevating writers connect. There is a consensus of aspiration between nearly weightless paper planes and Warner Brothers cartoons as they take turns patrolling indeterminate space. There is a spiritual principle on display in the tug of the kite whose string goes taut and cuts into the fist. It is in the mind of the child who makes a cape out of a blanket and bids Mommy watch as he flings himself, flying without doubt, from the bed. It is in the urge of the surfer to squeeze as much play as possible out of the dying wave. It is in the oratory of the tragic hero as he scales his awful fate. Each exertion is a prayer for an extra second's sense of release from the mundane. The sacred waits just above the brim and, except for cherished, fleeting stretches, forbidden.

At one of those midnight movies, a few students much the worse for beer broke into the projection room and toppled the equipment. The projector continued to grind away for thirty seconds or so on its side, so that people were walking, chasing, loving, grieving vertically, frame by frame literally rising to the occasion. The rowdies let loose, as you would expect; but still, it was a reprieve from the familiar story of exploding vehicles and exposed fleshes. As I say, it was less than a minute before order and linearity were restored. But I bet that I was not the only one who was a little disappointed. I feel it more keenly now that my last midnight movie ended some twenty-five years ago. I wish it could have gone on longer. Well, such is life. I say, keep it up.

poetasting

Bringing the Poet to campus is a project. Like one of the cartoon dirigibles wafting over the Macy's Thanksgiving Day Parade, his transcendent presence has taken many hands on many lines to conduct here. Before the Poet begins reading, he thanks the Campus Activities Board, the College Arts Council, the English Department, the Live Poets Society, the Faculty Development Committee, as well as the College President and all members of the campus community in attendance. Think of the men of the *Pequod* bringing a whale to bay. Think of the Lilliputians scrambling over the sleeping Gulliver, thread by thread lashing him down. There was a lunch to buy, and tonight a dinner and reception. Thanks to the Lunch Committee, to the Reception Committee. Someone had to drive to the airport to fetch him. Someone has taken care to set up the table where the poet's books will be signed and sold. Gratitude makes its systematic way to the far wall, in that take-one-pass-the-rest-back manner that is customary in classrooms. Has anyone been missed?

❐ ❐ ❐

Back in his hotel room are the notes he brought from home and which have dogged him from venue to venue. On the plane he brought out the old standbys—birds, sea, trees, light—to try to settle himself on this bad bed of a page. The stanza he had arranged for them, however, was slack and nondescript. It was, he knew, a temporary holding pen for the usual suspects.

He is telling his audience about dogs. Sometimes composing a poem is like taking a dog for a walk, he explains. Sometimes the dog has to be dragged away from distractions or out of its doggy daze to do its business. Sometimes he chuffs along right at your side and at your pace, and writing seems as regular and reliable as any other errand. Sometimes he gathers speed and purpose you hadn't counted upon, and you have to release the leash and let him run to save your hands. The Poet waits to let the image set. Of course, he continues, he is either chasing squirrels or hurrying to a favored spot to relieve himself, and neither instinct does much to glamorize writing. Two, three, four. This is the sort of urbanity and charming self-deprecation the Poet is renowned for. This is what makes him a tour favorite, and he does not disappoint this evening.

◻ ◻ ◻

The Poet has needs. Here are some of the things the Poet needs: fresh coffee, Ecuadorian preferably, but a lower Caribbean alternative will serve; a competitive tennis partner, no worse than a "B" player from the 35 to 50 age-bracket on a standard amateur ladder; a tobacco-free space in which to prepare and, later, in which to give his reading (his having only recently given up the habit). Otherwise, a lectern, a table, a pitcher of ice water, a glass. The constrained amenities of performance.

◻ ◻ ◻

The new poem is no poem yet. It is an incontinent slump of a thing so far. Listless, unregenerate, it shames him, that lazy off-spring that pulls up the covers against the daylight, refusing to find decent employment. He cannot talk about it yet.

❏   ❏   ❏

The Poet extracts chapbooks from his briefcase like a magician unpacking his trick birds. Like the wings of birds, too, or like porkchops, or like the courtesans in Italian films, forever weary and available in their beds, his books have a permanent splay to them. Their covers, wearing titles like *More Light* and *A Gape of Days*, are permanently creased from the year's reading tour; they are richly feathered with bookmarkers, themselves strategically numbered—an oral batting order. The Poet carries himself like the week's load of laundry, but he has this down, the rhythm of poem-generative anecdote-poem, the accomplished shamble of the credentialed bohemian. Poise and dishevelment; eminence no necktie shall fetter, nor suit suit.

❏   ❏   ❏

The Poet does confess his misgivings. There was a time when the poem "Tunnel Vision," for instance, played Angel to his Jacob, and it seemed that he would never wrestle that figure in the second stanza to the ground. This, too, is scripted; he told the same story on another campus just a week ago, sighing at the same cue. The Poet goes on to describe his compensations: those happy, unbidden times when the phrases tumbled in bright packages before him. He says that writers are hunter-gatherers at heart, letting their instincts range over the land-scape. Writers tune in, happen upon, overhear, he tells them.

Some are taking notes. Most are smiling knowingly, not knowing how even now, even as he dilates about the accom-plished, anthologized fate of the poem he is about to read, he is working over the gristle of a stubborn metaphor somewhere in the metaphorical back of his metaphorical teeth. Our best writ-ers were all magnificently bothered, he says, before he submits a new poem for their approval, and from the cozy universe of wannabes and hangers-on, of those who posted the ads, baked the walnut chocolate chip cookies, or chose the creative writing elective, comes universal approval.

◻ ◻ ◻

The way an octopus spews a cloud of ink to cover his escape, he thinks. Or is it a squid? He will have to check. Isn't it the male octopus that breaks out in stripes when it encounters a potential mate? He will have to remember to remember to check. Then the octopus tumbles aqueously off into indefiniteness. Or the squid does. An ooze of mood. A moody ooze. Oozing mood. Elusive. It bears consideration, and, in any event, it will be a reprieve from the fuddled poem at the hotel. Unless ... there was that poem he did about the viviparous lizard, which spurts blood to spook predators. Was this the same territory? How often has he skimmed legitimate disciplines for odd facts and phrases. How often has he, with his unwholesome appetite, raided the zoo.

It is the octopus, he later discovers, which, by the way, caresses the female with seven deft tentacles while inserting the eighth, laden with sperm deposits, through her breathing hole and into the vital chamber for fertilization. Splendid, he thinks, rapping the book against the table edge. That will work some-where, surely.

◻ ◻ ◻

Question: What advice would you give to young poets?
Poet: Advice? Since when do poets take advice? But don't worry. I have never met a young poet. There is no such thing as a young poet.

◻ ◻ ◻

Balance in all things, always. The Poet has a lump that worries him. Not a lump exactly, but a definite hardness, which is either new or has gone undetected until recently. He does not cancel his appearances for the week of the 15th, but he makes an appointment for the day after he returns. The compromise seems to him practical without being alarmist, and altogether sensible.

◻ ◻ ◻

Meanwhile, there is the ongoing world, the world of vigorous, dependable, and studied functions, which he knows only enough about to tap for jargon. He has a guy to do his taxes; another guy does his gutters; another his grout, not the gutter guy, the gutter guy being a specialist who doesn't descend. There is a guy who drags himself elbow by elbow beneath the Poet's house every November to change the furnace filter, and although he has felt his subterranean exertions beneath his feet, the Poet does not know his last name.

The ongoing world goes on, and the poet has no alternative but to trust. His brother, an attorney, is his attorney. When the sitter used to come for the kids, he would return to tend manuscript unashamed. On the other hand, one of the reasons he enjoys going to the gym is for the how-about-those-Giants and the damn-Chevys and the hard-frost's-comings; it is an hour's ducking out of responsibilities at the desk, eluding for a time what for everyone else is elsewhere. Also, health is a regimen like everything else, and he does have a family history of coronary disease to contend with. ("I got the pressure," his father used to say, a resonant mantra that found its way into the elegy "The Gentlemanly Doom," a shifty favorite at readings.) An hour, then it's back to offices, appointments, company trucks, and, for him, the regular stroke, stroke, stroke across the medium.

◻ ◻ ◻

The Poet winces inwardly at an easy figure from an early poem. I have never finished a poem, not really, he once told an interviewer for *Outpost*. An honest poem never stanches the flow of blood for long. It was a graceful way of putting it, all things considered. That line found its way into *Their Words' Worth: A Poet's Companion*, and it had since become a common touchstone for introductions to his readings. The review of *Final Notice to Disconnect* in the New York *Times* explicated the reference: "Particularly in 'The Horses of Instruction' and the volume's title poem, the bloodstains show through." Awkwardness, arbitrariness, misgiving—even the scandal of futility must be arranged as elegant expression. A writer's crisis must still make for good copy somehow. Words desert, but, so far, quotably.

❐ ❐ ❐

Here is a partial list of awards that the Poet has not won: the Nobel Prize, the Pulitzer Prize, the National Book Award, the Pushcart Prize, the Yale Younger Poets Award, the Lannan Foundation Award. He has, however, won a Guggenheim, three fellowships, a grant from the NEA, awards from several contests (the Hamilton Galbreath Illumination Award, the *Local Imperative* Annual Prize, the *Plead the Fifth* Honorary, a check from *The Way Always* for the year's best poem about Christian purpose, a check from *Game Seven* for the year's best poem about a sporting event, the *Word Up* Poetry Achievement Award and Medallion, the *Green Thoughts in a Green Shade* Prize for a poem about protecting the environment for the next generation, among others), which he has alphabetized for a promotional flyer. He has also resided eminently as a guest artist at four universities, with a fifth plum residence pending. He has also been granted an honorary doctorate from his graduate university, with which he has contracted to store his papers, but thinking about that vaguely troubles him with intimations of mortality. The papers will be all the more valuable and sought after once he is gone. The thought of his manuscripts, notes, and letters absorbing radiation in the elite company of the Special Collection does little to console him on that score. The price of eminence has always been too high, he believes, but it sounds too crafted and unworthy a statement, and he lets it fade.

◻ ◻ ◻

In the course of years of responding to questions on his reading tours, the Poet has compared himself to the following: carpenter, false prophet, public liar, termite, carnival barker, good liar, bad politician, exterminator, snake oil salesman, antidote, hopeless liar, rash scratcher, erudite masturbator, word cop, clown with a dictionary, ham to be egged on, thief, disease. His going rate for readings is now up in the neighborhood of two thousand dollars per appearance, plus expenses.

◻ ◻ ◻

Question: There has been a lot of talk in literary circles over the past couple of decades about the so-called death of the author. What is your take on the death of the author?
Poet: Good riddance.

◻ ◻ ◻

What the Poet loves best about his work is the scraw of his fountain pen against the page when that page is supported by the leather face of his notebook. It sounds and feels like the tearing of thousands of tiny threads. It is no mere affectation to write this way in the age of computers, not if one truly loves the sensations. Precision, intelligence, expensiveness. The self-indulgence. What began as a mannerism is now a necessity. When the writing is coming along, working and repose seem to him indistinguishable. When the going is hard and the page stiffens against his progress, he seems to see himself in his chair like a study in brown. Then it is harder to love. So is he. On those occasions, he relies on the trick of spending a fresh sheet of paper, one that hasn't had all the possibilities scraped off of it yet.

❑ ❑ ❑

From the Poet's *SubText* interview: "At times I despair of transmitting abstractions altogether. Well, 'despair' may be wrong, but I am skeptical. Instead, we might do better to restrict ourselves to physical sensations. Let us not speak of longing but of sinus pressure. Our relationship with God is like our relationship with the strawberry seed that impacts in one's back teeth and resists the most diligent efforts of the tongue. You want to know grief? Try sciatica. Better to wiggle the sprain or scratch the rash than cast lines into empty airiness."

The Poet was given the opportunity to look over the interview in manuscript form before it went to press, and it was this passage that most troubled him. Not that it wasn't accurate, but his hesitations seemed pre-filtered and his uncertainties self-assured. Not that *that* wasn't accurate. He ultimately decided to let his comments stand on their own and let others decide what they revealed about him. It seemed, finally, the mature thing to do. The worthy thing. So much of his time was like a review of the troops, all guarded moments. All of this self-editing, like picking one's scabs. Stop it, or they'll never heal. He mailed the damn thing back: wrong, but to his credit, unmarked.

❑ ❑ ❑

Question: Who are your favorite poets among your contemporaries? What other poets have influenced you?
Poet: I read haphazardly, with delight, and at my peril. The worst and best gifts I ever receive are books of poetry, which publishers, colleagues, and other poets send me regularly. I

never buy any. Other poets influence me by pissing me off, which helps.

□ □ □

In the dream, a virus has broken out in the language. Every utterance seems an acronym he cannot divine or, like the condensed messages on vanity license plates, part of a private code to which he cannot find the key. Words lie broken like accident victims along the road, or they have gone soft as Dali's melting clocks and drape uselessly against the few nouns in the vicinity. With the unnamed catastrophe having spread so far, he realizes that soon it will all be grunts and moans only. He finds himself longing for the familiar chafe of meter, the static cling of alliteration. He opens his mouth to cry or comment, invoke or intone, but there is nothing but the O his mouth surrounds, and it gives off no sound at all. When he awakens, he finds that none of this works as a poem, a situation he eventually turns into another poem.

□ □ □

The Poet is an excellent driver. He also mows his own lawn. He also coached Little League for two seasons. His cooking is, admittedly, only serviceable, but he built the shelves in his front room himself. His reputation for irascibility and eccentricity has survived these facts. In addition, according to his *SubText* interview, he is a fan of the San Francisco Giants, several progressive rock bands, and *Seinfeld*, although he admits that, owing to the demands of teaching, writing, and travel, he has not been to a game or a concert in years and only catches the odd rerun.

□ □ □

Question: How would you characterize yourself politically?

Poet: All writers are conservative by nature, I suppose, but really, I am not political in any systematic or deliberate sense. I am not all that tactful, even. I do vote, however. I reserve my rotten citizenship for the page. On the other hand, I cannot remember ever refusing to sign a petition in my life. Not once. And always, so far as I am aware, without repercussion.

❏ ❏ ❏

With a subpoena, with an eviction notice, with a complaint signed by all of his neighbors, the poem-in-waiting waits for him in his hotel room. It wants to know where he was on the night in question. It has compromising pictures of him. It has been waiting for a long time to take its revenge. It has the papers on him. The drop. The goods. When he opens the door, it will be glowering there, smacking a rolling pin menacingly against its palm.

❏ ❏ ❏

A photograph of the Poet's study appears in a coffee-table book about the places writers do their writing. Looking through his complimentary copy, the poet finds that his study keeps more or less to the general decorum of what the photographer/editor calls in her introduction "dependable dishevelment, in which the seeming chaos is revealed as flourishing possibility." The basic premise of the book is that writers' studies will relinquish their magic to lingering inspection—a point the photographer/editor makes when she connects her visual artifacts with the verbal artifacts that make us wonder about the circumstances of their production. Comparing the black-and-white photograph to the study itself, the Poet recalls Mavis Gallant's comment that she has "lived in writing, like a spoonful of water in a river." What the photograph is missing is the stratified smoke on the walls and ceiling, the carbonizing layers of dead plant and animal

matter—he is slow about tending to the ficus, and he has had
two cats in the past eleven years, both gone now—and the odor
of time. The Poet never confessed to her that the poem of his
she singled out for admiration during their conversation was
partly produced in a restaurant bathroom. Nevertheless.

◻ ◻ ◻

Question: Do you worry about the future of poetry? What, in
your opinion, is the future of poetry?
Poet: I am not worried about the future of poetry. Poetry has
invested wisely over the years. Poetry has been alert to fluctua-
tions in the market. It has a diversified portfolio. We should all
be so lucky.

◻ ◻ ◻

The Poet is an event. His campus escort is also reporting for the
campus newspaper. She quotes to him from the back cover of one
of his volumes, which promises that his poems are "teeming with
insights and intensities." The blurb was provided by a friend,
another poet, for whose volume the Poet later provided a blurb
of his own. "I blurbed for you. Now it's your turn to blurb for me,"
he hums to himself. His escort is too young to remember the tune
he is remembering. She is part expectancy, part accusation. Oh,
God, the Poet thinks, she is waiting for me to teem.

◻ ◻ ◻

A mountain of notes is waiting for him. A mogul of notes. A note
mogul. He works this over at the buffet provided by the English
Department, a limp geometry of sliced meats and cheeses. There
are brownies, too, baked by undergraduates. The hallway is
lined with posters, which feature xeroxed replicas of his book
jacket photograph, now a slur of grays—the I-strain of infinite

division and duplication—and the promise of refreshments. He selects a morsel from every partition and every plate, so as not to offend. Woozily he bears attention, praise, sheepish ministrations. Is "mogul" the word? It is difficult to correlate some days, and the Poet gratefully accepts a chair. Some days you can't get anything to snowball out of the slush, he thinks, choking off the conceit, but he has said this aloud, and the young woman who found him the chair straightens, decides whether she has been edified or insulted or if they should have gone, budget be damned, with the caterer after all.

◻ ◻ ◻

Poet: The rumor, and it is a rumor to which both writers and their readers consent, is that poets take on their topics the way dentists handle their appointments, grinding down edginess into smooth, tractable syllables. That is not what they do, or at least, it is not what I do. It does not feel to me that that is what I do. Everything bustles by, and possibly something of that everything grazes you, and when you look for it, it is already past you, hooded, head down. You are maybe a bit mystified, maybe a little rapt—do not underestimate the value of raptness, the gift of mystification—so you bring out the words like the extra chairs for unexpected guests, and you move them around. You know, you play them off against each other, rearrange, inflect the essence. You want to encourage the world to drop a little something in your beggar's bowl as it goes on its way, that's all. And to get that much, you have to make the words perform first because they are as ordinarily self-absorbed as the world you want to accost, or enchant, or upbraid, or forgive, or whatever, you see what I mean? As for understanding, well, you don't really try to understand so much as make do. A poem makes do. But a poem is an apology, too. I think I can say that every poem is an apology. Of a sort.

I'm sorry, but does that answer your question?

❐ ❐ ❐

According to form, the Poet is paid before he leaves. The check is in a white envelope with the college letterhead. It is unobtrusively passed to him during dinner by the department chairman, with the conspiratorial cheerfulness of a corrupt banker in a melodrama or an uncle at a bar mitzvah. The first time he ever played out this ritual, the Poet excused himself to use the bathroom and ran the water to cover his tearing it open. Today, as has become his custom, he will wait until his plane is in the air.

❐ ❐ ❐

We hope to make up time in the air, the pilot announces. The Poet settles back to make up time. The plane shreds sumptuous veils of cloud, maintaining altitude, and rides a steady vector as the Poet dozes. When once or twice he lifts out of dream, he sees a spill of golden hair over the arm of the seat in front of him—a child is sleeping in the collapse of innocence, or so poetry would have us believe. Poets should know better, the Poet thinks, and he works his way out of his drowse to locate his briefcase on the floor and position it on his lap before drifting off again. The pilot burbles something about moving about being free. If he cranes his neck, the Poet can just see the line of horizon receding over the slope of the world, faster the faster they go.

a gambler's chance

As a premium for lasting out a junket in Las Vegas many years ago, my father received from Caesar's Palace a dozen metal golf tees tipped in white gold, which were housed like a dandy's cigarettes in a white gold case. Every year the host casino came up with a different bit of intricate plunder as a parting gift for the visiting aristocracy. A pair of dice with ruby pips, jade facsimiles of thousand-dollar chips, cufflinks shaped like roulette wheels in whose miniature channels spun tiny diamonds—the annual valedictory munificence, as though the high rollers were luxury liners to be littered with confetti as they left the docks.

While my mother, inverately practical, a list maker all of her life and as reliable as the tide in reconciling the checkbook, held my father for questioning about wins and losses, my brother and I stole off with the more exotic booty. Even as children we realized that those jeweled dice would not roll out cleanly or lie flat, that the roulette wheel cufflinks could not be wagered on or worn, that the commemorative chip would not stack or spend. Gaudiness was an impasse and an end in itself. Dad's prizes were preening and useless, which is to say that they were works of art.

Usually Mom was able to enjoy the ingenuity behind these bits of super-concentrated capital, but somehow she could not comprehend the gold-tipped golf tees.

"You don't intend to *use* them, do you?" she asked.

"Of course. They work. You can't hurt them, you know. I already shot eighteen with them. They're golf tees."

"But, Bob. I mean, no one even sees the gold. You put them in the ground, right, and ... Bob, *no one sees the gold!*"

"Nevertheless."

"Nevertheless" put the pin to the blimp, as it often did. Rational argument was no match for it. Logic found no breach in the shield. Had my father sported a heraldic crest, "Nevertheless" would have been emblazoned across it, or better yet, would have ribboned in the mouth of an eagle clutching a gold-tipped tee in each talon. Dad was a prodigiously stubborn man—*stu-boor-REN*, as my mother would pronounce it, as though the word were a dress shoe that the dog would not let drop.

"Nevertheless" meant that the point was not the point. King Lear wanted his knights because he *wanted* them. I remember the question posed years later in a class I took on British literature: why, when Cordelia refused to play along with any public display of daughterly affection, did Lear not shut it down? It was, after all, his party, his performance, his play. Top billing must count for something. What was a king if not the embodiment of prerogative? Ah, but that is not the sort of thinking that gets you comp'd at Caesar's. Perhaps it was not righteousness but risk that filled monarchy's dimension. When Lear warned the obstinate Cordelia that "Nothing will come of nothing," he also unwittingly provided a creed for every gambler who draws for the inside straight. Tragic heroes always take the long odds.

So if Shakespeare's heroes could be outfitted with dictions as excessive as their destinies, Dad could sport tees of gold. When the prodigal Prince Hal proposed to mend into Henry V, he paved his premises with iambic pentameter. When Cleopatra barged into Act II, an entourage of worshipful modifiers led the way. For Shakespeare, majesty came down in a drenching reign of alliteration. As his sundry Caesars and numbered Richards roused, as they rose from grand to grander agitation, only the

overdone would do for them; and only death began to deflate
the high sentence they regularly ascended to. When ruling force
is shorn of ornament, its subjects bow but never can adore. That
was Dad's determination, too—Dad, who always kept his bills in
a silver clip, the highest denomination facing out, and who used
a silver lighter etched with an obscure crest that nonetheless
conferred substance upon him as he lit the cigarettes he wasn't
supposed to smoke.

Bluffs are exciting because they are dangerous. Being bluffed, however, can do no worse than embarrass you.
              —David Winkler, *The Compleat Gambler* (1951), p. 31

You know the joke: my father kept reading about how cigarettes are bad for your health, so he decided to cut down on his
reading. Look, he might have explained, men come in two sizes.
There is the sort of man who counts calories. He purses his dried
lips over the monthly budget. He preaches economy like an
evangelist; he would Walden the family in. His sons are made to
wear sizes big enough to last an extra year. His wife makes religion out of making do; she wears only white cotton underwear,
which some day will decompose into rags for swabbing down
the kitchen. For instruction, he recommends the Shakers, who,
strictly tucked in bare rectangular beds, coffin-stark, could fart
their sheets and never wake a sniff. This man's thrift subsists on
thinnest gruel. A few sips suffice, after which he is asleep by
seven and still a pauper in his dreams.

That is one sort of man. Then there is the sort who purples
without apology. The sort who finds bare necessity barren—the
mother of nothing but prevention. Necessity issues stern memos
about office supplies, which must be spent cautiously and segre-
gated in proper slots in the desk. Necessity snatches back the
hands of children who lean out of the grocery cart to grope for
candy. Necessity would have us copy out her lessons as she
spanks a palm with a straight rule. How she would have

blanched to see my father slash his broad swath through the hall. What would she have made of Caesar's trinkets spilled onto the bedspread for the kids to leer at while my father, flushed like a hunter who'd bagged the best buck, beamed in recounting his adventures and reasoned not the need?

The craps table and the poker table are not exactly hospitable to rational action. But it's worth a try! Whenever you're feeling confused or uncertain about strategy, ask yourself what's sensible. It is not fool-proof, but it's the most reliable recourse you have in that situation.
—*The Compleat Gambler*, p. 17

By the end of the first week after we had moved to our four-family co-op in the suburbs, my father had torn out the tulip bed next to the building and cemented in the plot. When the cement tested dry, he invited some of the men in the neighborhood over to shoot crap on the fresh surface. I remember a gang of five or six big, beery men hunched over their guts on a Sunday after-noon. Dad hadn't known anyone to call, not so far as I knew, but here they were, mysteriously drawn from softball and television and mowing and barbecue by the unmistakable chitter of dice. Later that summer, because Dad had taken such pains to level and smooth the cement, I used it to practice my marbles; by the time I was eleven, it became the ideal place to pitch nickels, until someone's mother got wise. But on that first Sunday afternoon, the playing surface was reserved for adults.

While their children hung over the porch railings to watch the men bet—children who knew that their fathers held some vague jobs that kept them fed but had never seen their fathers throw real money down—my father called the shots. For almost two hours, he announced the numbers to be made. He directed dollars to the Come and Don't Come lines he'd marked off with sidewalk chalk. He served as croupier by plucking and distribut-ing funds after each shooter had finished his turn. Time and again, as a public service, he repeated the basic rules of the game to bring the novices up to speed—those who had come only to watch, not to gamble, but who steadily edged closer until, won over by the urge, they finally kneeled.

The rules were as opaque as long division to the other kids assembled with me, but personally, I could not think when I *did- n't* know that a seven was good on the initial throw and doom ever after. I already knew about boxcars and snake eyes, about the friendly eleven and the cripple three. I knew what came, if it came, on the Come. I knew about all the hard ways.

After a couple of hours, all of the other fathers had cleared out, returning to their own co-ops with their own sons. My father asked if I'd met anyone interesting my age. "I guess so," I told him.

"You have to guess?" he said, smiling, and ran his knuckles gently over my head.

"Yeah. There were some nice kids."

"Yeah," he agreed. "You'll find that people are pretty much the same wherever you go, even in a new place. They're ready to be your friends. You just have to give them a chance."

Blackjack inspires more optimism than most other games do because it holds out prospects for an authentic edge. An expert player who has mastered a sturdy counting system may think that he has greater control over the proceedings. But the employment of multiple card shoes, memory lapses, errors in calculation, environmental distrac- tions, the vagaries of play, and the gambler's own anxieties all con- spire against that edge over time.

—*The Compleat Gambler*, p. 129

Poker is a game that you must play for money to make inter- esting. Whereas the intellectual challenges of pinochle or bridge are sufficient to sustain a friendly game, you have to be able to cash in your winnings in poker to bother with it at all. So there is no such thing as a friendly game of poker; a group of friends may play, but do not be fooled by the snacks or the chummy

ribbing or the innocuous conversation about the merits of the
Yankee pitching staff. Poker players suspend their friendships
when they play, and when they play, they play for money. When
my father taught me the game, he made it clear that whatever
counters you used—peanuts, saccharine packets, whatever—
they had to translate. ("Fun" is only the first syllable of "fungi-
ble.") Of course, Dad and I never played for money. I was nine
years old or so and, like any kid, cash poor—an hour at an
arcade could break me. What funds I did have came from him,
which meant that no matter how we'd have shrunk the stakes, I'd
still be in his pocket, so to speak.

Instead, like pathologists we dissected scores of sample
hands together. I became an apprentice to Dad's subtle aptitudes.
He patiently explained the hierarchy of hands, the logic of when
and how much to raise, and the great debate over whether or not
to keep the ace kicker. He lectured me on the moral turpitude of
sandbagging and the unmanliness of declaring deuces, or anything else, wild. He let me in on the advantage of having your
bluff called early in the evening so as to inspire recklessness
among your opponents as the night wore on. He mentored me
on the cardinal sins of staying in too often and too long.

Seven-card stud is one of the hardest games to analyze or to reduce
to reliable tactics. Because so many conditions interfere with every
turn of the cards, each game dictates its own terms. Stay alert!
—*The Compleat Gambler*, p. 152

All over America fathers were taking their sons into book-
lined studies to unpuzzle sex, while after-school specials drama-
tized the dangers of drugs. But in our house, the crucial confidences were poker strategies. Emily Post devoted paragraphs to
folding napkins but not a word to folding before the second pull
in five-card stud; you could reference her etiquette for maintaining the order of forks, but you'd search the home library in vain
for the importance of maintaining the order of calling raises or

going out. Doctor Spock knew all the pre-school poop, but he never mentioned doubling down any eleven you're dealt in Blackjack. ("Splitting tens is as suicidal as sticking a knife in a toaster." The good doctor omitted *that* essential childproofing tip, didn't he?) Wholesome households may have kept Holy Bibles on prominent display, but the straight skinny was that the real world worked according to Hoyle.

So if gambling was also a game, it was never only a game. Every amenity and insight derived from this central lesson. It must have amounted to hours that we spent deliberating over the cards. Child psychologists now call this kind of consolidated attention "quality time." So this was our quality time, our version of fathers laying them in to their sons all over the city until well after dark because keeping their swings level the next time they came up with bases loaded would somehow decide history. Each delivery bristled with consequence, as did every deal.

But because Dad and I could not play for money, we did not play at all.

Money isn't everything. When you are in the middle of the action, it is easy to forget this simple but essential point. So have a good time. Enjoy the play, the food, and the company, and always be on the lookout for a game that gives you an edge.
    —The Compleat Gambler, p. 194

There are no clocks in casinos. Although there are no thermostats to verify it, the temperature is always seventy-two degrees. The world is set on lull. The light is the light of pre-dusk in late autumn, and it never varies. If you drop a chip from the blackjack table, someone is there to retrieve it for you, although not the same person who sidles by every so often to offer to freshen your drink. Only the most scrupulous dream of heaven could live up to the upholstery or compete with the ergonomics. Pampered, regulated, plush—being in a casino is like being in a vault, extravagantly preserved like dollars or the dead.

A casino is the most modulated acreage on earth. Forget what you've read about mobsters. Forget the macho outbreaks in a thousand Saturday afternoon Westerns, with black-jacketed strangers twisting their mustaches, wizened ranchers covering the last raise with their crumpled deeds, or vested dudes laying cocked derringers down upon their draw. Forget the Scorcese films. The science of civil procedure and serenity governs the modern casino. A secret system of angles, baffles, and insulation ensures that whatever triumphs or tragedies occur, sound never exceeds the levels reached at board meetings inside mahogany walls or at evening prayer service. Gently battered by dice or supporting the crisp tectonics of poker chips, the betting greens have felt no scuff and betray no scar; deftly tended and brushed every hour, they constitute the most expensive pastoral imaginable, and better policed than *Lycidas*, more dependable than Brigadoon. Seen from the upper balcony, the gaming floor is a perfect, quilted terrain: the gleaming, geometric fields stretch out like plotted farmland.

If the craps player narrows his focus to exclude all the perilous propositions, the ancillary bets, and the aura of superstition surrounding the game, he can find a small, quiet spot in the midst of all that's happening and maximize his capacity for endurance.

—*The Compleat Gambler*, p. 106

A casino seems to be all about money, but it is also about time. Time is another currency and another deficit that drains surreptitiously away.

If you think about it, you realize everything conspires to keep you in place, to keep you gambling, but you do not think about it. Although you know better, nothing you do here seems like risk. You come to Vegas full of swagger and dare, but in the long view afforded behind the smoked glass of the mezzanine, everything is predictable and, from the larger perspective, changeless. The slots pay off at eight percent, tops; it is the worst gamble on the strip, and the most popular—amazingly, the slots alone, endlessly fed from paper cups, pay for the whole operation. Meanwhile, employees deal the cards, and they take cuts from every pot the moment that the last bet is made. The double-zero on the roulette wheel gives the house the odds, sufficient to withstand any sheik's wager or tourist's hot spell. Like a birthday party at a nursing home, the proceedings are monitored and—the casino's books confirm it—stable. Invisible day fades into a night that feels no different. It seems that there is nowhere else, and so you stay right where you are, where it's all taken care of, where everything wants to keep you.

And all the while, it is leaking silently, imperceptibly really, silently leaking, under the table, perhaps, where time finds you, where the losing oozes out. What do they call the guy in the movies who's in on the racket? A made man? The same thing they say when your cover's been blown. They've made you. You're a made man.

Events are unaffected by any given card's condition or location unless that condition or location is known.
—*The Compleat Gambler*, p. 12

Here is one basic secret to gambling, no charge.

You must cultivate a poker face. Work the furrows out of your brow; bleed the tension from your jaw; soften your aura and bake Zen into your complexion. Practice it in the mirror if you have to. Cards come and cards go, but unflappability will carry you through the worst stretches and lend virtue to the best. If every ace you buy guns your pulse, if the last card down cracks your countenance as it busts your straight, you will never become a consistent winner. The trick is to maintain the stoic's features while enjoying the epicure's indulgences. Learn to be Brutus at the baths. Reduce your humors to a finely tuned phlegm. Keep yourself to yourself.

While you polish your demeanor to an impenetrable reflection, take a course on the science of tells. Keep a glossary of coughs and flinches the way a hitter tracks pitches from the dugout. The casual player's face is a veritable tarot of indications; the way he clutches his cards gives them away. Does he flush from his flush? Does his posture show straight? Is his low hum the soundtrack of a high spade in the hole? Poker most shows a man, lays bare his means and his mettle. The successful gambler is opaque to others but never surprised, or if he is, he does not register that surprise for the rest.

Remember that "things always even out" is a fallacy. Probability is a theory that governs expectations, not real-world outcomes, which are not obligated to statistical distributions, especially not in the short run. And however long you play, in terms of probability theory, we are talking about the short run.

—*The Compleat Gambler*, p. 44

We know the mythology of luck. There is the one about the guy who held the dice for four solid hours, completing pass after pass in a dream of divine election. There is the one about the guy who did not know that two pair of nines meant four of a kind and in ignorance bought bliss. There is the one about the guy who came to Atlantic City just for the shows or for a cousin's wedding or for a welders' convention and figured, what the hell, I'll drop three dollars in the giant slot machine just to say I've done it, and you know the rest. There is the one about the guy—the one schmuck in all of North America—who did not know that it made no difference in what order you chose your lottery numbers, so that by returning to reorder the numbers he'd based on the ages of his mangy pets or on the birthdays of family members only he held dear, and thus to correct the mistake that out of the whole human species only *he* did not know was no mistake, won himself a *double* share of the multi-million-dollar jackpot. We have heard the legends, the tales of lucky bastards and fortune's fools, and because nothing much in the world breaks fair or makes sense, we believe. For if life itself were a bet, you would not take it. Our very bodies are strange, random conspiracies of atoms we've never seen. Probability runs us, and we are not probable, so it must be luck. Life is won on the come; each day is another unlikely, difficult pass you have to make. We believe in luck because what else is there to do but believe?

And anyway, as my father used to say, the horse doesn't know he's forty-to-one. You know it, I know it, the Green Sheet says it's so. His owner has other investments to offset this one. His trainer can read a stopwatch as well as anyone. Even his jockey knows the drudge that's under him. But the horse? The horse doesn't know the odds. Hell, the horse may think he's going to *win*.

Dad believed. It freed him from having to total fat grams like some hunched Cratchit stuck in a dingy circle of bad light. It saved him from wrestling with seatbelts or fishing for his reading glasses to make out warning labels. Hey, if your number's up, it's up. No need to track the package, trace your check, or pester the editor. You're in the system. Someone has your file. So, basically, go ahead and resume what you were doing. When the time comes, your fate will find you.

The longer you sit at a game at which you will eventually lose— what we call a Type L game, such as craps, roulette, or the slots— the more inevitable it is that you will not only lose but that you will lose what you are mathematically predicted to lose. So-called swings of fortune may feel incredible, but mathematically speaking, they are anything but.

—*The Compleat Gambler*, p. 80

By the time the pain was persistent enough to force Dad to see the doctors ... well, doctors are professionals. They know the signs and are seldom surprised. There were doctors who made useless adjustments to the monitors. They cast their cold eyes on life, on death. Still, you could not help but read their disappointment, although they tried to reserve it for the machines themselves. There were doctors who watched my father's inner slosh ossify on glowing screens. There were doctors who showed him pictures of his wasting bones, of the Stonehenge of wasting bones that cancer had made of his chest. A shambles of calcium. The leaching of years. All the decayed and fallen bones. There were doctors who did nothing but consult like kibbitzers at the card table or strangers lured by the shooter's hot streak, leaning in to nod and confide. They talked over Dad's dull, reluctant vitals, their voices odd and heavy with consequence, like loaded dice. His disease resisted procedures, overcame the bluff of every drug they administered. Stubborn, always *stub-boor-REN*. They let him in on his body's bad bets.

Sometimes a hand is not played the way it is dealt.
—*The Compleat Gambler*, p. 155

But at his best, Dad was always a tough out. He lingered like the guy who, throwing good money after bad, stays in anyway for a shot at the one jack that hasn't shown. We asked the doctors for a prognosis. You never know, they would say, knowingly. Try to believe, and try to help him believe. People recover, unaccountably. They beat the odds. You have heard stories, surely. It doesn't look good, but anything can happen. Nevertheless.

Before the "flop," any blind play is risky, although you do have the advantage of viewing everyone else's activities before you go. Certainly, unanticipated "miracle cards" are possible. How many of us have won on the big blind with hands we would never have played out had we been occupying any other position?
—*The Compleat Gambler*, p. 160

What comment do the handicappers make about the horse that's going off at forty-to-one? He has a gambler's chance. The experts had inspected the charts and gone over the forms, and they gave Dad a gambler's chance.

And I looked at my father, dying from the inside out, and saw nothing in his expression to tell me what he was holding.

Never lose sight of the "element of ruin." When you're out of funds, you're out of the game, and no savvy can save you. Being cashed out—that is the gambler's ruin.

—*The Compleat Gambler*, p. 22

When we collected his things, my mother folded his pants over her arm, and Dad's silver money clip fell out. A clump of hundreds spun out. Twenty-three hundreds, dropped down on the floor like the shooter's last-ditch risk to recoup. All he's worth. Everything, bet the hard way.

tales from the border patrol

First, try not to picture a horse. A little Zen exercise. Clear your
mind of horses. Abolish the equine slopes and the odors that
knife through the sinuses. Free all those expensive thorough-
breds from your imagination's paddock, and lock away Dobbin
in the stable. Round up the prize recruits from Owen Wister and
Zane Grey. Round up John Hawkes's horses, including the one
that took ten pages to be winched onto a boat from a pier,
including another that narrated its autobiography. Round up
Cormac McCarthy's horses, striding and stamping and dying
through the Border Trilogy. Don't forget to forget George
Stubbs's horses, flayed to satisfy anatomical passions. Picasso's
cubed horse in *Guernica*, arrested in wild aria, silently, invisibly
blistering the air—banish it. All the horses that pose or trot or
take the sun in all the Victorian novels, all the standing, stu-
porous, tolerant, indifferent horses that suffer the dreamy tra-
vails of the heroes they bear, the heroines they convey, delete
them all. Exterminate the brutes.

    Be relentless. Erase the iconic memories of Saturday west-
erns, bronc-bustings, and stretch runs. Drag Silver off with all
his pomp. Disjockey the Triple Crown hopefuls; unhitch them
from your handicapper's hopes. Rid yourself of Trigger, whose
intaglio on your metal lunchbox reared beneath Roy Rogers'

signature in a yellow coil of rope. (Better yet: tuck the whole lunchbox out of sight.) Pen the macho breed of *Bonanza* in medium shots, so that when the sundry Cartwrights rise up with the opening credits in smug, rugged fraternity, it must be because they have floated horselessly into the picture.

All right? Have all mounts come in out of the reins? Nothing but abandoned bridles, marooned stagecoaches, and slipped rigs? Not a hint of horse in your head? That's the idea.

No, you can't do it. Of course not. As the poet Charles Simic put it, "A hole is invariably a hole in something," and something obtrudes. A flinch of withers enters, a flash of tail. A dapple off an Appaloosa, perhaps, or a blonde streak of Palomino. The familiar snuffing and snorting of the idling horse refutes your refusal. Components of horse take the stage like an ensemble cast at the close of the show. Horsehair tousles between pricked ears like a lifted gunsight. A skirl of tail twists in the myth-thick breeze. Then a leg, improbably angled and delicate, stems from a haunch swollen like a continent. Something molten in the massive shoulders, a supple tonnage, unmistakable. Although you tie the concept up outside, it balks, it bucks, it snaps its tether. Even the word "horse" won't be budged. It takes root as only horses can—no comparison can deflect it. The congregation keeps kicking at your diction. Dark horse. Gift horse. Horse sense. Horsepower. Look down, and you find fresh moons left by hooves in the mind's loamy floor.

Now reverse the process. Try to think of a horse, and see what does not happen. See what will not come when you call. Although you thrash about like Richard III bellowing his hyperbolic bargain, there is no horse to be had. Whether you determine to establish it centrifugally from the central heft out, building horse equity, or whether you begin by collecting appendages, no horse coheres. You wonder what mimetic strategy served the Greeks, who were able to gird a replica out of local materials sufficient to pass as a god's gift and gull Troy. Try to improvise a horse, summon it out of horse colors—tarpaulin, washwater, melanoma. Coax one from the blur of insignias, ads for beer and cigarettes. Extrapolate from the glamorous pounding in the rolling dust that drifts up from ten thousand films. Think horses, not zebras, as William of Occam advised. Take back Blake's dismissal of the horses of instruction; offer to stay after class to heed them. Hopeless.

Meanwhile, who dreams of you? Consider the ebb and flow of God's conjuring. Out of some invisible circumference comes His inspiration and retraction, His peal and repeal. What about the forensic enterprise of your own existence? Perhaps you, too, are emerging grudgingly out of some unstable concern, congealing into a credible self only to recede, as if you were being inhaled out of that amplitude, only to be reduced into a primal gesture, into a faded terrain of bones and blemishes, into the single breath it takes to say "you." What if you are a frail project of continuity, a little turbulence, your embodiment built like a casket on a river? What if you are the fool of some distant enchantment and distraction, until you flicker, you hang by a nail, by the ledge at the base of your neck, by your Cheshire smirk like the rind of the moon, your last ineradicable vestige, floating, fading, but still there?

Still there? Hold on.

◻ ◻ ◻

When I was around ten years old, before the child care industry had become serious business, before sponsored recess, play dates, and all manifestations of mortgaged recreation; before we were wrested from our scattered activities and rescued from the hazards of our own invention; before we were systematically encamped, teamed up, uniformed, and Boy Scouted, one of the modest solitary pleasures my summer afternoons afforded was swatting stones over the blind wall of Harding Metals. I would begin by selecting as straight and bat-like a length of downed oak or maple I could find in the vicinity. Then I would snap off offending growths until I had a reasonable facsimile of half a broomstick (actual broomsticks being harder to come by than one's nostalgia might suggest). Then I went about choosing stones. The best pellets were somewhat smaller than robins' eggs but somewhat larger than acorns, and they had a certain indescribable heft that experience alone could validate. Happily, there were long beds of just the right sorts of stones fronting the factory: a smooth, generous ration spread like jewelry on a blanket on Broadway, in a fetching variety of fall colors.

The object—*my* object, rather—was to fungo them over the wall, which was perhaps fifty yards distant and some thirty feet high, onto an imaginary Addison or Sheffield, depending on which Wrigley Field vista I was whimming at the time. Admittedly, most of my swings fell short, so that after fifteen minutes my pings, tips, tops, skulls, fouls, and dribbles made a significant litter on the blacktop. But those I happened to catch flush cracked the way fastballs sent "back, back, way, way back" cracked off legendary bats. I watched them rocket into respectable arcs of high flies that had a chance; hung out, mid-summer, mid-sky, they cleared the bricks of Harding Metals like the rim of dream, gasped their last, and touched down soundlessly and out of sight.

It was about as close to Norman Rockwellian activity as I ever got, I guess. At the same time, it was the closest I ever came to delinquency—hardly enough to alarm the social workers, who in the 1960s had plenty to keep them busy without bothering with my harmless strafing of Harding Metals. I was ten, remember, and out for what might at worst be termed a little shiftlessness, or handy vandalism. I was just Tom Sawyering, suburban-style, spattering the rooftop the way, at worst, lice stippled the back of an indifferent bull.

This is what I was up to, and I promise you that no one at home was fretting or running for the Dr. Spock, because I was ten, which, so long as I kept my grades up and washed before dinner, allowed me to pass beneath the radar of concern. When a teenager comes home and answers his mother's "Where were you?" with "Nowhere" and her "What did you do today?" with "Nothing," well, one might legitimately worry about hidden legal fees; but my ten-year-old nowhere and nothing were pretty much as advertised and certainly not worth noticing. Until someone noticed.

It turned out that someone owned the stones. Someone got wind of what I was doing, whacking bits of property about and, evidently, disturbing the delicate equilibrium of Harding Metals. No Cubs had clustered for me at the plate after my last blast; no line of dignitaries had mustered to receive me on the tarmac. It was just one harried fellow in a brown suit—I presumed he was something on the order of Vice President in Charge of Terrestrial Distribution and Deployment, and years later I cannot come up with a likelier office for him—who found me despicable. He explained through his outrage that these stones cost money. They had been selected with greater discretion than even I brought to the batter's box. They had been spilled and tilled by landscape architects (there were such jobs, there were such men). Basically, there was nothing on the premises which was not the premises. And anyway, he complained, his voice like gravel in a pan, didn't I have anything better to do?

So I walked cautiously away, realizing that every step in any direction was another unavoidable trespass and knowing, now, that, notwithstanding childhood, I couldn't pocket a dropped dime or kick a pop can without consequence.

❒ ❒ ❒

"Show me a man who worries about edges and I'll show you a natural-born winner. Cardinal Y. agrees. Columbus himself worried, the Admiral of the Ocean Sea. But he kept it quiet."
—from Donald Barthelme's "See the Moon?"

❒ ❒ ❒

You are looking at a painting in the museum. Any painting will demonstrate the point; any museum will suffice. To get the full effect, you pull back, and the frame of the painting intrudes into the evaluative field. You now see the frame around the painting the way you see the painting. Art is a verb whose force implicates the frame, which is claimed by the canvas it encloses. Pull back, and the wall on which it's hung surrounds the painting in a swarm of beige, like an atmosphere, which the room contains and contributes to. You pull back, reaching behind you for a chair, but you hesitate because it is a chair in a room in an art museum, where there is nothing certainly, safely separate from the displays, and you dare not sit on what might also be art. You mean to withdraw into perspective, but aesthetics are contagious, calling dibs on the light switches, the stairwells, the signs above the suspiciously filigreed door jams.

A seizure of charged perception follows you into the street, from which the Institute looms: a massive accomplishment. Too late to get out of the way, you discover that someone behind you is taking pictures. You cannot flee the scene. You drive home along Lake Shore Drive, a route so renowned, so picturesque, that people regularly pull off to photograph the Impressionist sunset.

Tell the guests at a party about this sensation. Make it one of those parties predicated on the set of *High Society*. Smoke like Sinatra next to someone who drinks like Bing. Decide to treat that imposing reef of marble you've been trying to interpret on the glass table as an ashtray rather than a work of art. When you do, pay attention to the relief of grateful Grace Kellys who stab out their cigarettes after yours. Grateful, because they now know where they stand.

Did you make it an August night, warm enough that one frail drape plays like a veil over a window open wide to the night air? Did you? Pull back.

◘ ◘ ◘

"We have died, Vallard and I, we have entered the shadowless realm, region of erasures and absences, kingdom of dissolution. Clumps of cloud mist enter my mouth like smoke. Here on the other shore, here at the world's end, give me the sight and touch of things: shape of a hand, curve of a chin, weight of a stone; the heft of earthly things. Edges! Edges!"
—from Steven Millhauser's "Balloon Flight, 1870"

◻ ◻ ◻

The Scholastic Aptitude Test (SAT) will not accept any answer penciled outside the proper cell. The instructions are quite clear on this point. Part of the lesson is learning to stay within borders; part of the test is staying inside the prescribed lines. Even now, in some obscure, airless office in New Jersey, trained and tireless graders are umpiring the latest batch of aspirants. Improper marks—malformations suggesting gibbous moons or mold spores, as well as any mutations betraying horn or hump or tail—are rooted out like damaged chromosomes and disqualified from the future. Students must not underestimate the importance of filling in their answers fully, of producing nests of clear, perfect periods. No smudge, no errant blot will do. (Certainly the ability to accommodate boundaries is a sign of intelligence and bodes well for success in higher education.) Thus the truth is riveted in, in a series of snug absolutes. For beyond these walls lies annihilation.

◻ ◻ ◻

They are guarding their optimism, but the initial report is that they may have found Noah's ark. They are keeping their optimism in check, but the rumor is that the remains of an ancient structure—quite possibly massive at one time—have been located on or near the peak of Mount Ararat, where the legendary ark purportedly came to rest. Their optimism is being held without bail and is not speaking to the press, but sources close to the search team (strategically comprised of rabbis, endowed scholars, and expert mountain climbers) attest that their optimism is in favorable condition, that it is sitting up and taking nourishment.

Of course, its passage through the centuries and the Deluge has taken considerable toll on the ark, rendering it unrecognizable to all but the devout. There is no planking to speak of, and most of the hull, if you could call it a hull, has been eaten away. There is not sufficient deck to measure against the Old Testament. Frankly, the discovery comes down to a few cubits' worth of material. The Bible is mum about mast and rudder, so their absence among the salvage is to be expected and occasions no additional doubt.

Together with other experts (those whom conditions of health, intrepidness, or funding kept nearer sea level), they plan to repair and reassemble the ark. Consensus about the working blueprint has been as hard to come by as the vessel itself, and practical construction problems have also hampered the project. For instance, we have heard that some of the wood was damaged further in transport, and at least one recorded section has not been accounted for. Shards have had to be reshaped to fit flush; worn, warped, and ragged edges have had to be reworked to accommodate the carpenters' efforts; some of the pieces would not take nails and had to be replaced; a few disintegrated altogether. Nevertheless, the prospects are good, and a spokesman for the team is expected to announce that a new and satisfactory ark should be available for public viewing in two to three years.

❏ ❏ ❏

Chicago is a city of walls. In every neighborhood, schools and factories and apartment buildings turn their broad backs on the community. Kids make do, adapting their play. Whereas Coloradans assault their topography with toboggans, sleds, and skis, and Oklahomans flood their flat plains with soccer balls, as soon as the sun drifts in from Lake Michigan on a Saturday morning, as if summoned in Genesis, Chicago boys gather two by two for wallball.

No one has seen them made or heard them made, but the walls of Chicago are chalked and scored with squares—a playground version of the Lascaux cave paintings, commemorating similar strivings. Custodians long ago have stopped sponging away these strike zones, which merely reappear in a week anyway for the next outbreak of wallball. The game is a distillation of baseball, pared down to pitcher and hitter. A bat, a rubber ball, gloves, perhaps team caps to anchor pretensions, but basically a basic game, rigorously simple enough to satisfy Thoreau. There are none of the vile cryptics of other games that take longer to explain than to play. Occasionally you'll see a third player, typically a younger brother a parent has forced the players to endure, who is exiled to the putative outfield beyond the blacktop, but his job is not fielding so much as retrieving. In fact, although the pitcher will occasionally snare a pop-up or flag down a scuffed grounder, it is pretty much all hits and strikeouts for nine innings.

The pitcher calls balls and strikes. This is key. Over and over his pitches scald the bricks, and the batter he is trying to fire past or fool must trust his opponent to judge fairly if that last one caught the border. Was there a burst of chalk on the three-two pitch? Did anything kick up but dust? Perhaps the slightest puff, like flour off a breadboard? Hard to say in this sun, but it is up to the pitcher to say. The ethics of the game depend on it, as does the character of the friendship.

In "The Unmaking of Modernism," art critic Suzi Gablik wistfully considers the commitment of minimalist Josef Albers, "who woke every morning with the implacable knowledge that he was going to paint squares." Whatever his reputation in his own discipline, whatever the nature of his contribution or damage to the definition of art, there is no denying his claim to patron saint of wallball, which, like any art, perceives its edges through several converging factors: convention, examination, pleasure, consensus, and faith.

◻ ◻ ◻

Many of my friends married at opposite ends of a hyphen, vow-
ing to teeter-totter together for eternity. Prenuptial agreement
never had much to do with finances in my crowd—melding
properties among grad students was more or less like mixing
inert gases in a tank—so surnames became the primary bone of
contention. "What's in a name?" wondered Shakespeare's Juliet,
so blithely wrapped in luxury against the star-crossed night that
even professors have to pause to remember that she'd have been
listed under the C's in their rosters. As I say, it was quite another
matter for the peasantry. For them, a hyphen was often the sta-
ple of marital compromise. Thus, Herzog married Walton,
becoming Walton-Herzog, and Walton, marrying Herzog,
became Herzog-Walton. Out of that equitable deference a baby
arose: Jessie Herzog (the novelist-to-be) or Jessie Walton (the
inevitable wide receiver), a delightful boy either way, and who
by either or any other name smelled as sweet. In truth, geneti-
cally speaking, underlying every zygote is a hyphen.

Thus the hyphen is a splicing, a soldering of selves.
Consider the actor-director, the player-coach, or the singer-
songwriter—amalgamated essences devised to extend the ego
and confound the IRS. A sizeable percentage of *Who's Who* inhabitants, barnacling with more and more accomplishments in each
new edition, require multiple designations to do justice to their
cultivation in several fields. For them, hyphens neatly accommodate their status, which collects the way coral reefs do.

Political negotiation gave the world Austria-Hungary and
Bosnia-Herzegovina, hybrids that, like scientifically engineered
microorganisms, do not long survive their coinages. Speaking of
science, we have that discipline to thank for space-time (now
there's a concept to limbo under!), not to mention the complex
temptations of mango-tangerine.

Among poets, none so notoriously rides the hyphen as
Emily Dickinson does. Hyphens appear throughout her

collected poems like rickety bridges over existential chasms;
they are ledges left for us to slide along and not look down from,
lest we fall. And there is so much awful distance to traverse: loss,
hope, truth, eternity, and the Divine, Who may be designated
by that fatal dash from G to D.

Descending to street-level (specifically, in metropolitan
Chicago), we find ourselves driving through a confluence of
major highways which is known for several miles as I-90-94, an
oddity that seems to illustrate, with apologies to Heraclitus, that
you can't step in the same river *once*.

◻ ◻ ◻

Perhaps you are toughing out a dare or trying to impress a date
with your composure. Perhaps you are simply trying to stave off
nightmares. Regardless of how you ended up at a horror film,
there is a way to minimize your fear: sit as close to the screen
and as far to one side as possible. The effect is that no matter
what is lurching out of the mandatory fog, swamp, psyche, or
other intricate darkness to bare its baleful appetite, it will be
reduced to freckles. Wrenching your vantage and your neck
awry reveals how everything is really a conspiracy of illuminated
dust. Every movie comes down to the same bright particulate
hosed onto a blank screen. Stay vigilant, and you may even be
able to detect the soft sway of the screen in the air conditioning.

Once the monsters are flattened, of course, no dimensions
are safe. Castles implode and landscapes deflate; love is a
mirage, a meeting of peels on a heap; adventures swash and
buckle like optical illusions in the morning surf, which is precisely what they are; and every creature, humanoid or not, is an
incredible being of lightness. You are free of them. What is
more, by moving about the theater, playing hide-and-seek with
essences, you can theoretically resume and repudiate the spell at
will. Now a human drama is detonating; now it is a shaft of drizzle suspended in someone's headlights. If you have ever driven

through a steady rain on the highway and literally driven *through* it, so that all of a sudden it was going on entirely behind you, you will not be thrown by the sensation. Or if you have stood at the famous intersection where Arizona, New Mexico, Utah, and Colorado come together flush as a parquet floor. Or if you have let yourself strobe over one of those vision tricks, which is impossible to resolve as either duck or bunny, or which cannot be seen for certain as a white goblet or two black facing profiles. Or if, falling in a dream, you fall out of it into wakefulness and the surprise of your own embedded weight. Odd, possibly, even unsettling for a moment, but nothing to be afraid of.

When a film of a train pulling into a station was shown in an African village to an audience that had never witnessed a film before, people dived screaming to the floor. They were either panicked about being run over by an image, or they were afraid of the repercussions of unleashing such powerful magic. This is to slip a reminder past our own film-drunk sophistication: every film is a horror film.

And yet, the odds are that not every native ducked for cover. There must have been one, anyway, the one I imagine with his face nearly nuzzling the screen but whose curiosity slanted in from the far right flank, who crept to the curved edge of the charmed space, who dipped his hand into the variegated stream of light and did not withdraw it until, wonder having gotten the better of him, he drew back the screen to find the secret source. The one who, when there were no movies to distract the tribes from battle, handled reconnaissance. He may have been the bravest among them, standing up to the magic and the mechanism of shadows. Or he may have just been following an instinct to locate the radiant seam between worlds, watch for the next flutter, and slip through.

◻ ◻ ◻

They were discussing near-death experiences on television. There were sociologists, ministers, pioneers who'd been "beyond and back." It was an unfortunate phrase because it sounded like a basketball violation. But there was nothing humorous about the program. Initially, amiable skepticism and collaborative bliss were the sole reactions available to the panelists to choose from. After the first half-hour, however, the critics subsided before the more consoling, more generous visions of people who had misplaced their pulses during surgery, who had been struck solidly by taxis, or who had been touched by downed power lines.

By all accounts, the porch of heaven was a magnificent cliché. These people had returned from death and, as specialists in brinkmanship, could speak evenly about it. Indeed, as one of them (a housewife from Santa Barbara who had slipped and cracked her skull on the bathroom sink, of all things) assured us, she had *been* returned to tell people about it. Their testimonies seconded what testimonies on previous programs of this sort had taught us to anticipate: tunnels furred with light, a slur of indecipherable but soothing sounds, gentle exudations. Even given the periodic annoyances of commercial breaks, the mood was, for a weekday afternoon talk show, impressive. In such august company, the show's host had the earnest, jittery mien of an assistant principal. But she summed up the hour with poise: "We will all of us one day know what happens after death. The important thing to learn from our guests today is just how amazing and how precious *life* is." Well … yes.

Anyway, the day was waning, and there were the kids to be picked up from school and dinner to be made. But even so, there was the slick spot on the linoleum, the red light run, the gas leak, the inexplicable clot that makes a break for the brain and stops the world for you mid-sentence as the host looks genially on. As John Lennon once sang, "Life is what happens to you while you're busy making other plans," not long at all before he was dropped by a bullet on his own block.

One way of making sense of evolution is to say that nature never folds a winning hand. This is the spirit that lifts John Updike's young protagonist out of his spiritual funk in "Pigeon

Feathers." The intricacy of dead bird design implies a Designer. Out of the pigeons' mass grave and a little rearview logic, David contrives an ineradicable purpose for himself: "As he fitted the last two, still pliant, on the top, and stood up, crusty coverings were lifted from him, and with a feminine, slipping sensation along his nerves that seemed to give the air hands, he was robed in this certainty: that the God who had lavished such craft upon these worthless birds would not destroy His whole Creation by refusing to let David live forever."

What better question to beg? (David has to murder the birds to get close enough for revelation to graze him, but let's not quibble. As Wordsworth wrote, "We murder to dissect.") What trickles down through Updike's image strata is this prayer: Let me not be negligible. Surely we are cast for more than low comedy. Surely there is something to be said for the stamina of one soul flexing in the mirror.

Nevertheless, it sometimes seems as if every other bolt of lightning ignites a forest. Our toxins minute by minute rust the food chain. Rivers thicken and jungles cringe. Check with the Sierra Club: whole species wink out constantly. There is no direction that does not lead to the crumbling edge, and sooner all the time. Only germs seem assured of any habitation at all. And don't look past this planet for hospitality. As Annie Dillard reminds us in *Pilgrim at Tinker Creek*, "We estimate now that only one atom dances alone in every cubic meter of intergalactic space," which, it turns out, has expanded over the past century by a factor of one *million*. That atom dances, presumably, like the nut on the subway doing his dervish best down the aisle.

The morning papers are full of paleontologists finding man's final, entrenched positions. Our own ancestral compost, whose heaps we only temporarily exceed, grows and grows below us; our passage over the dead just barely tamps them down. A cross-section of earth is a submarine sandwich of civilizations. Like Jason, who sowed dragon's teeth to sprout an army of skeletons, we breed demise. Samuel Beckett has it right in *Waiting for Godot*:

"Astride of a grave and a difficult birth. Down in the hole, lingeringly, the grave-digger puts on the forceps." Beckett uses the hyphen to open the pit.

The talk show was ending, the credits were rolling, and everyone was hugging, hanging on. A near-death experience? What *isn't* one?

❏ ❏ ❏

The physicist Werner Heisenberg maintained that we do not interpret Nature; rather, we interpret Nature's responses to the questions we put to it. Thanks to modern upgrades in our technology and scholarly methods, we are hearing different answers than we once did. Satellite photos of Mt. Everest have compelled us to raise its official cap by seven feet, thereby adding approximately two strides to what was already the height of earthly achievement. Higher-fidelity analysis of ancient times has convinced many historians that the two thousandth year of the Lord was likely attained about four years earlier than conventional wisdom has it, meaning that those millenarians who perched anxiously at the extreme edge of 1999 were gathered for a train that had already left the station. And if the latest scientific projections are to be believed, our typical description of the physical universe is off by seven dimensions. But as any good wallballer knows, fair territory has always been a product of ground rules that alter with each new field of play.

On a related note, there is also some confusion over the last words of Captain Edward Smith, the doomed commander of *Titanic*. They were either "Be British" or "Every man for himself." Possibly Smith was responsible for both statements, although it must be allowed that the order in which they were uttered could make a crucial difference to posterity. In any event, it is not surprising that the survivors, who were undeniably preoccupied at the time, could not say for sure what he said, what with the water running.

centers of gravity

When you are an undergraduate at a major Midwestern university that is attached to a small city, you are not surprised to find that the city succumbs like a cell to the invasion it hosts. Our school colors oozed through the community, bleeding over block after block as if a new football jersey had been tossed in with the whites. Our mascot, an Indian chief sporting a full headdress and resolute enough to withstand any ambush of irony or political correctness, was absolutely everywhere. He glared over gas stations and loomed over laundromats; he graced movie complexes and presided over dry cleaners; with sober diligence, he guarded restaurants and banks. Law firms, Realtors, print shops, furniture dealers, and taxi companies labored in his name. So it was easy to imagine, for a student whose theater of operations was for the most part restricted to it, that the university, with its professors grown solid with scholarship and advanced degrees, its library sustaining so many million volumes that the weight had sunk it twelve stories underground, and its every building deep-seated in regular endowments, pulled enough g's to determine every orbit in the vicinity.

And for that reason, I was sometimes surprised to realize that to this land grant university not all of the land was granted after all. There were rumored settlements, further out in the county, where no one bothered with the football scores; there were legendary ghettos whose inhabitants never saw the Quad; there were tribes in which biological clocks were set to some mysterious alternative to the academic calendar. And it was on one of these distant, uncultivated fields that the same carnival docked each spring. With two dormmates in tow, I caught the first bus I'd ever needed in that city and set off to learn what lay beyond the reach of in-state tuition and the lights of the campus.

If this particular carnival specimen were any indication, Americana begins in kitsch and dies in grime. Each spring the sideshow proprietors limboed beneath an ever-lowered budget. They were reduced to tattered bills and ratty booths, to costumes that showed bare spots where they'd shed with each performance a few more spangles like heavenly dandruff. They had to make do with a few animals that wheezed asthmatically or winced with gingivitis. They put up with stunted stunts.

The carnival oddities were more septic or sorrowful than shocking—a cow that dragged a withered fifth leg beside it like an IV rack, a rubber man who bummed smokes between contortions, a line of vague deformities in vile jars, a gruff dwarf. Times being what they were, it was little wonder that the sideshow had come to count on acts that lit so little wonder. Staying solvent meant hovering just above the ordinary. There was the gypsy who wrung vague data from your hands, decoded your cards, or picked about your skull with painted nails as though it were lousy with clues. There was the man in the Vandyke who swallowed more indignities than any underling at the office ever had to, but especially fire, swords, and their limited permutations. There was the malodorous close-up magician, who, like the dubious jeweler splaying his trade on a New York avenue, relegated his marvels to a spread scarf or velvet square; the juggler who grimly adjusted to new shapes and hefts as volunteers tossed debris into his ever-condensing arc of wobbly triumph; and all manner of human deference to low overhead. And there was the guy who took punches.

With all the evangelical fanfare one overworked manager with a bullhorn could muster, Rockwell the Magnificent emerged. It must be admitted that his magnificence did not extend to his wardrobe: unlike the other performers, he eschewed a leotard and dispensed with cape or crown, opting instead for blue jeans and a flannel shirt. Disrobing, he revealed his knotty, redoubtable midsection and did a slow-motion veronica to ensure that everyone in attendance—perhaps fifteen of us—could satisfy his curiosity. His manager (who was also the ticket seller, the supervisor of the Shetland pony rides, and the top kick among scrubbers of Elvis, their lone elephant) drew us in with practiced pitches. "Check out the seasoning of that splendid meat! What a paragon of petrifaction! What a princely corset of flesh!" Then Rockwell lay down in the dirt.

Once all were gathered, the first test was summoned: a motorcyclist, who revved his engine menacingly, then urged his bike over the speed bump of a belly. Rockwell did not rise, but only lifted a hand to receive our uncertain applause. Next came a quartet of clowns piling onto a single deftly positioned stool, which earned the same casual gesture from Rockwell. Then two of the clowns returned with cinderblocks, which they stacked on Rockwell; the motorcyclist reappeared with a hammer and, with considerable ceremony, smashed them, again doing no damage. Finally, Elvis entered, cajoled by his handlers like a freshman at a frat hazing to arrange a front foot on our hero and bear down. After this last stunt, Rockwell worked his way to his feet to repeat his original turns, showing his abused middle, like the moon following an eclipse, still intact.

At this point, the manager began working the crowd with a professional insistence reminiscent of the temptation of Elvis moments earlier. While Rockwell enticed us, smoothing and patting his belly like a prize sow at the fair, the manager proposed an offer and a challenge: for two dollars, any one of us— any *real man* among us, as he put it—could take a clean shot. For five bucks, three. While I stared at that revolving planet of a man, my buddies were already eagerly, nervously pooling resources.

⊐ ⊐ ⊐

Don't believe what you see on prime-time television. Most teenagers have never been in a fistfight. I was just as tanked on testosterone, just as stoked by action movies and the NFL as the next guy ground down by midterm exams, but that is where my experience of fistfights ended. Although I'd stuck my chin out bravely on occasion and on occasion stuck my nose in where it didn't belong, I had never been struck on the chin or the nose for my troubles. I may have been involved in a couple of brief bristlings on the basketball court and one rough shove in a locker room, but that was hardly the stuff of legend. And in my crowd that was pretty much the norm. Oh, sure, there were a few exceptional Hemingways who'd cruise the local bars for the imagined insult or the odd dare and, like Bert Lahr in lion's hide, try to take on the room. There was one bowling alley incident, which led to some errant slugs and a series of mutually accusing phone calls between the parents of the two combatants. There was the time Mike Matuszak forced Jay Cohen to the floor in the school hallway and slammed his head two or three times against it for a grievance not even Jay could understand (or so he complained). But that was about it.

For fistfight etiquette, I continue to rely on John Wayne. When I was a teenager, kung fu films were all the rage, which gave rage a foreign flavor and, to my mind, a bad name. All the jittery deceit and artful dodging of kung fu—the transistorized incitements and staticky action—was, in the end, silly and shrill. The choreographed strikes seemed lethal, all right, but there was still something disreputable about all that flash and dazzle. I sometimes feel like the Luddite who brandishes his fountain pen against a humming sea of office computers, but I still maintain, for the naked nobility of fisticuffs, give me John Wayne.

If you looked past the orchestral accompaniment and wrecked property, you could recognize a ritualistic composure at work in John Wayne's fistfights. I am thinking of movies like *McLintock!* and *The Sons of Katie Elder*, with Duke at his most strapping, standing forth like the prow of the ship of himself. Even those bandits shagged with desert, who hadn't been to town in weeks, whose voices rasped and whose features were crushed by the sun, were aware; even rubes knew the rules. They knew they were going up against the most celebrated brawler of them all. When they charged howling with raised chairs at their lone adversary, they were taking on an institution—they might as well have tried to topple the Washington Monument or to shoulder the Statue of Liberty into the Atlantic—and there was a sort of decorum at the heart of the chaos. Thus they never swarmed John Wayne like ants covering dropped candy; they came at him one at a time, like guests moving through a reception line to congratulate the groom, to be flattened.

Duke did not so much throw punches as hoist them, as if his hands were sledges he lugged around. Certainly his were not hands for doing taxes or knotting ties. It was painful to see him do the mandatory love scenes, to watch him sweeten for Maureen O'Hara or lumber dully after Angie Dickinson, like watching a circus bear being forced to spin about in a ruffled skirt. John Wayne was ungainly when he would be gallant. He could rouse but not caress, and you worried when he'd chuck a lover under the chin or smooth her hair with one of those ponderous hands, just as you'd worry whenever a party guest would set the good crystal down on the stone hearth.

Talk about telegraphing a punch! John Wayne positively prepared to deliver it as though it were a presidential visit. He built up his punch like an overture. It was as if each fist were being readied for an expedition with heavy, marvelous cargo. Forget athleticism. Forget maneuvers. Forget the indignities of duck and jab. The blows he brought were frank and matter of fact. His roundhouse swings showed the same obvious, virtuous effort of a farmer hurling hay bales onto a flatbed. Duke did not feint or flinch or work the belly. No, John Wayne's rights were so downright *righteous* that you could almost consider it a privilege to receive one squarely, then to show the scar like a shard of the True Cross. And when highly billed adversaries, having been knocked over the bar or through the railing, were chosen to be hauled back to their feet and pummeled some more, well, they were marked with distinction.

❐ ❐ ❐

We had enough among us for three turns. After a short caucus, I agreed to go last. Smiling broadly, Roger, an architecture major from Granite City, strode to the batter's box and, without even so much as eyeing the target, suddenly fired a strike. His fist seemed to glance off the slick sheath instead of sinking in, and it barely sounded. Rockwell registered nothing more than a slight increase in his indifference. There was some laughter and cheering for Roger, who was still smiling, as if *he* were the one who'd endured. John, a sophomore in accounting who had grown up within walking distance of Wrigley Field, stepped up next. He peered in, straightened, revved his arm, and reared back. As he threw his punch, he twisted his arm, karate-style, as though the air it passed through were rifled like a gun barrel. It found its spot and stuck for a second, like a child's suction-cupped arrow hugging a wall, then slid off. Again, Rockwell was not impressed. Roger was nodding vigorously at John, suggesting that he was now in on the same joke. John looked at me and shrugged, possibly to indicate something about how little entertainment five dollars could buy these days. Or possibly not. Meanwhile, we had one punch coming.

❐ ❐ ❐

In the 1970s, when Joe Frazier was champ, Jerry Quarry was a perennial challenger. He was just good enough to lose well. Truly, it seemed to be Jerry Quarry's lot in life to serve as a stepping stone for legitimate challengers to the crown or as a tune-up for a more significant bout. Waggish journalists referred to the aptly named Quarry as a Great White Hope who was neither great nor hopeful and who, after the eventual beating, was no longer even recognizably white. But if he was not gifted, he was game, and he made a better living than most by just hanging in there.

The way I remember the Frazier-Quarry fight, they had felt each other out for a few rounds, which is customary, until in the middle of a middle round, Frazier suddenly, unaccountably, dropped his guard. He simply lowered his gloves. Quarry was momentarily startled by the opening, then he let loose with his best left. Frazier staggered a little, recovered, and raised his hands again. Well, the fight was over. It went on for another couple of rounds, but it was over. Frazier knew that Quarry could not hurt him, and now Quarry knew it, too. And eventually, inevitably, Quarry went the way of all overmatched and battered flesh.

I can picture him heaped in his dressing room afterwards, with his wounds leaking and bruises taking root, realizing that at least he had taken his best shot. As the saying goes, that's all you can ask of someone. That must have been some consolation to him after his loss. Or possibly not.

◻ ◻ ◻

I approached and looked upon the great man's median. I had reached equatorial Rockwell and gazed upon it. I observed his venerable belly, his grand maw. Here was someone whose gut-level ethics were laid plainly out there. Life was a brunt to be borne, so toughen your bark—that was the message he stood for. His skin shone bright and leathery as a new valise containing unfathomable organs; in fact, it was easier to assume that,

unlike other men, Rockwell hid a solid core. Perhaps that was his
secret: one goes stoic from the center out.

Maybe then I thought of Ahab lashed to that notorious
bleached bulk. Or I may have revolted at the sensation to come:
like booting with a bare foot a wet bag of mulch. Or maybe I
caught a glimpse of Rockwell's face and saw it just begin to fill
with ruin. Whatever the reason, I pulled my punch. Grudgingly
begun, it dudded against him like a dead shell.

And I had no one to apologize to. The manager did not lead
a chorus in scorn. Instead, what remained of the crowd had
quickly dismissed me and already turned their backs. Roger's
allegiance was shaken—his smile had shifted down to a smirk—
but he understood enough to keep quiet. John simply noted the
time: we had to get moving to catch the last bus back. All around
us the carnival was packing up for the night. The booths were
shutting down. It seemed the whole place was imploding,
although I know that it was only self-consciousness that made
me believe that I was the one who'd stuck the pin in it. I glanced
back at Rockwell, who was occupied with buttoning his shirt,
which he did, at least as it appeared to me, almost modestly.

◻ ◻ ◻

Today I am teaching an eleven-year-old boy how to box. My
friend, his mother, has been a pacifist since college, when Viet
Nam brought that conviction to the surface for her. But she lives
in the world now, as she puts it, and she knows that you don't
have to look for a confrontation for one to find you. She knows
that society is divided into hammers and nails, so her son needs
to know how to defend himself. Even at eleven. Especially at
eleven, really. But she knows nothing about boxing, and, as a single mother on a strained income, she cannot afford the martial
arts classes offered at the fitness center. So she phoned me to
step in and just give him some of the basics. After all, I was the
one who had shown him how a right-handed pitcher brings his

left foot forward as he throws, how a proper quarterback snaps his wrist past his ear, how a basketball player puts backspin on his shot, and why, in every case, it is essential to follow through.

"Even if I could help, he'd be embarrassed to let me try. But he'll listen to a man," she said, pausing after this to let me catch up to the implication, which was that she herself had listened to a man, and look where it landed her, unable to buy professional protection for her son. "He'll take it from you," she said.

When I get there, he is waiting for me in the backyard. It's June, but he is wearing his winter gloves, which would have to do for boxing gloves. I flash on an image of the two of them, mother and son, rummaging through his closet, making a mutual project out of this crisis of vulnerability—the latest in the endless series of exposures that constitutes every boy's maturation, although I do not say anything of the sort. I smile at this kid in the T-shirt and winter gloves, who wants to fight, who wants to make it fun. But I do not criticize, and I do not make light of the situation. We do not credit our teachers nearly enough. Any education is a weighty business.

So while his mother watches—"Let him show you, honey!"—I show him what I can. I start by sculpting, moving his legs and shoulders for him. I help him take a valid stance, straighten out the loops and flails in his punches, and tell him always to follow through. "Where's your center of gravity, huh?" I keep asking him. "You always need to find your center of gravity. That's where your power comes from. That's how you maximize your force." And so we spar for fifteen minutes or so, until we are summoned for lunch. "You have to stay for lunch. It's the least I can offer you." It is not an easy life, and I don't think it gets any easier, but you have to eat.

So I watch her watch him, her son who now knows how to throw a punch, as he works his way toward the crust he'll abandon. His gloves are next to him on the table. I wonder what he makes of the whole weird business of preparing for a fight he is not supposed to want or have. But of course, I know what is

going through his mind: he's rushing through lunch because he's
eager to go at it again. Mom's look says something like "This dis-
turbs me, but you can see why I needed your help." It is no more
than five minutes since we've sat down, but he's already up with
his gloves and bolting for the back door. "Are you ready yet?" he
calls from the yard. My own mother, who had the burden of two
sons of her own, had a habit of looking up to the ceiling on
exhausting days (and which were not?) and crying "Strength!"
But the look I get from this boy's mother says something like
"Boys will be boys," meaning me, too. Or possibly not.

Anyway, I go out. I still need to tell him about the importance of having a clean fight, if you have to have one, and about
obeying the rules of boxing, which may not always be clear but
which still exist, and about keeping your hands up at all times,
because you never know, and about getting the good lick in
when you can, and about saving face when you can't. It's a lot for
a boy to take in, but the consolation is that no one expects you
to get it all at once.

body language

Fronting the university library is a set of human statues, one on each side of the main doors. They are not sentries or welcoming officers. They do not suggest camaraderie or academic employment. They attend to no one.

What consumes them is a predicament of beginnings: they have been caught at the task of tearing themselves out of rock. Each beleaguered figure seems a Hercules in hopeless rage against a lethal robe; each is forever half-embedded in its granite sheath, forever unable to be fully born, and heaving beneath the knowledge that the self is an impossible and agonizing haul. It is as if fate had caught them at the larval chore of every muscle and joint. Or perhaps the argument is reversed, and they are being digested by their origins, swallowed inexorably back into the block. Whichever the intent, the hard fact here is that embodiment cannot be taken for granted. It is shown to be a vicious ruse at their expense. Even in their shared travail they do not regard one another, for a sense of otherness is a luxury beyond them. Between them lies a channel of steps, which custodians daily sweep clean. Each of these figures is obsessed with the body's bad dream of itself. The tension is fierce, cold, absolute: you are confronted by works-in-progress in final, useless rage against unnegotiable stone.

Aesthetic distance reveals the library's own groaner: in the
end, there is no transcending the concrete.

Whatever his charge had been—something allusive and con-
ventionally majestic, no doubt, befitting a solid library endowment—the artist has provided a difficult lesson: the body is an
unresolvable conflict, which we engage and deny, engage and
deny. The statues imply motion—there is still ongoingness going
on, still the imaginative possibility of their maker's returning to
finish his work—and at the same time, all along their great resistant surfaces, there is the burden of arrested development and
checked desire. A Pompeiian spell has been cast against them.
Impacted, they strain eternally against solid welds. Anonymous,
they wear out the seasons, with some rough, unspoken judgment
relentlessly at their backs, the shadow of bone on bone.

All that gravity eating light.

The library steps are scooped with use, like lower lips drawn
down by invisible fingers, in earnest consideration of the students
passing there. But because they are made from a different stone
than the steps, the statues do not relax with age. Only they pit
and stain. They have grown leprous with distress. One has a thin
crack through the hip that disappears into the carapace; the other
has at some time during the past century dropped a toe. The
wind seems to pick up as you descend the steps, so as you leave
the library it is easy to think of dissolution licking at them under
that stifled tide they carry—merciless, and mercilessly slow
about it. During a typical Midwestern November, when a brittle
light lies against the bare branches veining the Quad and Time is
a tongue flicking at your ear, you draw up and batten down your
thickest scarf, taking what cover you can.

For Delmore Schwartz, the body is a heavy bear, clumsy and
stifling and inescapable in its appetites, "Dragging me with him
in his mouthing care." For William Matthews, it is a rented house
to rummage about in, which he toasts: "Here's to the body, then,
our only real estate, / our squander, our hoard. Long may it contend." An athlete jogs on a treadmill and tries his pulse for a

favorable report. A woman in her empty apartment still locks the bathroom door behind her when she checks her breasts for consistency. They are like the poets sounding themselves, tending their imagery like Zen gardens.

Most all of the poets you read have long since gone under.

If you fasten on the right undergraduate, you can follow him out of campus to the local Snak-Atak, whose patrons cower in comparable postures against some cold they cannot shake inside. So many merchants have given up on the downtown area, with its denuded Green Street, its forsaken Main; so many stores fail to put up a brave front. Meanwhile, this is the sort of low simmer capitalism has come down to. In the parking lot the unemployed have shambled to a halt and talk about coffee. They remind you of the way race cars after collision coast onto the infield to steam, the competition over for them now. What inverts two of the customers into the folds of their coats—that same student is bent in study next to an older man, who is separately absorbed—is nothing so cerebral as the research library suggested. No resonant myth invades their discretion. Here the curriculum is soft pornography, and in these magazines all savor is professional and the bodies blare. The women strapped and pinned to the racks—a caricature of bondage to intimate the contents—are always too crass, too opulent about their offers. Sirens of the homeliest aisles, they are all slick business. They imitate the Snak-Atak they inhabit: obvious, predictable, aggressive, a carnal assault. Convenience is the key here. (THIS IS NOT A LIBRARY, a handwritten sign taped to the top shelf warns.) Get in, get it, get out, and get going.

Tradition would pimple the boy and ravage the man somehow, sharpen the lines about his mouth, say, or coarsen his hands. You see no evidence, however, no furtive pantomime. They are both solemn and locked in, lulled and, perhaps, faintly rocking.

Feminist contentions to the contrary, no one fantasizes that the women in skin magazines are looking at them, panting to be taken under their covers. In fact, their virtues are impenetrability,

falsity, and a forgiving blindness. Do what you will to it, Sharon
Olds explains, "and it will not care, it is shameless, no honor / is
innate to the body." No, whatever violation happens, happens
outside, where the working world boiled over years ago and
dried up. As they expertly dare and adore you, the pictured
women suggest that you can perpetrate nothing of consequence
against them. Nothing about them asks for possession or change
or understanding or remembrance. Nothing says stay.

It may be something about the glossy paper and the shivery
light of the Snak-Atak, but it seems as if something looms just
past the skin of the women, like the skin's implication. Call it
costliness—a commercial aura. The eagerness they affect in the
photographs is the eagerness of commodities to be consumed,
yet they pronounce nothing more political than plane geometry.
They merely masquerade as bodies, bodies that cannot break
down, Platonic despite their incitements. This is thanks to what
might be called aesthetic distance. They promise love condensed
and sweetly undeceived. They cannot be betrayed. What you are
doing, huddled in your collars and cuffs, working your sheets, is
penance, ah, but not to them. Regardless, they let you off.

The boy leaves without buying anything, not so much as a
pack of gum to justify his stay. The guy behind the counter is
not offended; he cannot be bothered, not for what he makes an
hour. He has been cultivating his indifference all shift long. The
place is in the hands of part-timers, whose reflex is to surrender
the keys to any culprit or, in case of a fire, to walk out and not
look back. Once outside, the boy churns in his coat like a crab
snagged on its shell, repositioning. The wind occasionally finds
its way inside, swelling a sail at his back. He stops to zip up, and
when he does the coat deflates to conform a bit better to his
body. But it is his father's, and the fit is never right.

The doctors had hooked his father up to half a dozen monitors, trying to translate his motives. But by then, everyone
already knew what his body was saying.

When his father died, his mother took him on a tour of the

walk-in bedroom closet to try on clothes. The closet was thick with shirts and sport coats, all stiffly pressed together in silent ranks against the single light and stiffly vigilant as mother and son passed between. Some of them had never been worn at all. They had been purchased just prior to his father's having gone into the hospital for what turned out to be his last weeks. New clothes were a hedge against his death; or, better, they were a ransom paid out to get his body back in one piece. Now they would only go to Goodwill, to strangers, his mother told him, unless he could get some use out of them.

The body is a record of the past. It is a savage culmination that remembers everything. His father's body had become a slum, his prospects a neighborhood gone bad. In the end, his only option was to sell short.

She found it consoling and proper for the son to take whatever he could upon himself, but his father had been a much heavier man, and not even long illness caused him to dwindle enough for his last shirts to work. The pants, shoes, and ties were impossible, of course, too clownish for commemoration. The silver ring required thicker fingers, while the watch hung impracticably, perilously slack about his wrist. Smoking had done the man in. What good would a gold-plated cigarette lighter do his son? Nylon socks, reading glasses, hypodermic needles. Scores, literally, of unbroken frames of pills, in graduated arrays—seven the first day, five the next, then three, then two, then one—as though they were performance graphs of a failing stock. The residue of obligation. A dead man's dregs. At least the money clip could be taken—his father, like so many of his generation, firmly believed in paying cash—and the son accepted its outlandish weight in his jeans pocket. But his father was for the most part, and inevitably, abandonable. The rest of the possessions, which were growing lighter every day with his departure, awaited donation or the landfill.

Any memory is love, but even to spare memory, only the one coat could be managed at all. But he has never been

comfortable with it. It slants and chuffs on him constantly, an
extra lung; it swarms about him, making him look derelict or
retarded, so he thinks. However comical he looks, he is committed to his father's sake, but his father's sake defies interpretation. What he has sensed ever since the funeral is that his father
includes both the man and his absence, that hollow he hides in,
that remoter self, and it is too much to absorb. That billow, that
swag that catches at him from behind. His father is an amplified
silence, an invisible Anchises riding Aeneas out into the street.

When he was four or five—he could not have been older
because it was on weekdays without school—he would occasionally get to go with his father downtown to pretend with the
office supplies. The adding machine and the date stamper were
particular favorites, part of some densely serious commerce that
the child knew nothing about. At the end of the day his hands
were smeared with ink, the heels mysteriously bruised blue. On
the streets of Chicago he was a faithful colony of his father's,
only and always his father's son, and he hung anonymous and
assured against a pants leg as they crossed Dearborn, Clark,
LaSalle—massive avenues named for military leaders and explorers. At that point it had not even been a year, surely, since he had
made a practice of scuffing up and down the hall in his father's
slippers, which was always good for a laugh. There was a photograph somewhere of him, too, with his head swallowed past
his nose in his father's hat. So it was long enough ago that men
wore hats like that.

Gripping the coat in at the collar and belt, making a bale of
himself, gives the boy the sense of taking in more space, of taking more space on. It is an effort always: refocusing, gathering
dimension. He pulls himself together the way a photographer
manipulates an image for better resolution. The space between
him and his father is a kind of aesthetic distance: that unoccu-
pied zone where the first hints of infiltration are expected.
Anyone who bothers to look would see the boy as someone who
has been hit in the chest or who is trying to hold his organs in.

The coat slobbers over him, as if some appetite were still alive in it.

He makes his way down the street, tacking into the insistent wind, which according to the regular winter's miracle in Illinois is always in your face. Only after he turns the corner does he ease his grasp on the coat and extract the stolen magazine. It was an easy matter to stash it and go. The counterman never looked up. The man at the rack with him, whose own little infidelities were enough to absorb him, never moved. In the open air, in what light remains of the waning day, he imagines the magazine expanding in his hands, but still no one is looking. Nothing follows his crime—no bustle of law enforcement, no accusation from a second-story window, no blame at his back. He riffles indifferent pages, smudging his fingers.

The smuggled images are flat in the flat light and blurred. They answer exactly no need.

Where he stands he is shielded by the blunt architecture of downtown Champaign. Where is the broad, grieving ghost of his father now to scold him or show him mercy? But the usual ragged traffic passes unremarkably through as usual. No matter. Not a trickle of interest, and the wind between buildings is calm. It remains, somehow, a rumorless afternoon.

Actually, he had had the money on him to pay for it, and possibly the nerve, too, to brazen out the lurid purchase in public. Stealing was never on his mind. It was one of those involuntary actions, the body's blurting out, reflexes speculating on their own. And all the while, there is this consensus of neglect. And yet, there is penance in any flesh you carry.

No one watches, makes him out a vagrant, presumes against him. He has been left in his own custody. Exile is when everything in the world gives you aesthetic distance.

For all of its diminishment, the city still maintains its steel garbage baskets. At the next one he reaches, he shoves the magazine in as deep as it will go. He has to shake his sleeve free of orange peels as he pulls it out. November in central Illinois concedes nothing. It is one of those days when daylight drops like something shot in the forest. The way the boy bulks up again, he might look determined, but really, it is just so cold out.

Will he live forever? Sometimes it feels that way. And in just this form, hovering over himself like a match struck in the weather. Hunching toward the street again, he makes his slack and darkening return to campus.

call waiting

I am eating breakfast with Al at The Pie Stop, a corrugated steel bunker that opens at 3:00 a.m. and is closed before noon. The place caters to truckers and cabbies. I may be the only person here who doesn't drive for a living.

It's 7:30. Certainly I'm the only one who hasn't just gotten off shift. These are men who cash their paychecks every week. It is December, and most everyone wears denim. One guy has his denim sleeves pulled up to reveal that he's smuggling wrenches in his forearms. Another one has a neck whose pimpled slubs keep coming untucked and oozing out of his denim collar. You can see the arduousness of everything in the way they grumble over the last election and the Bears' miserable excuse for an offense and the impossibilities women pose and money—money, especially. These are men who down three cups of black coffee before filling Thermoses with more. They believe nothing in the world is going to change much, unless it gets meaner, harder, colder. Colder, especially. When they come in, they stamp off crusts of snow and seethe through teeth that they'd gritted against the winter's merciless probing for weaknesses, for openings.

Life is persecution and black coffee, over and over, and the waitress puts down a full cup in front of each man before he orders anything. From table to counter to table and back again, she dodges and accommodates, making one shaky radius after another.

In less than a year, The Pie Stop will be out of business. I'll get to see the tractor flatten it. The place has no foundation, so razing it will take about fifteen seconds. A florist will replace it, then an insurance firm. The last time I made it back to the city, it was a photo shop.

This morning, Al is talking to me about hash browns. He wants to write a book about hash browns in the greater Chicago area, and he's asked me to meet him for breakfast to talk over how to go about getting it published. I'm the only person he knows from our high school "who has anything to do with books, job-wise," and since I'm back visiting family over my winter break—I'm the only person he knows who still divides the calendar the way we did in high school, whose time, in fact, observes the same tides as time did thirty years ago—he left a message for me to meet him at 6:30. I negotiated for an extra hour's sleep—it is my vacation, after all—and when I arrived he had already finished a plate of ketchup-smothered eggs, toast, and hash browns, which left a moist, vaguely menstrual debris between us. Now he is chasing it all with coffee, paving the way for pastry. Al is a guy who *really* works for a living, for whom hunger is something you took care of like your kids.

"I eat them every day, anyway, you know? And over the last few years I've been in probably, what, forty different coffee shops and truck stops all over Chicago, so I've got the lay of the land, you might say, as far as hash browns go. I know where the best ones are made, and the cheapest, and the fastest. If you like 'em especially greasy or burnt, I know where to find those, too. *An Insider's Guide to the Hash Browns of Chicago*, or something like that. I'm the guy to do it. Anyway, what's the saying? Everybody's got at least one book in him, and I think this one's mine."

Al has no illusions about wealth and fame, mind you. He is by nature and situation a modest man. "When worse comes to worse," he says, signaling the concluding strains of the day's

complaint. "When," not "if." Al faces the hard facts like traffic on
the Dan Ryan and, like the resourceful driver you *had* to be, tacks
into it, probing for openings the way the weather does. I still
recognize in him the high school sophomore who once bummed
rides, desserts, and quarters for the pinball machine. Once I saw
him snatch a fistful of fries off a stranger's abandoned plate on
our way out of Morry's. (Even then he betrayed his preference
for diners over fast-food franchises. Why eat off paper when you
could enjoy the real clatter of real silver against real plates?)
That one spring break we drove with another friend to Florida,
Al used two plastic drawstring garbage bags for suitcases. No, he
clearly isn't in it for the money because he hadn't ever been in
anything for the money.

A bear claw arrives, with its dandruff glaze, along with more
coffee. Never much of a morning eater myself—a can of Slim-
Fast is all I can manage before lunch, and that only recently in
deference to my having read an article about the irreplaceable
health benefits of breakfast—I watch him intently as he swabs
the plate with his pastry to recover the sweet fallen dust. My
own first meal takes forty seconds on average to complete, and
that includes the additional couple of seconds it takes me on
alternate mornings to wash down an aspirin (yes, in deference to
another article about staving off heart disease). Meanwhile, Al
has been sitting here for over an hour already, combining a
Rabelaisian appetite with monkish deliberation. "Research!" he
explains in a couple of gusts of wet crumbs, and his smile widens
to display the latest entries.

❏ ❏ ❏

What greater gift is there than the early, incontrovertible evidence of a calling? If only our chosen occupations chose and
occupied us like willing little Italys. If only vocation always
showed as clearly in the mirror as eye color and bedded down as
deeply in the genes.

For most of us, unsponsored, unmoored, forever barking elbows and shins in a pathless wood, Fate is a flirt. As she bats her lashes at the end of the bar, we wonder if she is beckoning us or suffering from allergies. We cannot tell through the smoky distance if she is signifying loose behavior or a loose contact lens, so we hang fire, running a nervous index finger around the rim of the glass. But life is an entirely different matter for those chosen few who know that they *are* the chosen few. From their day-planners lifts the aura of a master plan, and they fill in their autobiographies with the assurance of Ben Franklins or bosses' only sons. There is the prodigy who during a bout of toilet training hums his first symphony, or the adolescent who tops six-foot-seven before junior high, or any one of those lucky bastards for whom bushes burn without burning down. Fate sidles by and takes his arm, making a claim so clear as to shock the palmist or startle the astrologer like an ambush of regimented stars.

❏ ❏ ❏

At the start of college, I gaped my way through New Student Week with the rest of the freshmen, all left to our own dubious resources and creeping about the Quad with incentives dark and genital, with the exception of one appointed afternoon. On that day, with a thousand other newly hatched and deposited peers I sat in the Armory, which was temporarily devoted to the testing of interests and aptitudes. This particular day's test, the KSIE (or "kissee," a label that helped make the ordeal less forbidding), was an elaborate, exhaustive inventory consisting of six hundred multiple-choice questions cunningly designed (with subtle repetitions, deftly altered phrasings, and Moebius strip overlaps) to ferret out of us our unconscious desires, hopes, and intentions, which in turn would clarify our respective best directions. Questions like: Would you rather attend a) a play; b) a baseball game; c) a concert; or d) a museum exhibit? Questions like: You have fifty dollars to spend any way you want to. Do you spend it on a) books; b) clothes; c) stereo equipment (we had barely scratched the 1970s, after all); or d) a party? Questions like: Would you rather be a) mean; b) lazy; or c) stupid? Like any multiple-choice test, None of the Above, or Some Other Option, or Guilty with an Explanation was the missing cell, which is to say that it was an exasperating five hours for all of us.

I took heart from noticing that the tests had come from Iowa, where similar tests administered approximately every two years from first grade onward had likewise been devised. (I have still to this day never visited Iowa, but in my mind it resolves as an endless checkerboard of plotted fields alternating not between squares of red and black but between squares of corn and standardized tests. I envision inseparably nuclear families, shot heroically from below, contentedly presiding over dreamy tides of corn and billowing pages of pristine tests, their covers unsmudged, their seals unbroken.)

And so, after my six hundred impeachable answers had been entered into the digestive system of the best university computer 1971 had to offer, I received my career diagnosis: Questionable. I was questionable. After the regular expenditure of considerable intuition and fees, my future was questionable. I was then assigned an adviser, who suggested I play the percentages and stick to required courses: the 101 in which I would learn about irrational numbers; the 101 in which I would learn that measuring the location of a charged particle altered its speed, and vice versa; the 101 in which I would learn that poems were onions made of endless layers and endless tears. There was the 101 in which Aristotle defined true happiness as doing the right work and left it at that, which was the 101 in which I learned that God had taken sabbatical a century or so ago and hadn't shown up for office hours since. Basically, I was tossed into the deep end of the general curriculum and told to swim for it.

And while I was contending with college, trying to make it to one shore or another, Al was already making his living, *this* living, and eating the most attentive and intensely researched breakfasts in the greater Chicago area.

◻ ◻ ◻

An actor is being interviewed on *Entertainment Tonight*. He is promoting his book about his life in film. Asked if it is a "kiss-and-tell," he simply smiles the famous and still mischievous smile he has smiled on screen for thirty years, the smile that sells.

On *Oprah*, an animated counselor maintains that every component of self-esteem, from job satisfaction to communication in marriage to a favorable body image, is connected to every other, as she outlines in the book Oprah is holding up and slowly sweeping over the heads of the audience. Camera One zeroes in on it until it passes out of range, at which point Camera Two picks it up, so it is never out of sight.

Over the course of two weeks in a year featuring a presidential election, *Today* gives equal time to all of the principal candidates from both parties, as well as to the Reform candidate, the Libertarian candidate, the Green Party candidate, and a self-funded candidate who owns one of the two largest chains of shoe stores in North America. Each has published a book outlining his vision.

Every early afternoon talk show has its "house psychologist," a levelheaded woman brought in during the last quarter-hour to referee family squabbles, get in the faces of smugly arrogant teens, or shepherd the desolate, the deformed, and the dispossessed through their complimentary makeovers. Each has a book, and each book has a full-length picture of its author on the dust jacket, who looks creamy and polished and confident and sympathetic and unconflicted and inevitable, all at once.

Chefs. Secretaries and custodians and barbers who have eavesdropped on the prominent. Reformed addicts, as well as relapsed addicts. Spiritualists, as well as those who have lost God, as well as those who have found Him. Dietitians.

Professional wrestlers. All have produced books. Blurbs announce variations on the belief that this is the book each was "born to write." The Pope has a book out. So (ghosted by the First Lady) does the President's dog.

❏ ❏ ❏

"Do you believe in the life to come?"
"Mine was always that."

This is from Samuel Beckett's *Endgame*, which we covered in Introduction to Literature. (Yes, another 101.) The burden of this interchange is typically misunderstood, which is not at all unusual when it comes to Beckett. It is supposed to be funny.

In that same course, we covered Henry James's "The Beast in the Jungle," which is about a man who spent his life avoiding prosaic attachments (including a discernible career, including love) so as to remain available to the special, momentous destiny that he could not define but did not doubt loomed in the thick-eted distance like, well, a beast in his jungle. So the guy squanders his life putting off everyone and everything—keeping the line clear, so to speak. And the punch line is that no beast comes. Nothing pounces. It's all nothing but beastless jungle.

In this instance—literature can be slippery—it is not supposed to be funny at all.

❏ ❏ ❏

To anyone with an appetite for connection, let me suggest going to a major university. A campus is a repercussive hive, resonant at every level. In my mind, the throngs of students crossing and recrossing the Quad create an invisible thatching over the years, uniting building to building, integrating curricula, increasing the synaptic voltage. One massive network, one endlessly spreading correspondence course.

For my own part, I never threw away any of my papers from
any class, for there was nothing that was not potentially ger-
mane. Just as distant cousins still pump the family blood, vagrant
bits from the nether disciplines could claim affiliations to one's
major field. Who knows which Amazon flower heedlessly
crushed underfoot held the irreplaceable serum? One could dis-
pose of nothing with impunity.

As if in seizure, I was constantly flashing on correlations
from day to day, class to class. I could not see without *see also* or
study twenty minutes without sensing *cf.* During certain periods
I could no more separate a finding from the referential pile than
I could with all my wits about me isolate a single wit. Every note
or phrase seemed the tenor of a vehicle I'd noted or phrased the
day before. My notebook pages were pocked with so many pairs
of parallel lines indicating kinships that every paragraph looked
like a slalom run that had borne the slashes of miniature skis. Or
it was as though my thoughts had all been hopped upon by precise little birds. Both, really.

◻ ◻ ◻

I found out from my grandmother that my father had once studied to become a doctor. I'd had no idea. He was already an attorney when I was born and had never wavered or craved otherwise, not so far as I knew. That what I presumed had been his
uninterrupted twenty-four-year journey toward engendering me
had once eddied around some alternative seemed like wanton-
ness, or at least it sent a brief bubble through my metaphysics.
Anyway, Grandma saw me flinch.

"No, he never told you that, did he? It's true, true enough.
He studied science in college. But he couldn't be a doctor. He
didn't have the hands for it."

She was stuffing kishke, kneading ground sausage into skin
casings. Her own hands appeared to be perfectly suited to it, a
born kishke-stuffer's hands: thick fingers with wide, round

knuckles and stubby thumbs sheathed in pitted bark. I had never seen anyone else perform this task—never considered the task then or since apart from my grandmother's pressing and pressing the greasy meat through. They were my father's hands, too.

"So Dad became a lawyer."

"And he's a *good* lawyer, too. Doctor was out of the question. He would not have been a success. He would not have been a happy man," she explained, all the while working the skins. I never even bothered to offer to help her anymore. Kishke was her specialty, and anyway, she had long ago made it clear that this was no job for me.

Perhaps I examined my hands.

◻ ◻ ◻

A giraffe can pick out its kin from the herd by the subtle uniqueness of its reticulations. A tiger can pluck the right cub on a dead run. A starling can slip bird by bird through the flock during rush-hour commute and find its mate. Everywhere in nature, tabs are alert to their proper slots.

There is a human counterpart to this, and he is a fixture of Restoration comedy. The hero, a young man whose sprightly manner, winning appearance, and nimble diction do him little good in the opening act, slaves anonymously away for most of the play. He continually proves himself bold or clever or gallant, but alas, these star-power endowments cannot change his station. Luckily, after his virtue is demonstrated, a gentleman of means is somehow moved to confess the secret of his lost son. He mentions a special locket or defining blemish, and our hero is unveiled as our hero. When it comes to Restoration comedy, this device, however hard it may be for audiences weaned on realism's sugar-free diet to swallow, is not negotiable. First, virtue is proved to be its own reward, then virtue is rewarded with fortune. It's destiny's staged economy—a real crowd-pleaser, if we are to believe the records that have come down to us about the count of the house.

The closest comparison our century can muster may be the Horatio Alger story, whose typical plot structure, featuring a bedraggled kid's evolution out of larval confinement and general abjection into gleaming class and stature, was an inspiring arc of triumph. Mark, the Match-Boy, is serendipitously struck against some remarkable circumstance, lighting the way to a marvelous future. Out of the crooked timber of Ragged Dick a straight fate is magically made. They typically know about getting on with it, and they are typically spared the travail of wondering what the "it" is that they are supposed to be getting on with.

❏   ❏   ❏

I admit it. I cannot follow a detective story. Motives blear for me, and clues dissolve in the plot's hard boil. The cops congeal; the culprits coalesce. So I founder like a child stymied by algebra's variables and unknowns. I page back through the book for bearings I'd never gotten in the first place or blindly search the screen, which seems to have eaten all the light. I am always amazed that Humphrey Bogart has brought the case to bay before I've even sorted out the cast. Hercule Poirot takes complacent pains to lay out the mosaic of exposition, and although I cringe along with the gathered guests, it is not in my case for fear of being implicated. James Bond's urbane and tailored schemes are so much continental drift to me, and it feels as if every satisfied cry of "Elementary!" from Sherlock Holmes comes from a departing carriage.

My only hope is to latch onto the detective's trench coattails and trust in his instinct for coherence. If I'm lucky, he spends a scene with a gun trained on him while the evil mastermind—so *he's* the one, which means it must've been another one who plummeted to his death, and what happened to the brother, wasn't there a brother?—unpacks his dastardliness point by delectable point. But of course, the detective has prepared for this very eventuality, having snapped up the crucial clue earlier, remember?

Something is taking its course, I guess, turning back the pages, rewinding.

◻ ◻ ◻

Because I was not cursed with sufficient athletic talent as a boy to postpone certain fundamental realizations—that I would never play centerfield for the Sox, that the stars could not reconstellate to land me in the Bears' backfield, and that too many laws of physics would have to be repealed for me to enjoy the lift or speed or court sense to sink a winning basket for any franchise, ever—I moved on more quickly than many of my friends to other fantasies.

For a long while, I thought paleontology would be it for me. *The Big Golden Book of Dinosaurs* was for months the only book, and, like any believer's bible, it contained all necessary revelation. At seven years of age, I could hold my ground against any species, withstand their barrage of statistics and syllables and come up smart-assed. A savvy host, I knew how to keep the meat-eaters and the plant-eaters apart. I could recite the major eras quicker than my peers could manage their multiplication tables. I had weights and measures down.

A particular mystery that defied even the august squad of doctorates on the editorial board of *The Big Golden Book* had to do with stegosaurus. One of the enduring pleasures regarding stegosaurus was the "Fun Fact" that it required two brains to operate its massive bulk—one in the head, one in the tail. (Each brain approximated the size and appearance of a chewed wad of gum. *The Big Golden Book* even provided a picture of a chewed wad of gum for ready reference. It was pink, though there was no reliable conjecturing about the color of stegosaurus's brain.) Years later I would recall this bit of information when I attended a conference at Ohio State University, whose campus was so large that it required two union buildings at opposite ends to coordinate its enormous student body.

The mystery concerned the function of the double row of bony plates that ran upright along the back of stegosaurus. One school of thought surmised that they served as a sort of radiator, regulating temperature with the changing seasons. According to another, their primary purpose was to protect stegosaurus from predators, such as tyrannosaurus rex (height: up to twenty feet; length: up to fifty feet; weight: fourteen thousand to sixteen thousand pounds). A third theory speculated that they were used for mating displays. Do not imagine a combative atmosphere at the offices of Golden Book, however. No side was adamant about its position. For everyone involved, stegosaurus's back was a hedged bet. And there was consensus in this regard: whatever those back plates stood for, they served a definite purpose.

❏ ❏ ❏

As I write this, I am divorced. When I finish, I am going to meet my girlfriend and another couple, all of whom are also divorced; actually, we have had six divorces among the four of us. We're getting on.

Nor is this very unusual among our circle of friends. Nor, report the weekly news magazines, throughout most of the country and my generation. If you believe the conventional wisdom, ours is an age rife with disavowal. Some pundits of evangelical inclination contend that this is a symptom of our civilization's demise. (They often hawk books about this on afternoon talk shows.) Most of them maintain that it is too late to save us from the fate of the dinosaurs—at least, this is the conviction of the ones who believe that dinosaurs once existed. Some of them positively look forward to that day, for on that day, eschatology tells us, all things will be made plain.

As I write this, my grandmother is gone. So is my father.

Sometimes I see them, or aspects of them, begin to emerge in my gestures, my opinions, my fears, my prejudices, my face, my phrases, my child. They don't arrive with advice the way they always did in life. Instead, when they subside, they seem to shave away the thinnest layer of bank from me, so that it is not only them I find myself missing.

As I write this, I am thinking about an article I came across recently about a substantial revision in scientific findings culminating in the renaming of brontosaurus. That animal is now officially known as "apatosaurus." We are no longer to use the designation "brontosaurus," which is being systematically expunged from schoolbooks. Evidently, brontosaurus per se is and always was extinct. But scientists are not embarrassed or dejected. In fact, they assure us, science often requires the temporary adoption of mistakes to guarantee a later accuracy. Like proponents of spontaneous generation, the discredited discoverers of brontosaurus performed a service, compelling their descendants to rule them out.

In other words, sometimes you have to go a long way out of your way in order to come back a short distance correctly. That is a line I remember from Edward Albee's play *Zoo Story*, another fossil from my 101 notes.

The new edition of *The Big Golden Book of Dinosaurs* will also have to make amends. This will not be the first time, either. Years ago, in response to a flurry of letters from teachers and other dinosaur aficionados, the picture I remember best, which showed the attack on a humble, grudging stegosaurus by a tyrannosaurus rex, was eliminated because those animals never coexisted. As numerous experts wrote in to point out, tyrannosaurus rex was a creature of the late Cretaceous Period (roughly sixty-five million years ago), while stegosaurus concluded its browsing some ninety million years earlier, in the Jurassic Period. As to what did them in—a giant meteor, possibly, or a change in the climate—that may be verified in a future edition. Maybe they died of darkness.

As I write this, I am a college professor and so, in a sense, still in school. There are doctors, and then there are doctors who can do you some good. It's a family joke. A Ph.D. is a ticket to tenured adolescence granted to those happy, happy few who went through school singing beyond the genius of the C. (Name that tune.) While the rest of the world rushes past, catching cabs, next year I start forty-first grade. Get it? It is supposed to be funny.

And when I get a chance, I will check the World Wide Web, as I do periodically, to see if Al's book has come out yet. Nothing so far. Possibly, of course, the book is out, but in so small a supply from so local and cozy a publishing house that it has escaped the attention of Amazon.com. On the other hand, given our conversation that morning in the dearly departed Pie Stop, you'd think if it had, he would have called.

variations on a gift horse

When she saw her great-granddaughter for the first time, Eva suspected that the baby was a boy.

Undeterred for once by the stingy procedures and stale halls of the Ravenswood Care Facility, we had maintained buoyancy as we passed the residents docked in their wheelchairs against the wall, variously damaged and straining. We had not stopped to peek through the open door of the permanently knuckled Mr. Weisburg, nor slowed down to heed the daily keening of Mrs. Klein. Our new daughter was precious candy, and so we swept through that gauntlet of the gaunt, bore our baby girl past all the spilled sense and vague hungers, to make sure that Eva would be the first to get her fill of her.

A regular at temple for decades until this most recent illness laid her out, Eva had announced her sole defiance of Hebrew convention: despite the dictate that children be named exclusively to commemorate the dead, she asked that should we have a daughter, we name it after her. With a stroke, all the trendy onomastic aids and etymological primers were swept aside, and nominations ceased. Chloe, Jennifer, Rebecca, and Sarah were tabled, for the once and future Eva had the floor. For Chava, the baby would be Chava.

And now the old woman peered at the child out of her

stanched aptitudes and stymied will and would not believe. We
who had pried her away from her own room and forced her to
stay at Ravenswood, where everything was abrupt and strange
and stank of hygiene; we who had retreated into lockets and picture frames on the bureau, the wrack left in the wake of her life's
contraction, now too far away for her to see; we, her beloved
and treacherous family, had come to her to lie about the baby.
Our plot? To make her feel better. We could be that cruel, and
to someone whose only crime was to grow old and to love us
down to her last wit.

In his poem "Losing a Language," W. S. Merwin considers
people whose lives had unspooled like that; he refers to them as
"wrong and dark." Presents are predicaments for them, and
"when there is a voice at the door it is foreign / everywhere
instead of a name there is a lie." Eva's strange, expanding family
was making a gift of itself, blocking the doorway.

"You have a beautiful family, Eva," the day nurse concluded.
Chelsea was her name, if you can believe it. She was younger
than I was, and yet she called our grandmother by her first name.
I don't think she noticed the old woman pucker at the
familiarity. (We were all of us in on it, she knew.) "Your great-
granddaughter looks like you." Eva, with her bad eyes, had to
take it on faith. Oh, it was insidious. The family knew her needs
and weaknesses like flaws in the china or missed stitches in the
quilt. Age opens the chinks in us, eats at the seams. An inevitable
clutch of others, it was her family who bungled in, flanked the
bed, intercepted the mail, colluded in the corner, put her here
and told her this was her room now.

She regarded the changeling like another unpronounceable
pill to swallow down. (Ninety-four, and sensing a conspiracy here
to try to get her hooked on drugs.) I came close and heard her
"Tsk, tsk, tsk" at my daughter, who was an odd bit of tin in her
beak. I went so far as to take off the baby's diaper and show her
that we were not just trying to make her happy. We would never
do that. "You see, Grandma? She's a girl. Look, look at her." But

she was looking away, unable to face this latest indignity I was laying upon her. The extraordinary will that had seen her across two
continents and sustained her through two world wars, that had
not let her rest until she had saved enough out of her ridiculous
earnings to bring her whole family over from Russia—even if we
could forget the story, it would still define us—had now tapered
to testiness. Doubt rose from our Eva the way lavender rose from
storybook grandmothers. There was still energy enough left in
that ninety-four-year-old body for tenacity, for festering, but not
enough to be more than a bother. She was a residue of enterprises
and pathetic means, surrounded by an invalid's washed-out
economy: some jewelry and makeup she wore only when Chelsea
decked her out for company, the purse she no longer carried full
of cards she no longer consulted, a comb she never used,
Lifesavers should the children visit, tissues. A trace of saliva bub-
bled out of her, making an ellipsis as she drifted. She had outlived
the need for manners, weather, or verbs. She wept for a hundred
reasons as I braced her namesake against her in her lap.

The fact is, I come from skeptical stock. Disbelief is more
than characteristic of members of my family; it is encoded deep
as any gene. We address the world with narrowed eyes because
we know the world for what it offers and for what it is. "Trust"
hides "rust," so be vigilant, we say. We positively abjure being
positive. When it comes to presidential candidates, recent films,
the death penalty, Zionism, or dessert, we may be irremediably
divided—enough to make us table Thanksgiving—but in this
essential sense, all of our backs are aligned against the same wall.
Unrelenting, we live life like a reconnaissance mission, slanting
like crabs about the boundaries of the unfamiliar, pincers out.

Our Eva, who understood even after she had forgotten
everything else that time is a concussion, that death is always a
mugging, that it waits to ambush you when something is still in
the oven, would not know my daughter, but she knew this.

◻ ◻ ◻

Every spring my elementary school used to hold a carnival. For one Saturday each year, thanks to the spasmodic magic of a few earnest mothers, the revenant custodial staff, and crepe paper, the gym was transformed into something vaguely Arabian. "Carnival" was too ambitious a term for so resolutely wonderless and fizzless a place as Middleton Elementary School, not only because of the meagerness of the scene and its formidable resistance to glitter, but also because there were no rides, no animals, no displays, and no shows. The entirety of the operation was given over to half a dozen or so games of chance, each manned by someone's mom or a (presumably) untenured teacher who had been pressed into weekend service.

From one perspective, I suppose, the distillation of the carnival into a kind of adolescent Vegas showed integrity. There were no claims to moral elevation or higher purpose here; the genially enforced wholesomeness of the event did not distract from the fundamental attention to getting and spending. There was not even a bake sale to soften the acquisitive impulses. We had taken James Joyce's "Araby" to the suburbs: the perpetually strapped PTA craved our quarters almost as intensely as we needed to risk them. That was the annual carnival: sunny, shameless, antiseptic, and naked.

The most alluring of the games was the string pull. Scores of prizes—whistles, baseball cards, temporary tattoos, cap pistols, kazoos, Tootsie Roll Pops, keychains (but what grade schooler carried keys or responsibilities requiring them?), colored pencils, punch puzzles, as well as a blizzard of red Sorry circles like a bloodied field of vision—dangled tantalizingly out of reach. Their tethers meshed in a thick tangle at Mrs. Arbus's shoulder. For a quarter you could take a crack at this mercantile empyrean, or it was five chances for a buck. If your pull made one of those red suns rise, you got the consolation of a butterscotch disc and Mrs. Arbus's assurance that your contribution to the PTA would benefit the school in some unidentified yet tangible way that you some day would come to appreciate.

Out of everything, I wanted the coin box trick. It was a flat wooden contraption which, by virtue of some (I assumed) simple yet cunning mechanism caused the patron's coin, which the magician placed on the bottom panel, to disappear when he slid the top sleeve over it. The rube would stew a bit, then a second pass, and his coin would return intact. It was a deft and cheap little miracle, the finest commodity in the exchange, and I wanted it. So I spent a good half hour spying on the game, watching the kids, some giggling, some anxious, some somber and tactical, select their strings and draw them gingerly down. I watched rings, tops, wax lips, onion gum, a rubber mouse, and a dozen red suns ascend. The coin box trick remained in place, undisturbed in the firmament. The arbitrary and final reward.

It was time. I approached Mrs. Arbus at her table and plucked out, one by one, my clammy cache of quarters, then fanned them out for her. "Tha-at's six, honey!" she said, sprinkling an octave with cheer. "But, really, they're worth *seven* chances. You get five for a dollar—that's four quarters—and two more quarters make seven chances." Mathematics and fortitude—crucial lessons of grade school.

Believe me when I say I had no expectation of winning. I had no faith, nor even the expectation of faith. I tried to follow the coin box string into the deep, indiscriminate braid. Mrs. Arbus swung the ends toward me. I dipped my thumb and index finger in. I pulled, lifting my first red circle. Then a second. Then a third. Mrs. Arbus grew a bit uneasy for my sake, and she encouraged me to stay with it, by which she meant not to cry. But when the fourth red circle came up, I found that I was nowhere near tears. I was absorbed. It was more than that, though. I was even—and up came the fifth red circle—gratified. Confirmed. It was the way I figured the ant felt when winter seized the imbecile grasshopper in the fable my mother used to read to prepare me for a world that gives nothing for nothing. (Although the irony was lost on me at the time, the systematic disappearance of my quarters into Mrs. Arbus's Maxwell House coffee can represented a pretty impressive coin box trick itself.) It was an awfully big truth for a dollar and a half. Six red suns, then, on the seventh try, a candy cane, which I did not refuse but gave away. I was convinced that, the agreeable Mrs. Arbus notwith-standing, the fix was in. Some fix was. And in the minute or two it took to be relieved of my money, I had matured into skepti-cism. I came into the family inheritance, and, existential already, I did not complain or grieve, which was the family way.

That is the way I remember it: an hour's slumming among the gullible. *Everyone* must have yearned for the few truly worthy prizes—the coin box trick, the fountain pen, the pocket flash-light, the green jackknife. *Everyone* must have been wishing on the same brightest stars in the gymnasium sky. The baited lines that hid the switches. The treasures we were never meant to have. (Which of us would have been *allowed* to bring home a jackknife anyway?) The prizes we could never claim because those in charge could not afford to lose them. The prizes—I decided—that were not even connected to any of the strings at all. And so I circled my psychic wagons and muttered, by way of a parting shot, the family vow: won't get fooled again.

❑   ❑   ❑

Telling stories at graveside is like landscaping. The soil is not the best. You plant what you hope will grow.

The story that implicated all of us had to do with Eva's ninetieth birthday. After a prolonged and surreptitious exchange of phone calls, the family settled on buying Eva a new mattress. After some twenty years of use, hers had grown stale and, frankly, embarrassing. We used to try to convince her that there was nothing extravagant about seeing to her comfort, especially in view of—no offense, Grandma—her ever-increasing relega-tion to her bedroom, but we might as well have been talking to the furniture. It was no use trying at this late date to chase the fears that forever nested in her head or to budge the bigotries that like the oak bureau sank its clawed feet deeper each day into the carpet. "It's *my* bed," she would say, simply. Or, sometimes, to clarify, she might add, "It's my *bed*," shifting the emphasis as though trying to situate her body on the awful thing before sleep. Clearly, the only way to make her succumb to our love would be through subterfuge.

The plot was to have the main battalion of relatives massed for the occasion take her out to a birthday luncheon, where they would distract her with waves of endearments and smoked fishes. Meanwhile, a select squad of uncles broke into the house, wrestled the old mattress into a borrowed truck, and drove it to the dump, while the point man—me, actually—waited for the delivery of the new mattress. That was our plan—compassion's sneak attack.

When they drove up to the house, Uncle Stanley helped Eva complete her ascent of the curb from the Buick Regal. (Those politically dissolute relatives from out of town who had driven in with Japanese or German cars parked further from the house for fear of setting Grandma off.) At the very moment she saw that the front door was open, Eva began to wail. She immediately realized what had happened, and the truth knocked her back against Stanley. It was the Klan. The Ku Klux Klan. They had been waiting for months, for years, for her to let down her guard. Now she had left the premises vulnerable. Now they had struck.

They had taken the mattress, in which she had been steadily stashing away ones, tens, and twenties, so that no Klansman, Nazi, or Cossack, no product demonstrator or wily neighborhood kid, could get to her valuables without going through her. When the sky fell or the bombs dropped or the banks failed again—had we forgotten *all* of our history?—there would be something to fall back on. Her mattress. And now it was gone.

It did not matter that the same platoon of us was dispatched to the dump to retrieve the bills, which we picked out like ticks from the clumped and runny innards of the old mattress. This was not *her* money we were pressing upon her, she knew at once, and our insulting her by substituting our own bills for the stolen ones was, well, it was just like us.

◻ ◻ ◻

Weighing the potential for trauma against the need for certainty and closure, experts disagree on the advisability of letting young children attend a funeral. After some debate, we decided to bring along our two-year-old daughter to Eva's burial. What had made our decision for us was a conviction about the long-term value of including her in the ceremony. It was healthy and right and proper for Eva's namesake to contribute her small presence to the murmuring pack at the edge of the grave. And after all, she was family, too, as much as any of us were.

Actually, she was very eager to see what was going on. As the casket was lowered into the ground, she shook in my grasp, which was her usual signal to hold her up higher. No child likes to feel cheated or to be sent to bed just as the party is starting. She wanted to miss nothing.

We watched life's primary coin box trick. First, someone's body is inserted into a casket before the eyes of the audience, then it is covered over. Then, through a sleight of nature, she is gone. No matter how many times you see it done, death is a showstopper. It is the trick that never lets you down. It is the part in you that you cannot betray.

"Where is Gamma, Daddy?" I told my daughter something. I told her she is up in heaven. That was not enough to keep her down. She wanted to see, and she wriggled against me to get higher. I told her heaven is past the stars even though you cannot see it, just as the stars are always out even in the daytime, but the sunlight keeps us from seeing. I told her that Grandma Eva was not in the ground, that what we saw was not really her. I told her that she has risen among the angels.

And she gave me this look.

priced to go

You have to know the jargon to appreciate the culture. For instance, the folks who arrive an hour earlier than your advertised opening are known as "early birds." And they are like birds, scrabbling about your yard, pecking at the sill before you are dressed and ready to receive them. It is the expense of celebrity. No grievance committee petitions so assiduously, no rabble rouses so unquellably, as that presumptuous dawn patrol. Like epileptics—which some of them undoubtedly are, you think, not ready to feel generous before seven—they smear windows, probe latches and handles for diversion. There is nothing arbitrary about their Saturday skulks. Experienced prowlers, they have all circled the same classified ads and mapped out assault plans; coming here is only the opening act in their theater of operations. Mostly older men and women, they drive up in scabrous trucks and station wagons already laden, testifying to perpetual enterprise. They are in the know, and once you have raised your garage door (after a petulant interval that teaches them nothing about courtesy), they move in swiftly and, as best they can in your cluttered and rudely avenued garage, fan out to rummage and scour.

The most practiced are called "garage sailors," and in their precise, parasitical sweeps they call to mind, by turns, movie pirates, demolitions experts, and attorneys. Once the garage door is up, they move immediately upon furniture and baby clothes; any of those items in reasonable condition are gone by mid-morning. You batten yourself to a card table by the driveway, where you preside over the cash box that, like the newspaper ad and the day-glo signs you set out the night before, must be offset by the first dollars of profit. Like a street musician, you have seeded the box with small change, hoping to coax others to follow that anonymous lead.

The night before, when the last of your silt had been divided and punctuated, there was a moment when you wondered if anyone would come at all. Who would contradict this abandonment of yours? You went to bed anxious as a bridegroom, reflective as one, and with a bridegroom's second guesses. In pajamas you went out to check the garage again and reconsidered your inventory, altering the price on the toaster oven and snatching back the cardigan. But these doubts have proved foolish: your debut is a success. Business is brisk and addictive this morning, and every purchase buys you space, which was your main purpose in having the sale—to subtract from your store as if stripping calories from an indulgent diet.

A garage sale must represent the most casual sort of transaction on earth. How much aggression could there be in the lazy tussle over a couple of hand towels? None of the strict you-break-it-you-bought-it consequences apply. There is none of that bald and driven commerce. Here, instead, is a minor-league haven for consumers, where they are welcome to move about unprompted and pressure free. Still, the way they ignore the sticker prices perturbs you. You do not want to haggle, but rather had intended to sit back, a fatted capitalist, indolent and dreamy as Sidney Greenstreet in *Casablanca*. But they take you on and draw you out, challenging you to shave a few cents off a flowerpot or bent trowel. (You have to admit that you do not garden and never have. That was her hobby, her effort to reclaim the backyard from the negligence of the previous

owners. It is an embarrassment to look at now.) It is your property but their depth you're in.

It amazes you the way they want what you do not want, that
despite value's disintegrating molecules, some value somehow
for somebody still keeps. Your negotiable past tense. Plastic
baby bottles. A scarred picture frame. A box of fittings that fit
nothing you remember. An unspoken coalition of appetite drives
them. They seem to have to touch everything—a ritual laying
on of hands, perhaps, a reflex of consecration. "How much for
this?" asks a woman scarved in orange and red, scalps won at
other sales, and it is not until after you come up with a number—
by now, you no longer bother to direct them to the stickers—
that she asks "What *is* this?" While for you all riddance is good
riddance, for them the worth is in the having. Pipe cleaners.
Crayons in a coffee can. A roll of insulation. Underwear. For the
dry salvages of six years in this house, someone will bargain; for
a tattered coat upon a stick, someone will bid. Somehow, all of
it goes. Even half-empty bottles of bleach and motor oil go.
Someone wants one shoelace. A low-level urgency abides. A
child that's been dragged along with the promise that he can buy
something if he behaves wants your old license plate. (It wasn't
even for sale; you'd just neglected to remove it when you were
cleaning out the garage. You size the kid up for dimes, hazard a
price. He has just enough.) They are more sensitive than you,
you suspect, more capable of care. They know how to make do
with the done for.

There must be fifty garage sales going on all over town during this first decent spring morning of the year. The ads all seem
bound to the same strategies, the same seductions. Obsolescence
sets in like rust, and on any block you can find, like random
dinosaur teeth, blades to food processors they no longer manufacture. Whole stereos go for ten dollars, outsized amps for five.
Every six weeks the doomed Apple II computers are displayed,
but no one bites. And yet, the tricycle with the bad wheel finds
favor. The same guy who went for the nineteen-inch RCA

television comes back an hour later for the fourteen-inch Zenith. You warn him again about the bleared color and the lost remote—your ethics transcend the few extra bucks coming to you—but he waves it off. What are you missing here?

Among the disposables are bits of property that were left to you in the settlement. The dictionary is more flexible about this term than the lawyers were. A "settlement" is an establishment, as of a person in a business or of people in a new region. It can also be an adjustment or other understanding reached in financial matters, business proceedings, or the like. Today's sense of "settlement" is contained in "or the like." ("Or the like" is a convenience, a catchall—a garage sale of implication.) Some of these things fell to you in the settlement the way the hot potato in the party game falls into your hands when the music stops.

It turns out that your garage is a hospice. You realize that you have never seen any of these people anywhere else. Some are probably neighbors, or they shop where you shop, or you have excused yourself as you bumped them in the public pool, but you recognize no one. But they have found you, the ill-mannered and the poorly dressed. Their need is reliable, comprehensive, and opaque. Here the ravaged still inherit, as the wretched assess your refuse, pick through your shallows of acquisition. Their trick is to temper inspection with mercy. Tarnish does not deter them from moving like holy men among lepers through the makeshift aisles. So there is something to your slough after all. You think of the boxes the police bring down for the bereaved to cling to or that detectives nose through for clues. Even the jetsam of the dead retains a pulse. A watchband. A broken clock. A stained dish drainer. Outcroppings of personality. To think that a mismatched batch of kitchen utensils had charisma. Something in your scruff calls out to them. Messages are read in your sediment, which like jewelers or pathologists they spread out to inspect. Your ooze answers some obscure demand. To think that something could still matter in those mittens. To think that a flat of needles could plead or a whiffle bat pine.

"Possession" is a word with a limited warranty. Won't some
of this stuff resurface in other garage sales? After the buyer has
thought better of it, or worse? You envision an ongoing circuit—
a friendly, reciprocal physics or stubble economy. There is a bac-
terial logic to the way that over time a given lipstick or paper-
back will pass from hand to hand.

A couple of girls are browsing among your ex's sweaters like
deer nibbling the hedge. They pull back quickly from your
glance.

You thought you were getting away with something, having strangers pay to weed the place. (In the jargon, this is
called "getting out from under." See "free.") In exchange for the
right to graze, they brush hog your past. They take up your
slack for you. So why do you sense, as they pluck the belts and
ties and carry off the crib, that with every sale you are selling
short? Perhaps the event proves your incapacity, not your ingenuity. While his wife plunges in among the old nylons, an old
man whose cap promotes a local union is weighing wooden
chess pieces like loaded dice. Appraisal worms his face.
Another man, whose T-shirt reports a rock band's itinerary,
peers deeper into the open metal shelves, and nods, and
frowns. A third man bags and shoulders his catch of flannel
shirts. You look back at the old people: with four hands, man
and wife are holding up a down jacket. An impenetrable
moment in the closed shop of regard. They have obviously
been operating as a team for some time; they handle their tasks
with the silent efficiency of couples folding their sheets at the
laundromat.

You watch desire rise and fall, and you begin to resent the
invasion of the privacy you have invited. You are being judged
for the life you have led and have chosen to leave behind. The
candleholders testify against you. The wedding gifts you let
go. The scorched clothing, the wallet, the letter opener—clues
from a crime scene, laid out as evidence. Or they are tea leaves
spread out to form a narrative you cannot read on your own.

A settlement can also be a transfer of property to provide for
the future needs of a person. Not to mention the property thus
transferred. Or the like.

"What are you asking for the paintbrushes?" You say that
they are not for sale. Only the marked items are for sale. "I'll give
you five bucks for them." Sorry, not for sale. "I can go six, I guess."
You flash on your younger brother's collections. When he was a
child, he collected collections. As an entrepreneur, he was more
relentless than selective, but because your parents realized that
there were worse ways to direct a ten-year-old's energies, even in
the generation before drugs found the suburbs, they did not dis-
courage him. He traded in and traded up among his friends until
he had the market on bottle caps, army soldiers, and Marvel
Comics cornered when few knew there even was a market. A
commercial call to "Collect 'em All" went out, and so did he, like
a retriever following his breeding after flung sticks. He had a full
squad of NFL heroes, which he lined up along the bookshelves
like athletic versions of religious figurines. When Gatorade came
out with depictions of team helmets on its caps, he kept a
progress chart, pleading with Mom to purchase quart after quart
in order to snare the elusive Eagles or for the sake of the missing
Saints. (Once when Mom forgot the chart he had prepared for
her and mistakenly brought home the duplicate Bills, he threw a
fit so magnificent that she agreed to exchange it the next day for
a legitimate bottle.) When he couldn't stomach the stuff anymore, he resorted to spilling out more than he drank, and finally—you know this for a fact—to unscrewing the wanted tops at
the store and rearranging the bottles to cover his crime.

The completed collections were bagged, boxed, and sealed,
filed into envelopes or tucked into drawers, as their size and
nature dictated, and they were never, never sacrificed. He pro-
tected them against cleaning jags and spasms of redecoration;
against moving day and maturity he kept them. You mocked him
on his way to college for his childish grip on childish things. You
scolded him for his constipation. You threatened to rat on his

packs. Do you want to be the ass of the frat? No girl would go for a grubber of rubble like you. But he held up and held on, and to this very day he still has everything. Basically, he was more persistent than you knew how to be. So is the guy who finally convinces you to give up the brushes after all. Were you really going to paint the bedroom again? A brief pang as you watch him depart, then you go back to stacking quarters.

She had never been able to throw out anything either. You used to take advantage of her absences by gathering up catalogs and magazines and taking the bundles, like heaps of slick fish, to the garbage. When she would return, you defied her to guess what you had disposed of, the point being that what she couldn't name she couldn't honestly miss. That was supposed to be the moral of the story, anyway. The problem was that whenever she couldn't find something, you took the blame.

A welfare center providing community services in an under-privileged area is also occasionally called a "settlement," or a "settlement house," but this is somewhat less common usage. Anything that comes to rest out of a solution may also be termed a "settlement." Remember your chemistry. Typically this results from centrifugation. Think of the garage as the extremity to which centrifugal force has driven everything that wasn't secured. Hence, your settlement is your spin, your scatter, your scat. See also "bottom." See also "dregs."

Relinquishment is a powerful drug, but it may be wearing off. What have you done? While you were under, what plunder has ensued? When your former wife called to suggest you sell the old clothes she couldn't carry off when she moved out, it all seemed so eminently sensible. The first trust she had placed in you for months was to price her vestiges and send a check. How sane and agreeable to think of the piles of clothes as pyres to honor household gods: Purge and Thrift and Necessity. So you have forbidden no valediction this morning. That's right—go to your puns and your poems. The art of losing's not too hard to master though it may look like (*mark it down!*) like disaster.

And if there is some oversight you're committing as you throw in the odd nail file or the extra thread, if there is some gem amid the junk you're bundling into the hatchback of a mother while her twins tug at her, if there is some saving magic or secret metaphor inherent in all that leaks out of your house this Saturday, it is all so much subtler than a clean garage and cash on hand. So as lunchtime approaches and the crowd thins to a trickle, you take off another twenty percent. Strangers are on the premises, but you let your eyes close anyway. You let others do your savoring for you. You may be called to account for reckless behavior some day, but not this particular one.

"Settlement" also suggests making the best of a difficult situation. (See "Appomattox.") For this is what give-and-take encounters come down to: a shared conceit, whereby all parties walk away, if not uncheated, undeceived.

The smart sailors linger just offshore to wait you out. Time is on their side: because it is almost noon, no offer is too paltry to refuse. Eventually you will want to consolidate your gains and get out with what's left of Saturday. Eventually you will be forced to settle.

After compensating for your costs, you calculate that you have made a couple of hundred dollars. Remarkable, when you think about it. They have whisked away your pittances, and there is now room to pull the car back into the garage without rattling the recyclables, and the car door opens freely for a change. You look around, and already it is hard to remember everything that's gone. In the jargon, you have "made a killing" or "had a good day."

the big interbang theory

Streamlining may be a virtue when the subject is cars or the Internal Revenue Service, but we at Interbang, Incorporated believe that when it comes to punctuation, streamlining is deprivation. There was a time when writers communicated with advantages whose very designations—*punctus elevatus, positura, cryphia*—show how it is necessary and proper to resort to Latin to deliver a poignant combination of elegance and extinction. In the course of his rapt and admiring review of Dr. Malcolm Parkes's history of punctuation, *Pause and Effect,* Nicholson Baker coins terms for bygone dash-hybrids—the *commash,* the *semi-commash,* and the *colash*—which, their ingenuity notwithstanding, have proved to be as evanescent as certain unstable compounds devised in the laboratory and lasting just long enough for physicists to name. Baker urges us to give thanks to Parkes for conveying something of "the flourishing coralline tidepools of punctuational pluralism that preceded our own purer, more consistent, more teachably codified, and perhaps more arid century." In turn, we give thanks to Baker for bringing the baton a bit further.

But for all of Baker's and Parkes's enthusiasms for punctuation's multifarious charms, their tone is primarily elegiac. One reviews with dismay the diminished ranks of punctuation which answer the call to inspection on a contemporary typewriter or computer keyboard. So much potential blown, so many options come to paltriness and grief. When Baker takes the roll of the nine basic marks of punctuation that gruff mandarins of standard usage still allow, one wonders how that starting nine, however formidable, can last an entire demanding season of expression with no bench at all to count on.

But here at Interbang, our business is to look forward, not back. We believe that punctuation's best, most productive years lie ahead. Our Research and Development Department is hard at work devising and testing innovative marks of punctuation equal to the complicated communicative responsibilities of today's most enterprising men and women.

Our company name, Interbang, commemorates our first major punctuation product, which linked the exclamation point to the question mark, as in:

Where did you get that revolting nipple ring!?

So provocative did that inaugural duo prove to be that within months we came out with a reversible version suitable for the subtlest shift from the emphatic to the interrogative:

Are you telling me that she means to marry that jackass?!

Remembering Yeats's complaint and prophecy in "The Second Coming" that "The best lack all conviction, while the worst / Are full of passionate intensity"—college seniors in the humanities, take note: there may be a place for you at Interbang—we wanted a sign that split the difference between the inability to commit and the inability to bend. And so we came up with this delicate interaction of rhetorical postures: the question mark tugs at the exclamation point, beckoning it to reconsider its stiff resolve; the exclamation point urges the question mark to buck up. It is a lovely device, really.

Sadly, certain entrenched interests engaged in smear tactics against the interbang, so threatened were they by its swift and growing popularity. (You may recall a spate of grammar handbook supplements denouncing "the unnatural marriage of exclamation point and question mark, like a cocker spaniel and a trout standing at the altar," not to mention a particularly ugly incident at a Conference of College Composition and Communication, resulting in the arrest of several tenured professors, including the featured speaker at the plenary session.) Furthermore, in a shameful display of conservative zealotry, Victor Borge, the comic pianist famed for the routine in which he used silly sound effects to denote the punctuation of a romantic story he would read aloud, suffered the cancellation of several college performances—this despite the fact that Mr. Borge not only never used the interbang in his routine but also was not and never had been employed by our company.

Although the interbang has been relegated of late to appearances in comic books and notes passed during high school gym, its pioneering impact is irrefutable. But we want quickly to assure the skeptical that despite our eagerness and inventive energies, our creations at Interbang are always user-friendly and consumer-oriented. Sensitive to the subtleties of human expression, which our products both honor and facilitate, we are also sensitive to the realities of the pocketbook. As a result, you will be cheered to learn that all of the punctuation additions we propose in our latest catalogue can be accommodated by even the most rudimentary keyboard.

For instance, consider the *ultimat*, which is a set of virgules leaning teepee-fashion upon a newel post or center rod: /Λ. It is designed to indicate a secret pleasure swelling beneath the words themselves, yet representing a more private appreciation than an exclamation point implies. Think of it as a shudder of pride or unutterable affection deep in the chest wall. (The prototype for the ultimat, by the way, was called the *kvell* by its originator, Steven Tannenbaum, who wished to acknowledge the Yiddish approximation of this feeling, but less partisan heads prevailed upon him, and *ultimat* became the de-ethnicized compromise.) Thus the ultimat-inspiring statement on the page arrows upward with higher fidelity to its emotional origin than was previously possible:

Yes, now that you mention it, my son does start medical school in the fall//\

The delicacy of sparing the audience one's boast while at the same time living up to the boastworthy moment clearly calls for an ultimat. Using an exclamation point for the job would be like plucking a hair from a mole with a needle-nose pliers.

Then there is the *voidant*, a closed pair of parentheses which can be inserted anywhere in a sentence to indicate the unexpected and seemingly unwarranted, yet unmistakable intrusion of angst. How many of us have had our smooth moods disrupted by such a sudden decompression, a preemption or premonition of impending comeuppance or mortality? Our random test groups noted its resemblances to an abscess, a bubble in the bloodstream, and a null set suggesting a present absence in mathematics, all of which felicitously coincided with the intentions of our R and D people. We already have seen ample evidence of the flexibility and usefulness of the voidant:

There is nothing like seeing your daughter getting her () driver's license.
We should finally have the house paid off () by next year.
Next year () in Jerusalem.

And as modern man gets more and more in touch with the complexity of his psyche, and with the seal broken on the new millennium, the entrepreneurial possibilities seem positively limitless. So it is not surprising that, although it has only recently been released on the market, the voidant has already become one of our most popular offerings.

Among our most recent products, the *waver* seems especially promising. It denotes a frank, studied lack of commitment; it says (in the spirit of open-mindedness, not muddled vacillation) that the author invites further evidence and ultimately can be swayed by reasoned argument. (Hence, please note that the mark is a *waver*, not a *waiver*, the latter bastardization emphasizing

a repudiation of involvement, which, while it has not so far led
to disputes rivaling the great *as* versus *like* controversy, much less
the civil war that continues to rage in the Language Change
Division of the Modern Language Association over the *that*-
clause, is a misapprehension that could cause the writer to run
afoul of proper usage.) Although it can, like the voidant, be
inserted anywhere the author deems suitable along the length of
the sentence, the *waver*, which unites a simple plus and minus,
can also greet the reader like a salute or welcoming banner at the
start of a sentence:

+-I recommend the broasted chicken, if you happen to like
broasted chicken.

So free of the belligerence that attends the exclamatory, so
free even of the absolutism that the declarative imposes, a sign
of "wavering" planted before the first word also prepares the
reader for launch the way a Spanish interrogative does with an
inverted question mark at the start of an impending question.
For not the least of the contributions of Spanish culture is this
indication of a tone-in-progress—the punctuation equivalent of
"Men at Work" or "Open Trench." Admittedly, there are detrac-
tors of this Spanish convention, too (see the rather cheeky dismissal of Aaron J. Chamberlain in his "The Spanish Inquisition
in Question: Questioning the Spanish Question," *Journal of
Linguistics* 27.1 [1991]: 12-29). Nevertheless, we at Interbang
believe that it is a mistake to equate a fair hearing with a faint
heart. Just as we admire the Spanish for the pliancy and hospitality of their inverted question mark, which in a small but winning way indicates the appropriateness of terming Spanish a
Romance language, so do we endorse the waver and look forward to its growing acceptance. We are convinced that you will
agree, after reading just a few pages with thoughtfully placed
wavers, that reading a text without them seems like driving in a
town without traffic signs.

If you were to enter any one of the thousands of virtual discussion rooms on the Internet, you would discover just how

undeniable is the human appetite for adequate punctuation. There you find strangers trying to defy estrangement and distance by decorating their pages with all manner of slits and sickles, quasi-visages and jerry-built expressions, concoctions of commas, hash marks, and ampersands like an optometrist's delirium tremens. See me, they urge. Know me. Yet all the while the most trenchant desires dwindle down to the oblivion of the ill-conceived; for want of just the right conveyances, countless potential relationships are stranded.

At Interbang, Incorporated, the most experienced, most highly trained, and most typographically creative people in the field are working daily to make their, and your, communicative endeavors possible. Bringing accuracy to intimacy: this is both our record of achievement and our continuing goal. "Ah, love, let us be true / To one another!" pleads Matthew Arnold in "Dover Beach," as the poet perches perilously at the edge of a darkling, voidant-assaulted plain. We at Interbang applaud that sentiment, and we maintain that in order to be true to one another, we need an enlightened parliament of punctuation.

You would not lend your son a car with faulty brakes; you would not allow your daughter to go out on a date without a proper escort. Why send out a sentence that is less than fully equipped? In its unassuming, yet fundamental way, our latest product line helps to separate the modern interlocutor from the ungrammared masses. So before you trust another syllable to insufficient, worn-out punctuation, take a good look at what Interbang has to offer. Because at Interbang, we think we know what you mean/|\

the poetics of know-how

You don't have to sit through the movie to know that the girl is going to the guy highest on the marquee. But I'm convinced that if I ever lose my beloved it will be to someone who can pop the car hood, isolate the ping, whine, clunk, or wheeze, nab the right tool without hesitation from a compartment in the trunk I've never even bothered to look into, and tighten, splice, or disconnect whatever needs it. You know the type, with his aura of aptitude. He confidently appraises the situation, leaning over the engine like one of Cooper's Mohicans sounding the ground or a cardiologist detecting an arrhythmia his patient never suspected, much less fretted about. Or if his expertise does not rest in his ear, he has a nose that can separate compounds into their chemical components, an eye that can sight unerring vectors down a length of pine, or—pardon my projection—hands that can ratchet orgasms out of any woman at all. At the movies your date may sigh over urbane manners or crafted abs, but in the real world, to the worldly go the spoils.

I speak, of course, as a man who traffics exclusively in intangibles. I am a Ph.D., a title properly pronounced, like a Yiddish expletive, "fid." I am a doctor, yes, but not (in my family's parlance) a *doctor* doctor. When it comes to accomplishing something you can actually *point* at, I turn to the classifieds. Look, a

modern poem can accommodate hundreds of competing readings by restless young professors needing to publish—there's
plenty of room on the interpretive bus, no need to shove—and
no number of cooks can spoil the broth when it's *Burnt Norton*.
And yes, Wallace Stevens suggests that there may be as many as
thirteen ways of looking at a blackbird, but stray from the one
legitimate way of installing track lighting in your living room and
you've got trouble, my friend! So when I am faced with a task
that must be correctly and unambiguously completed, I rely on
the list of odd-jobbers at the back of the paper.

Here they are, boxed at the bottom of the page—the city's
permanent terrarium of low crawlers. Here are mechanically
minded men, men at home with hardware. Their advertisements
are matter-of-fact and more laconic than even Clint Eastwood
could ever hope to match. Will fix anything. Honest work at reasonable rates. Veteran for hire. (To such men, subordinate claus-
es, much less semicolons, would be as suspicious and humiliating
as a son who makes the throw from third like a girl.) Ezra Pound
argued that the main shortcoming and danger posed by someone
in my profession comes from the way we over-pack ourselves
with words: "The lecturer is a man who must talk for an hour."
How refreshing, then, to find men who just plunge their hands
in; who can find without hesitation the meter strangled by the
backyard honeysuckle vines and who do not have to ask where
to go to get under the house. If there are gutters to affix, third-
floor windows to wash, stumps to pull, leaks to seal, roofs to
scrabble upon, foundations to examine, or brush to hog, it is men
like these, not the esoterically and nth degreed, whom you count
on. No cum laude, however summa, may presume to come close
to them. Give me definite men, purposive and practical—men
with work belts and metal receipt pads, men who keep their keys
close by on retractable chains and jackknives in their front pockets for a score of handy strategies, men who have to go to their
trucks to get what they need and find it there. Listening to their
knuckle-down diligence, John Updike's furtive Harry Angstrom

is able for the first time in the "Rabbit" novels to get some rest: "The clangor of the body shop comes up softly. Its noise comforts him, tells him he is hidden and safe, that while he hides men are busy nailing the world down, and toward the disembodied sounds his heart makes in darkness a motion of love."

Once a plumber I called in to undo what I'd done trying to fix the kitchen faucet suggested that while he shut off the water—he knew immediately where this might be accomplished, whereas I, when faced with Mondrian prospects like electrical circuitry or intersecting pipes, became Hercules contending with the Hydra—I should get his Allen wrench from the front seat of his truck. I felt like a virgin in a fraternity, having to apologize for my unforgivable ignorance on the subject. (So let me get this straight: wrenches have *proper names?*) He was one of those men who want to be paid in cash to better duck the grubby paws of government, about which they have absolute opinions, for they know what it means to have a *real* job. I was not about to argue politics with him, so I temporarily turned Republican, seconded my guy's grudges, and paid him what he asked.

For reasons of ego, I guess, attention is the toughest price to pay. (This lesson is made clear in *Death of a Salesman*, in which Willy Loman is eulogized as a man who had the wrong dreams: "He was a happy man with a batch of cement," says Charley. "He was so wonderful with his hands," adds Willy's widow.) We tend to treat laborers as also-rans in the rat race; it may be more accurate to say that they have no interest in being fast rats. Sweat and grease are mere weekend pastimes for me and my colleagues, managed exertions like gardening, worship, or golf; for the repairman who fixed my furnace, taming what seethed like a beast in a fable beneath my floor, exertion is exactly what it is.

One look at men in work clothes lets you know that no poetry happens in their houses, no matter what claims Whitman made for the common man. Not ever. And yet, what superiority would I pretend to claim for myself? When have I ever assembled anything without ending up with a handful of extra nuts or without inexplicably falling a screw or two shy? I am no more likely to find the ground wire in the Amazonian thicket of a stereo than to pick the winning Lotto numbers, and I can only fantasize about getting fittings to fit flush or plucking fuses without flinching. Since I can be defeated by the humblest technologies in the house, anyone for whom tabs seem magically attuned to their appropriate slots will always overwhelm me.

I speak on behalf of the helpless tenured, for whom uncertainty is a principle and who sail daily through the cumulus. Ours is the privileged delirium of people who handle nothing weightier than paper. How can we not admire virtuosos of utility, who implicitly oppose our odd, groundless pursuits by plying a trade? What are our elevated devotions, our hothouse, frilly sympathies and classroom chicaneries worth when we murmur and shuffle like distant relatives at a wake before the broken copier that stops us cold? One glance at the respiratory confusion of an air conditioning unit or an automatic garage door opener's exploded view can make the most esteemed academic stash his diploma in the bottom drawer of his desk. There is nothing like the discreet charm of discrete challenges deftly accomplished. Oh, in the rarefied climes of the research university, the ranking deconstructive theorist may intimidate or inspire, but unless he is able to take apart a carburetor, he'd be wise to keep to his office and save his opinions for the back pages of PLMA.

For fixers may envy us professors our meager tax deferrals, but they do not reciprocate our dreams of them. As no administrator, accrediting agency, or literary critic ever could, they make us feel negligible. Returning from the plumber's truck that day, head hung and empty-handed, I knew true shame.

A friend in my department once told me about setting out one afternoon to buy his first lawnmower, a selection he'd arrived at after spending several hours consulting the annual buyer's guide from *Consumer Reports*. He had been working in his garage, and he had not bothered to change out of his Sunday grunge

clothes before driving to the hardware store. As it happened, the
key detail in his outfit was a cap he had inherited from his uncle,
which carried the logo of a local pipe fitters' union. The sales-
clerk noted that the brand he wanted included an optional main-
tenance contract. "But you probably do your own repairs," she
said. It must have been the hat, he told us at lunch the next day.
And, no, he did not disabuse her of her impression. If you're at
the gym and a pretty girl gives you the eye, exactly how quickly
do you hustle back to the locker room to retrieve your wedding
ring, anyway? No, my friend would not have traded that
moment's misassessment for a dozen positive student evaluations.
He still loves to tell that story, and it is worth his enduring the
anxiety that some day the mower won't start.

In *Catch-22*, Joseph Heller introduces Orr, Yossarian's mentor
and fool, as having "a thousand valuable skills that would keep
him in a low income group all his life." But it is Orr, we recall,
whose eccentricities prove to be survival tactics after all. After
the last bombs have dropped, it will be men like Orr who will
lead, jerry-rigging their way through the rubble. When con-
trasted with the neurotic compulsions and wholesale absurdities
that dominate Heller's novel, Orr's "craziness" comes off as the
canniness of "can do":

He could use a soldering iron and hammer two boards together so
that the wood did not split and the nails did not bend. He could drill
holes. He had built a good deal more in the tent while Yossarian was
away in the hospital. He had filed or chiseled a perfect channel in
the cement so that the slender gasoline line was flush with the floor
as it ran to the stove from the tank he had built outside on an eleva-
tor platform. He had constructed andirons for the fireplace out of
excess bomb parts and had filled them with stout silver logs, and he
had framed with stained wood the photographs of girls with big
breasts he had torn out of cheesecake magazines and hung over the
mantelpiece. Orr could open a can of paint. He could mix paint, thin
paint, remove paint. He could chop wood and measure things with a
ruler. He knew how to build fires.

As his name implies, Orr represents adaptability, alternative, and divergent thinking—crucial talents in a difficult environment. (That Yossarian ends up paddling to Sweden with a little blue oar is, surely, a pun designed to commemorate his example.) If one hopes to disengage from Catch-22, he would best load his every rift with Orr.

What bookish knowledge compares with the arcana of the toolbox? What linguistic finesse can match the declensions of socket wrenches, laid out gleaming in descending order of size like a grand organ in a cathedral? My favorite scene in the movie *Apollo 13* features flight director Gene Kranz, played to a crisp by Ed Harris, inciting a panic of expertise. He announces to the pack of engineers at Mission Control that they have to figure out how to modify the square lithium hydroxide canister used to remove carbon dioxide from the crippled spacecraft so that it will fit the round opening in the lunar module environmental system the astronauts now perilously reside in. They have to make do with only those objects and materials available to the astronauts, of course. And time is running out. I admit that the science escaped me, but I loved the frenetic improvisation of it all as, for all their lofty credentials, the ground crew Keystone Kopped about with plastic bags, cardboard, and duct tape to invent a contraption that would save our heroes. Why they never bothered to consult a janitor, I'll never know, but it pleases me to imagine the lot of them imploring a humble tinker to give a damn. In my scenario, like a parent putting down his newspaper to repair the mess his kid has made of the model tank, he would then lay down his mop and casually, calmly put things right.

It is a commonplace of freshman composition papers that we live in a fast-paced society, but I am convinced that it will never outstrip entropy. In the words of Robinson Jeffers, "You making haste haste on decay." And you can bet that anyone who has faith in the phrase "durable goods" has never owned any. Eventually, even your shiniest machines will have to be seen to. At some point, the refrigerator's compressor will fail, and you'll

return from a weekend in Kansas City to find it has become a
laboratory for devolving leftovers and mutant fruit. One day the
ceiling will show stigmata from a thunderstorm that exploited
seams in the shingles or infiltrated the flashing. Like the clichéd
soldier who buys it in battle but never heard the bullet coming,
you may not hear the pump sputter, the belt unbuckle, or the
gasket give, but the damned thing will be just as dead.

Hasn't having a car taught you that there is no past tense for
"purchase"? The hand the local dealer dealt you is one you have
to keep drawing to forever. Even leaving aside the mundane
demands—gas, oil, replacement filters, tune-ups, and scheduled
services that fill your owner's manual like a dance card in hell—
like the tenacious plate spinner on the old Sullivan Show, you
have to keep moving to keep things whole: just as you've
replaced the blown tire, a spark plug goes bad; the moment one
death rattle is muffled, another reports in; you've staunched
every wound you can think of, but from somewhere, something
still drips on your driveway.

Apollo 13's ad-line might as well be the mantra of the middle
class: "Houston, we've got a problem." If I may risk a fixer's infix,
this is not a bad dream but the way it absofuckinglutely *is*. For if
Yeats was right that the first sign of the Second Coming is
"Things fall apart," we'd better gather up our warranties right now
and take cover. And what is the image that approaches in that
poem? What impending shape out of *Spiritus Mundi*? What rough
beast is now on the clock? Let us pray: perhaps what resolves
through the wreckage is not the end of us after all, but a solid,
deliberate saint of know-how come round to save us at last.

primogeniture: 1962

You will not like me better after this.

As an older brother, I developed into a virtuoso of small torments and petty revenges. I perfected the pinning of my younger brother's shoulders to the floor by working my knees into the fleshy parts just below the armpits. I was precise and systematic: first the leaning in over his thrashing face, which pinched his arms that much harder; then the threat of spit oozing eyeward, which was when, like the fisherman in the fable blackmailing his catch, I exacted promises; then the climactic excellence of refusing to negotiate after all, followed by the awful dollop and plash.

Wasn't it Artaud who extolled a theater of cruelty? Make no mistake: the art of abusing is hard to master.

And there were the false confidences. Do you know what I heard Mom and Dad say about you? Just enough plausibility to plant the seed. Just enough to make him think that malice alone could not explain *every* account of their misgivings about him. (Like second guesses, second children are fretful things.) Or the broken deals. Proposing to exchange my toys for shares of the Halloween spoils he hoarded, I would discandy him first, swallow hard, then renege. Or I would hand over the jammed cap pistol or cracked and pea-less whistle he'd unwittingly bargained for. Hey, *caveat frater*. Let the brother beware.

You have to learn to keep your territory intact. Having come first, you go first, for the ur-text trumps future editions, and no sequel compares to the original. You call the front seat, double-cross the crossed claims, secure the bottom bunk, lay out boundaries and ground rules. You lick the bigger slices of pie for hungers to come. The first birth breaks the mold. You pull up the DNA ladder after you. There is a direct ratio between age and impunity. So you get permanent dibs. As for conscience, true art not only forgives arrogance, it positively necessitates it. Who would stay the author's hand or caution the sculptor to step back from the stone because it was not his turn yet?

But before you assign me blame like extra homework, keep in mind that there was often compensation in this arrangement for him, too. You say I only wanted him out of the way. But back when it was a Sunday morning before dawn and before cable, I would try anything to get my younger brother up. My brother slept in a damp splay, looking like a drowning victim beached by bad dreams; or sometimes he battened down in a clutch of covers, curled like a pillbug against the coming sun. True, it was usually a relief to have him unconscious, since he was the clichéd little kid who tagged along, forever shadowing me out of some muddled worship. So my mother said, at any rate, to soften my complaints. Since Mom could always claim superior bothers, she quickly trumped my exasperations with her own—would I rather have to cook or clean or put up with *both* of us than bear the small brunts of a brother's love?—and so I was made to suffer his baffled, pain-in-the-ass adoration. Yes, it would seem that having him asleep and out of the way for once would be a mercy.

But what advantage could I take, what with having to be quiet? Left to my own devices, I found myself deviceless. Surely early Sunday morning television held no glamor. The first show to flicker up out of the fissiony mist at 5:00 was *Mahalia Jackson Sings*. Unaccountably vigorous at this hour, with inflatable life rafts for lungs, she rang out gospel so alarming that I would have to rush to the Zenith to lower the volume for fear of rousing my father, who would have brought me his *unmistakable* version of the Word. Then came *The Big Picture*, an endless chronicle of World War II, which meant another hour's noise to muffle. Its most consistent image was of massive gray erections: long-bar-reled guns rising to prominence out of ship turrets, tarpaulins, ground cover, and mountainsides, as though *Satyricon* were being shot on every battlefield. Since I was barely nine years old and stood clear of the constant sexual undertow—that would not come for another couple of grades—the imagery was wasted on me. With the sound down, a thousand dying mimes on either side barely ruffled my boredom. Then came *Newsbeat Chicago*, featuring two subdued and civic-minded hosts who read the weather and interviewed aldermen. Even if I could endure this programming, with my skin chafing against the den's vinyl fur-niture, there would still be a wide, stagnant canal of religion to cross before anything decent came on. Wrestling wasn't until 11:00, so I determined to bring my brother in on the day.

Sometimes working the linoleum beneath my bare feet until it creaked was enough to rouse him. Otherwise, exposing a few toes to the cold or dabbing his ear with a wet Q-tip would do it. Occasionally it took my slipping a sour pickle past his nose, or just pinching his nostrils shut till he shuddered awake. Before he was able to rage, of course, I was urging him to hold it down. I'd play anything, I told him. I'd let him go first every game, be the black checkers or the racecar in Monopoly, choose the cowboys and leave me the rude and futile Indians. Hoping for Stratego or Strat-O-Matic Baseball, I plied him with his favorites, offered Sorry or courted him with interminable Careers, anything, so long as he would keep me company and not wake our parents, who had parents' lives and did not deserve the world so early on a Sunday.

All right. I admit that my need for his company eventually cost him. Typically I would manipulate him into that most invid-ious of pacts: a trade that made him my slave for the day. If I ever pocketed extra Oreos for us, ate his carrots along with my own to spring him from the sentence to clean his plate, or spared him in front of friends the mocking names he hated, he had to agree to be my slave for the day. He used to watch us play football on Christiana Avenue from the catwalk that served as our sideline. Hopeful and marooned as Crusoe, he stayed alert for the call to even up the sides when dinner or curfew claimed a player. If he was summoned to the street, he understood the look I gave him: the price was his next day's freedom.

All children are ravenous out of range of their parents, which, when you think about it, is most of the time. So you have to make your own ethics. That was the point of the slavery my kid brother could not refuse or cry about; otherwise, days would be added to the bill. It was only fair. Look, it was my burden, too. I had to come up with the parameters of his penance. I had to invent ways of keeping him agreeable while keeping him under. Make my bed before you do yours. Don't whine that you took out the garbage yesterday—today you double up. Hand over the gum. Desires are not always articulate and automatically at hand; it is wise to prepare them ahead of time.

Hey, don't Bible at me about it. Long ago I learned to side with Esau over Jacob. Every older brother knows the real lesson of *that* episode. Jacob exploits his being adorable to wheedle fate and bend the regulations of birth order. In the wake of betrayal, Esau fades from Scripture while the baby prospers. Older brothers keep reading in vain, expecting Esau to assert his priority, possibly by scribbling on Jacob's drawings after distracting him … but no, Esau disappears. There is only the memory of injustice to live by. It is one of the most exasperating scenes in the Book: Jacob fleeces his father while wearing a false hide like stolen turf.

Okay, sometimes you get greedy. It is only natural. You push the envelope.

❐ ❐ ❐

Even before anyone could predict that baseball cards would compete with other investments, they held clear value for every boy on the block. But only a moron would wager Mays. ("Moron" is harsh, I suppose, but this was Willie Mays on the table, come on!) No one would think to trade his sole Clemente or barter his Banks. Better to risk a dozen Mets than expose a single McCovey to the fickle currents of the lag. Ah, but the slave ... the slave lives without prerogative, and you raid his line-up at will, exclusively tricking out your own collection with stars like God editing the heavens.

In the final analysis, for the artist, hubris is the only sin.

One of the rival empires, Fleer or Topps, probably, came out with a special set of commemoratives that year. Silver packs gleamed at eye level like astronaut equipment—sleek, blinding, unaffordable, and stoking what lust adolescents could muster. And suddenly it was clear what my little brother was born for. The big score.

I didn't have the funds for the cards I craved, but I had *him*. I had gotten my brother up to a week's worth of indentured servitude, but I was willing to forgive all current and future debts for the Major League Masters Limited Edition (the name regally swollen on the side of each box, with its gaudy entourage of exclamation marks). Bring me such a box, I whispered, and you'll win a permanent reprieve from me.

That's right—I upped the ante on him. I escalated the stakes from stealing cookies from our own kitchen. I put him up to petty larceny with the promise (showing my uncrossed fingers) that I'd never put him down again. He would never again be emissary to any prerogative or dark design of mine. I dispatched him with plenty of sugar, I'm sure—You can do it! It'd be a cinch for you!—but without further strategy. Just do me this one favor, I said, and my disfavor will lift forever. In the Monopoly terms he could appreciate, I told him that he could earn him an eternal GET OUT OF JAIL FREE card for a moment's resolve.

Thus I launched my falcon to carry out my fancy. I may have

justified myself in my own mind with the conviction that he'd never *really try* to pull it off. Yes, knowing me, I must have rehearsed my testimony. I never really thought he had the mettle to test, Your Honor. Who figured him for so much stomach? And anyway, the brat would have to know I didn't really mean it, that I'd been spitballing—he'd seen me ball spit before, hadn't he? *I was only kidding, kid!*

As I say, it was not my shining moment. But over the next few days, whenever he was out of sight for over an hour, and as I fantasized about the line-ups those heat-sealed boxes held, I must have wondered whether he might actually be rising to the vile occasion I'd made.

❏ ❏ ❏

Must I describe the ritual of my brother's returning to the dime store with my father to return the stolen merchandise? By eavesdropping, I was able to piece together the discovery of the goods I'd godfathered him into taking. I imagine some collusion between my father and Friedman, the store manager, and the telephone conversation during which they hatched the morality play of my brother's humiliation. I can picture the gangplank progress to the store, the choked and prodded apology—"Look at the man when you speak to him. Speak up now"—and the long walk home. But this is all conjecture on my part. The fact is, I was never implicated. While I was working out a coppable plea, my pigeon never stooled. If Dad realized that my brother could not have masterminded the crime on his own, he never mentioned it to me. Never. And my brother kept quiet, hogging it all. And he has not referred to it since.

When I reconstruct the incident today, of course, I realize that the caper must have immediately come apart. (I am an adult now, with mature suspicions.) I bet that Friedman saw my clumsy brother smuggle out the box in the first place and called my father so he could stake out the little boy's breathless return.

Delaying the arrest let the guilt build. Possibly Dad was waiting for him to turn himself in.

Meanwhile—a "meanwhile" covering decades, remember— he keeps me hostage to his silence on the matter, having swallowed it whole like the last bottle of pop without spilling a drop. Diabolical. The genius of greed—I have to admire him for it.

He has two sons of his own now. My nephews are themselves rabid for baseball cards, and their collection features several from the sixties, which they keep pristine in plastic sleeves. Over time the cards have become an inheritance too valuable to lag. To be honest, I could argue that many of those cards actually belonged to me—it only stands to reason—but I let it go. The older boy shows them off proudly and confides that they will some day defray his college tuition. As I turn the protective pages with him, I notice that his brother is watching us from the door. He has an expression on his face that I can't quite read.

arrangement in mixed media

By sitting very still, he figured, nothing else would happen. The car had spun to rest on its hood, and the old man, still belted in and holding the wheel, seemed to be allowing the shards of the past twenty seconds to catch up to him and settle back together. Saturday morning television (though critics sneer) provides an analogy to help us connect: Sylvester, shaped like a punch clown but spry like one, too, game like one, is skulled by a blunt something, leaving his head flat as a landing strip; or he gulps a sparkling bundle of TNT, leaving his head a silhouette of ash that collapses; but he revives just in time to haul his nine lives, daisy-chained and dying skyward, back into his body by the last escaping tail. Nine paler versions of himself, each sporting a harp and angel's wings, rising into the afterthought of cartoon sky. Cartoons, those warehouses of shared imagery. How else does anyone imagine anvils or dynamite or the soul's blissful drift toward heaven apart from Warner Brothers' affable designs?

Now the old man, deserving better—and who does not?—was like a cartoon, too. What sound effects would have accompanied the accident? The brass section dropped down a stair-well, possibly. But there was nothing to compare it to because he could not for the life of him remember any sound. There was just this scene, served up, arrived at unaccountably and, in truth, without precedent. Some broken glass near the intersection, but that could have been there already. Gouges in the telephone pole, but they, too, could have been caused by anything, anytime. Stapled notices for a church picnic, a yard sale, a rally in the park—all of them obsolete, yet still flicking in the wind. Bits of paper no one ever bothers to retrieve. No, it takes an accident to bring out the authorities. Specialists in forensics and insurance claims who have to take everything into account.

It could not have been more than twenty seconds, but those seconds had contained much more than he could comprehend at once. At least by holding very still, he thought, concentrated on a still point, there would be nothing else.

He took stock. Upended and cramped by the weight of his legs foundering in his old man's trousers, the kind that need suspenders and suggest the ampler past of an ampler man, disoriented by the bunching of his organs and the sudden dump of blood into his head, he looked subdued, even contemplative. Old men ought to be explorers. He might have been imagining his lungs sliding over his heart the way late afternoon clouds swallow a hill. He might have been imagining his liver corrugating or his veins and arteries tangling like wire hangers at the bottom of the laundry basket. He might have been imagining his spleen nuzzling his stomach, if that was in fact the spleen there. How to imagine his spleen, or his gallbladder or his pancreas, for that matter, for he had no picture, no sense of so much of himself to go on. He waited the way that astronauts waited in their capsules to be fished from the ocean and pried out.

I was one of four who had parked our cars—as who would not have done?—and come to investigate. We converged like infielders hustling to cover a bunt. We pressed in from different sides the way people do to tackle a parachute after the jumper touches down to help him hold his landing against another gust. We moved tentatively upon the car as if we were the usual rubes closing inarticulately upon the alien craft in every fifties sci-fi film, sure to be doomed before the second reel. Or voyeurs,

maybe. We did not come too close. Similes can be wicked. I had
to kneel to the street to see in. Like a prowler. Pick a synonym.
You see how nasty it can get?

Perhaps, in order to keep his wits about him, he was
dutifully rehearsing the birthdays of his grandchildren or
considering—remorseful? reconciled? and who would presume
to judge?—how long it had been that he and his wife had been
living together like a couple of leaky pens in a cracked coffee
cup. Or an inventory of his bookshelves. Or a mantra made from
his resume to keep himself surrounded by a grace of sense. Then
again, he could have been considering how science might one
day reconcile relativity and quantum mechanics. Let our frail
thoughts dally with false surmise. Little rivets of decameter to
wind his nerves around. A bit of Milton to place, if it was Milton,
to work between the tongue and teeth and gently pass the time
until the extraction took place. A lifeline.

At any rate, he was talking. Not looking at me, not looking
at any of us, really, but steadily talking, apparently having something out. A turtle burbling in a terrarium. I don't want to be
unkind, but if you had seen him through the window, furrowed
like that, knuckled ... tucked in like a turtle, tenant with a dull
head, and burbling away.

A man is bottled slosh, he might have been saying. Or
thinking it and saying something else. Communication is always
a difficult business. It is hard enough to read lips right side up.

There was no precedent. Alliteration and metaphor make it
seem easier than it really was to take in. But who can speak for
him? Something familiar about his situation might have been
dawning upon him. As a boy, he could have been a devotee of
military models: plastic fighter planes, tanks, jeeps. One of the
last steps in putting them together was to attach the tiny pilot to
the cockpit or to insert the sitting driver into his seat, delicately
wobbling him like an LP onto the prong of the turntable and
snapping him into permanent place, the proctological effort
eased and rendered irreversible by a seminal gob of Tester's glue.

Possibly his predicament so obviously emulated birth position—
this latest trauma shaking loose the original one—that he
remembered Eliot. In my end is my beginning. The pelvic strain.
And all is always now. Eliot. And something, something decay
with imprecision. The still point in the turning world, and how
to stay in place, and how to stay still. Eliot, certainly, a memory
that credits him, I hope, returning with the drill of blood up his
spine, which now was down. A symbol for something he could
not keep intact, which broke down with him the way metaphor
does, and who was responsible for that? Not Eliot. And the old
made explicit, understood in the completion of its partial
ecstasy, in the general mess of imprecision of feeling. That's
Eliot, a bit tangled, maybe, but who could blame him, under the
overturned car, under the circumstances, which allow but a little
consciousness? Dim light, purifying darkness, in this twittering
world waiting for God like the late bus. That's him.

It had begun to drizzle. From his perspective, raindrops
were sliding up the windshield as if the sky were inhaling them,
drawing them back. The pattern is new in every moment. He
looked straight ahead, with the look of someone who is looked
at, but whether or not he was watching the rain was not clear,
not from what I could see.

Or he may have dreamed all of this before. Once he had his
bearings, it was no longer a matter of things becoming clearer
but of their taking on a vividness beyond clarity. Heaven, or a
dream he'd had, or at least felt as though he'd had: the discovery
of sensations and pressures, the point of view eerily restored.
Leaving one still with the intolerable wrestle with words and
meanings. Hold still. The poetry does not matter. It was not (to
start again) what anyone could have anticipated, and who could
blame them? A blessing that it comes back at all, sustaining him
until he is come for.

How much time had passed now, sliding up the glass? Some
of the drops were settling in a crack in the windshield which, to
be honest, could already have been there before the accident.

I tapped at the window to rouse him from what I presumed to be his daze. We're here for you, mister. He did not turn. He did not turn because he did not hope, because he did not hope to turn.

Where were the police? They always appear, but who ever calls them? They seem simply to show up and confirm the situation, nail it down. What is your name, sir? Sir, can you tell me your name? Can you move? Try to move. Can you? Do you know where you are, how you got here? Police were needed on the scene to get the story together. Manuals, forms, all the appurtenances of ordinance and regulation. Their gleaming, dentless, triumphal cars like new cosmetics. Their grackle-blue-black uniforms, skin-slick. Their swelling rectitude. Nothing happens until the police ask for it.

An ambulance would be coming, vulgar and blaring, bursting with urgency when defter touches were required. There was no crisis, only a progress to swell: an old man lodged in an overturned car like a sliver twisted beneath the skin. Officers would come in, affect propriety. Equal parts confidence and concern had to be registered on professional faces, and performed in the difficult line of sight left to the old man, who was either the perpetrator or the victim, or possibly both, a compound ghost both intimate and unidentifiable, and who could reasonably be expected to know? We needed the police—not only the man in the car, whose hat, collapsible umbrella, and pocket change rested over his head on the fabric headliner, but also our impromptu quartet in our various postures of supplication, in our constitution of silence silently accepted, needed them. To reel the accident back in, establish the facts. It was their job to cordon off the figured speech and keep the subjunctive back behind the lines. What was keeping them?

Meanwhile, here was a guy brought up hard against his biology and looking for all the world like an embryo going bad in its jar.

I went through a series of pantomimes, auditioning for

recognition. Both palms down and softly pistoning to indicate "Stay calm" or "Don't move," but which could have been taken for "Roll down the window," which in his case would mean raising it like a gate in a channel. Then right hand in a fist with the thumb protruding and thrusting sideways to indicate "We'll have you out soon" or "Do you want us to try to get you out, because you can't be too comfortable, and the police haven't materialized yet to take charge, and although we are not all that inspiring a sight, the four of us ringing round you like crows, makeshift and tentative and pecking as it must seem to you, we're what's available?" But this particular movement admittedly resembled a hitchhiker's plea or an umpire's decision after the slide, both cruel jokes in view of what he'd suffered, and I was not so callous as that—a crucial point to get across but for which I had no gesture at all. No way to say that was not what I meant at all. All the while I kept my eyebrows peaked to show concern, nodded vigorously to show hope. Inventing a pure and wild dialect. I was a baboon agitating over the grubs in his lunch, whooping, flailing to bring his brothers near or keep them off. He might have gathered as much and only that, and who could blame him? Trying to get through with shabby equipment always deteriorating.

He might have been praying. Praying that someone come for him or stay clear. Praying not to end, or for an end to it. "You are not here to verify, / Instruct yourself, or inform curiosity / Or carry report. You are here to kneel / Where prayer has been valid." Deferential, glad to be of use. And turning toward the window, he would have seen me: a poor attendant, a politic ape.

We thought it best to pull back. Other, separate motives were beginning to creep back to us, undoing our knot. One of us was late for an appointment. One quite simply didn't want to be bothered—and, after all, who does? One still had his baby boy clamped in his car seat and had to get back to him. He went to the open window. "Are you okay, pal?" "Ba." "You want your squeezy?" "Ba-aa." "What is it, Robbie? Some juice?" "Ba?" "Do

you want to get out? Out?" "Ba!" "And any action / Is a step to the
block, to the fire, down the sea's throat / Or to an illegible stone:
and that is where we start."

And now the cops, those concerned with every lawful traffic, were on the job. Breaking out the right tools. Finding the
signature of event, the right black scar on the road to measure.
Assessing the significant glass against the distraction fit. It was
training that made them, and we were not to be blamed for
belonging on the periphery. "Who are only undefeated /
Because we have gone on trying." If they were better able to
assess an old man's blather, if they could better penetrate an old
man's incapacities or better absorb the complicated odor of an
old man's stool, we were still men with jobs, men with families,
men who watched their neighborhoods, made their kids say
"please," sponsored fund drives, kept our weekly covenant with
the front lawn. We were involved with Little League, charities,
the PTA. We were good men, men who voted and spoke up and
spoke out. We were men who had stopped to check. Fellow
men. In a crisis, we had pulled over and taken off our coats, and
despite the desperate sentiments of *Times* editorials and all
trendy skepticism aside, who would not have done as much?
And now the proper personnel were finally on the scene.
Doubtless, society was not yet dead. Even now the old man was
being loaded with reasonable dignity into the ambulance,
which had arrived—mercifully—quietly. He seemed still to be
talking, except that now he could see that the right people were
there to take it in, which must have been a blessing.

A few others, drawn by the ambulance lights, had shuffled
close to have a look. Harmless opportunists and understudies
hanging about the stage—belated, but not to be begrudged. It
was the way that people were, wanting to take a little hit off the
damage, that's all. But moral men, all of us, early and late, shaking our heads, clearing our throats, shifting our weight. "If you
came this way, / Taking any route, starting from anywhere, / At
any time or at any season, / It would always be the same: you

would have to put off / Sense and notion." Out of the wild dialect of contingency seizing on an object lesson, craving a cue.

"Nothing more to be seen here. Go back·to your homes." The rest was not our business. "Either you had no purpose / Or the purpose is beyond the end you figured / And is altered in fulfillment." That's what we were waiting for. The director's cut.

Another official car would come to retrieve the old man's car, collect the fragments, sweep away the broken husks of the accident left behind. The dry salvages. "Dust in the air suspended / Marks the place where a story ended." Meanwhile, leaving the disfigured street, we could resume ourselves. And now we would have a way of putting it at the dinner table, a pattern for owning and disowning the past, with the whole family together and with the television off, the way we learned whole families used to be together on television (though sophisticates scoff) a generation ago. Every memory is a poem to be made, and every poem an epitaph. We had our story, which, for dramatic effect, we would reserve for the right moment. Right after grace.

the understory

Vladimir: I missed you ... and at the same time I was happy. Isn't that a queer thing?
Estragon: (shocked) Happy?
Vladimir: Perhaps it's not quite the right word.

—*Samuel Beckett,* Waiting for Godot

I think it must be something in the water. It seems as if everyone I know is depressed. A. is depressed, and so is B.; C. is depressed, and D. is depressed as hell. E. is depressed by all he has become and all he hasn't. So is F., who has the look of someone the atmosphere's betrayed, as if he senses something's secretly gone bad far back in the fridge. G. is depressed like other men, only more so, he claims, doing his Bogart. He says that life is a trial, and you're stuck with a lawyer who's unprepared, a surly jury, and a dozing judge. I agree with him that this is clever, and I agree with him that being clever doesn't help.

There's a veritable contagion of depression that's come over us. Some are vaguely depressed, lashed by cables so cunningly devised they leave no mark. Some are minimalist, barely leaking the odd sigh. Some are Rabelaisian, laden with inventories to audit their woes and ever ready to go off on jags of wrath. Some are slack with it, and some are rigid; some are listless, some keen.

Some are depressed notoriously, some operatically, some, bringing the earth's ailings in on it, altruistically, and some with foot-
notes. Some find each day a revelation of travail, while some get
used to the muck as they go along. But all in all, there's a consensus of depression, with practically all of us able to defy any
brilliance and mope, heads down, past any sunrise or blaze in
the stained glass.

Depression weighs on H. like a steady rain, on I. like a Santa's
bag of toys he has to suffer and give away, on J. like a barbell that
has him pinned to the bench. K., L., and M., a triumvirate of vex-
ation, all add to the sad, unanimous vote. N.? What do you think?
O.? Have you seen someone who tries to remove a permanent
tattoo and leaves a scar just as permanent? That's O. for you.

Speaking of burns, P. deems the sun a personal punishment,
which at least compensates him with some sense of election, in
that something massive has it in for him. However, Q., pointing out his own sores, quickly blows that pretension. Q. has
lately contracted even further than usual, having recently been
reduced to playing sex games and chess on-line. (What are you
wearing? Knight to rook four. Your move.) R., who is fond of
reminding us that his thesaurus offers eight more synonyms for
melancholy than it does for joy (a point spread, he says, that
only a fool would bet against), decants his depression into her-
metic verse, prods it into stanzas like rendering plants. His
attempts to put his ill humor alliteratively to bed basically
amounts to the longest eulogy on record—that is, if you don't
count what S. has been committing to journals for thirty years
(her invariable annuity, so to speak). S. tries to cheer herself up
by saying that she writes in order to persist more formidably
and more clearly somewhere, somewhat the way the grave will,
she adds, which, of course, depresses her. Then she gets to be
like Faulkner's Addie Bundren, dwelling exclusively upon her
coffin. That's the trouble with existence, T. says. No one gets
out alive. It's like trying to light an imbedded wit with the same
bad match, but he keeps saying it. He's almost giddy with his

gloom sometimes, even rakish, his overcooked complaints
tough as knots by now. And his hard heart bubbles like a golf
ball in a cup.

It's like an open audition for a Bergman film out there. Not
only are the people I know best depressed, but depressed is the
way I know them best. U. does not recognize herself apart from
her depression, and, frankly, she's afraid that if she ever loses it,
she won't be able to find herself in any reflection. She always
seems to be flinching from well-aimed insects, as she casts about
for whatever it is that throws the world so out of whack for her
that she can't imagine it ever being back in whack again. Try to
cheer her up, and a flock of suspicions come to roost in her
mind, their hooks sunk in deep, taking root. V., on the other
hand, used to make a real effort to raise his spirits. He regularly
took prescription drugs to combat depression—for years, in fact,
he swallowed multisyllabic pills, moving dutifully through the
pharmacy like a student in Advanced Latin—until he decided
that being dependent on drugs was more depressing than what
they were designed to counter. These days it takes all the deliberation of a barn raising to lift his countenance, and once it's up,
it is the only time that anyone, seeing the strain on his face, will
ask him, What's the matter? You can't win either way, I guess,
which is sort of depressing, too.

It's like triage close to the front lines, stepping as best I can
around my crestfallen friends without actually stepping on them.
A hemorrhage of depression. Come in close to console W. as he
humps his troubles through the dumps he's forever down in, and
you'll hear the resentments he's left on permanent simmer
carmelizing in his brain pan. How's it going, W.? Couldn't be
better. I'm sorry to hear that.

X., competitive even in his pangs, counters W.'s vaudeville
routine with the tale of the oldest preserved corpse ever discovered, hacked intact out of four thousand years' worth of former
Soviet ice, and who (so it is rumored) the claimants may divide
up the way that X.'s ex's lawyers have drawn and quartered him.

But these are the same old dolors X. has been dragging around on rusty castors for months. You'd think the guy'd be dead on his beat by now.

Y.'s is the very model of a modern major general depression. Y. notices that the close-up wounds of the most recent teenager gunned down in the local paper are precise little mouths about the bullets that did him in. They fit like lips around nipples. Kafka thought the same sort of thing about arrows, recognizing with the same rueful satisfaction how injury shapes us accordingly. Y. recalls for me one of the woodcuts in my edition of *Moby Dick,* which shows the whale's continental flank clutching the first black harpoon it received like an all-day sucker. She teaches literature to dour undergrads who, if they had the energy to muster druthers, would prefer, like Bartleby, not to. She works in a world where students can't read and the bombs are smart, she says. Your daughter is growing up in this world, she continues. Everyone's daughter is. Every other semester or so, someone in class asks her if all great literature is depressing. Do you want the long answer or the short answer? she replies. Both are yes.

Meanwhile, Z's depression is no center and all circumference. From time to time, Z. will vigorously shake his head as if trying to loosen a kite stuck in a tree. I suggest to Z. that he's obviously in one of his moods, realizing as I do that, so far as I know, he has only one mood. I'll tell you about mood, he says. "Mood" sees "doom" in the mirror. Look deep into those twin pits and you'll fall in. Hell, he says, sinking further into his chair, don't look and fall in anyway.

I have plenty of time to consider my run of sullen friends while jammed up on Chicago's sargasso, the Lake Shore Drive, where the cars keep clumping up and everything barely labors along. In city travel, as in comedy, timing is everything, and I stayed too long at the Shedd Aquarium. Now I am parked here. Parked. Literally. Parked and packed in with everyone else, and like everyone else wondering about the confused physics of our predicament: if the first guy is going the speed limit, and the guy behind him, and the guy behind him, why aren't we getting anywhere?

It was the octopus that had brought me to the Shedd and held me up. I had meant to leave well ahead of the city's infamous five o'clock rush hour (infamous for beginning at three-thirty), but I lingered in the artificial chambers of the sea.

For it had been the octopus, especially, which a television special compelled me to see in person. Even PBS could not domesticate it. The octopus churned and slopped behind my nineteen-inch screen like a heavy load of wash. I could barely bother with the murmuring mutual congratulations of the scientists who stalked and photographed the beast. These were unprecedented pictures of an unprecedented cephalopod, they burbled, then began to pun on "suckers." But flaunting expertise in the face of it was like trading stocks at communion. The octopus was an indecent exposure, frank and vile, convulsing like a bowel, and although the scientists, pressed against their dials, assessed and measured and compared— they commented about the thing's design marvels and its flaws as if they were inspecting a late-model car—they could not contain the amniotic thing.

I turned off the sound and doused the lights, increasing the sense of immersion. The octopus was a viscid, ghastly avalanche, a reticule of schemes, an enigma endlessly enfolding, which none of these associative snares could capture or arrest. But the creature was the very embodiment of nuance, insinuation—it was Wallace Stevens's "intricate evasions of as" winding subtly undersea. I could not help myself before the contradictions that the octopus, ever-blossoming, encompassed. It implied both drift and calculation, composure and craving; it kept coalescing but—oozing wound—never clotted. It was utterly biotic yet dreamy, seething up its indeterminate sleeves. It had me, and I had to see it for myself.

Standing rapt before it at the Shedd with a bunch of determined mothers and itchy kids—who *else* goes to the aquarium on

a Tuesday?—I remembered from the program that the octopus
is, for all its incessant slither, for all its undulating feints,
decisive. It is a billow of appetite, a grand organ unraveling its
mouths and stops and flues, yet somehow symphonic in ways we
cannot guess at. Constrained to robotic arms and diving devices,
we are arthritic and clunky by comparison. Even the scientists,
tacking in their clumsy tonnage, got the joke we are.

There was a steady thrum at work in the aquarium. Some
mysterious turbine winding, some concerted, perpetual effort to
steady temperature and pressure. On the program, the scientists,
alerted by a similar sound, had noted that a sperm whale, using
echo location, bellows over a mile for its meal. If that had in fact
been a sperm whale they heard. Like tenants in a distant apartment, the scientists were aware that something was going on,
but they couldn't make it out.

Anyway, by the time I snapped out of it, it was nearing four.
So here I am in my stopped car, with the windows rolled up and
the air conditioning laboring and feeling for all the world that
we are all fish caught mid-slither, sealed in cunningly controlled
environments of our own. Sounds of concern, sounds of frustra-
tion, sounds of amazement—we are stuck like smithereens in
separate ovens here!—rub against the glass. The sun erupts in
sudden flashes off hoods, windows, and mirrors—a desperate,
illegible semaphore. Some of the drivers uselessly pound their
horns. Some stick their heads out into the August heat for a
moment to air their angers, gape, or groan. One guy in a Firebird
has his radio set on blast, and my car shudders from the bass.

I am no prophet—and here's no great matter. No transub-
stantiation shimmers in the windshield. Still, like everyone else,
I wish for some indefinite something wonderful enough to lift
me absolutely out of sight of the inquisition of any mirror. Or
better, let some radiance break down the locked and barricaded
door to the cellar where I've been holding myself hostage and
free me from my own sick demands. Better still, remake me
entirely out of light and stitch me up in light, sound and sure as

a Buddhist bell. But for the clutch of traffic, to be delivered once and for all instead of undone! I remember the tiny pearl fish, which burrows backwards into the anus of a sea cucumber to avoid danger, and although I do not envy his situation, I can't help but think that I've had worse receptions.

I try to hold it together, but I keep worrying that if the Lake Shore Drive doesn't get unkinked soon, the car will overheat and I'll have to abandon it and scramble through a not-so-hospitable part of the darkening city—it's getting later all the time—to find a phone. I check the dashboard dials. I shut off the radio and ease the air conditioner to its lowest setting to lessen the strain on the engine. When a lobster grows large enough to have to shunt the casing in which it scuttled across the floors of silent seas, I learned, it is at its most vulnerable to predators. For an anxious minute I watched it roll about as if some surgeon has tossed a bad gland off the table and missed the bucket. Almost the moment after it made a break for it—how did they ever manage to film this?—other measly creatures fastened upon the shell and started to crunch away at its nutrients.

We've started to edge forward a bit, then after a few seconds, a bit more, in the exasperating peristalsis of Lake Shore Drive. The last mile has taken nearly forty minutes! How long before I can get to an exit? The old Malibu can't take much more. I am no mechanic, but I can imagine its innards seizing up on me. In sorry shape for years now, the car has started to move, but no faster than lunch through a digestive tract. I've turned off the air conditioning altogether and let all the northbound exhaust in. If I can just urge it on another hundred yards—what a humiliation, when we should be measuring our progress in miles per hour!—I can get out of this and shut it down. Then what? I'll have to call one of my friends to come get me, I guess. I wonder who'd be up for it.

But what is my plight compared with that of the male Trinidadian guppy? Pity him for his contradictory survival imperatives, the Catch-22 evolution has subjected him to. If he is too colorful and conspicuous, he advertises himself as dinner; if he is too drab and withdrawn, he fails to attract the procreative attentions of females. So he must balance the risk of being eaten against the risk of being alone. Either way, it's fatal. Which is to say that tragedy is cheap—somewhere or other, everyone is feeling the heat. Waiting helplessly in the impacted late afternoon traffic for the Chevy's fever to break, I'm no one special.

I've had better days, haven't I? I say aloud. *Haven't I?*

love among the stacks

I love libraries. This is not the same thing as loving books, a passion that is necessary but not sufficient to the love of libraries. There is much to love, of course, about books alone: their aloneness, for example. I am likewise enticed by their titles, their heft, their congregated gravity on shelves where they slouch in rank like soldiers at ease. Here one lies open on a tabletop as if basking in the sun; another waits next to the bed, full of promise, revealed as only half-discreet beneath the covers. (Invite me to a party at your house, and I will read your bookshelves. You may worry about Gary, who is taking too long in the bathroom because he is going through your medicine chest, or you may obsess over whether or not yesterday's underwear is out of sight when Roger goes to use the phone in the bedroom, but I am the one with the most intimate view of you.) Emily Dickinson wrote, "There is no frigate like a book / To take us worlds away," and in doing so she launched a thousand pastel bookmarks trailing gold yarn. I would add that if books transport us, they also increase our weight. In addition to taking us worlds away, books also keep us more formidably *here*. To read is to make one's presence felt.

I have just read a novel by Donald Antrim in which the citizens of some anarchic suburban future have fortified their homes with moats, booby traps, spike-filled pits, and other ordnance against neighbors and other strangers. In one scene, intrepid, visionary council members patrol the park for land mines by strategically hurling books from the now-closed library. *Biological Aspects of Mental Disorder* hits without incident, and the *Handbook of Classical Mythology* lands safely; *The Darwin Reader*, on the other hand, is blasted clean through the center, while *The Riverside Shakespeare* and *The Poetry of Robert Frost*, although they cause no explosion, compete admirably for hang time before settling like struck birds to earth. It is good to know that books retain value regardless of civil strife, but had everyone gathered in the library rather than plundered it for defense missiles, one suspects, life would have been less forbidding in Antrim's world, not to mention far quieter.

Then there is my friend Mike O'Riley from college, who played intramural ice hockey on a limited budget. Because he could not afford official hockey pads, he insulated his pants with paperbacks. As a goalie, he frequently counted on books in an immediate, intimate way. After one particularly difficult save, he noted that *The Scarlet Letter* saved *him* from having to see the urologist. Today he has a wife and four children, thanks in no small measure to solid literature.

But to redirect my focus, some would maintain that books, like love and faith, seem less sublime when they are institutionalized in a library. Perhaps they sense something more coercive than worshipful, more of the penal colony than of the cathedral, in the walled hush of the place. People who love books but not libraries look askance at library overstocks left on cold rolling carts for disposal or quick sale: they spy their now-obsolete serial numbers etched into their covers, and they think of ex-cons looking for employment outside the system.

Nor are lovers of bookstores necessarily available to the allure of libraries. People who love modern bookstores also love to mug and preen at newborns beyond the glass in hospital nurseries when they themselves have no intention of parenting. The mixed odor of transitoriness and mercantilism in contemporary bookstores in particular is deadly depressing, for their arcade glossiness degrades books faster than the acid in old paper. In bookstore windows, books vamp like underage strippers, awkward among the diet supplements and spring fashions that are born to the role. Hastings, Walden, B. Dalton's—books were born free, but everywhere they are in chains.

Ah, but in a library, books are bound for glory. What a relief it is to enter a library! What a privilege to prowl the stacks, where burrs of curiosity catch on cunning surfaces, subtle designs. A library is not only essential to democracy—how civilizing the civil service they silently perform—it is a democracy on display. For all its gathered erudition, there is nothing elitist about a library. It is not just user-friendly, it is downright promiscuous, its every aisle and index crying access. Numberless hungers flourish here. Even the section known as Permanent Reserve can, despite the pretense of that designation, ambush and ravish you.

My favorite librarian congenially reigned over the English Graduate Library at the University of Illinois. She knew every book in her keeping by size, color, and location. She made computer indexes obsolete before their invention. Who ever troubled himself with the card catalogue when she could say, "Wilson's *Axel's Castle*? Yes, that would be the third aisle, second row from the floor, a red and gray binding. It's in." I imagine her in her youth, although one could hardly imagine her younger, huddled with her lover in the perpetual flourescent noon in the corner recesses warmed by literary criticism, discreetly exuding the aroma of binding paste, whispering due dates and where he might touch, "a little more to the left and straight down, you'll find it." The librarian who narrates Elizabeth McCracken's *The Giant's House* confides that even as those who beguile us disclose a strange ignorance, ignorance is likewise beguiling. This is especially true for the reference librarian, who can kindle romance out of that endless circuit of needing and having information and turn *The Statistical Abstract of the United States* into her own private *Kama Sutra:* "Synecdoche is a literary device meaning the part for the whole, as in, the crowned heads of Europe. I love you. I could find you British Parliamentary papers, I could track down a book you only barely remember reading. Do you love me now?"

Some book lovers find libraries too public—but one more reason to have to wear shoes. But where else is what Emerson called "the infinitude of the private mind" so regularly, so effortlessly appreciated? What is more mindful than a library? Where is interest more reliably compounded? It is a veritable community of solitude. In a library we are substantially alone together.

But let me no longer crouch behind the plural. I am here to confess, to testify. My name is Art, and I am a library addict. I love to watch children settle their attention into a book like a warm bath and watch the raptness rise from them like vapor. As a child myself I would chase the bookmobile the way attorneys reportedly chase ambulances or Beatle fans their beloveds. I would take a trip each week to the library and be amazed at the utopian economy of the place: you can take this book home for free so long as you bring it back on time. What a sensible, humane sort of parole! Here in the library was where Doctor Seuss lived, the habitat of not just *The Cat in the Hat,* so I believed, but of the actual man who hatted the cat. My younger brother kept returning and reborrowing the same book—*If Apples Had Teeth*—which began, "If apples had teeth, they would bite back" and showed a carnivorous fruit latched onto the nose of the unsuspecting consumer. This was too good to relinquish, and my brother would follow the book from the return desk through its course of circulation back to its shelf, where he would snatch it for another go-round. There was a children's section at the library—think of the grandeur of that acknowledgment, unprecedented and unimitated outside of day-care anywhere else in the city. In the garish plush of the children's section, where each volume had been rubbed by hundreds of small and grubby thumbs, a child could dream of anything, and the dreams counted.

In Herb Gardner's play *A Thousand Clowns,* the hero's nephew, who has been in his uncle Murray's unofficial and eccentric custody for eight years, has been granted the luxury of changing his name as often as he wishes, to whatever he wishes, for as long as he wishes, with the provision that he must select a permanent name for himself by the time he reaches his thirteenth birthday. He goes through an impressive array of dog and comic book hero names, not to mention "Chevrolet" and "Toulouse" and "Raphael Sabatini," but the point is that in order to authenticate each reanointment, to really road-test it, he takes out a new library card for each new name he adopts. Know Thyself, we are advised by needlepoints in kitchens across America. Where better to know thyself than in that fundamental context of texts, the local library?

A library is such an optimistic structure, isn't it? How reassuring to watch readers compose themselves for study, arranging their table like a vanity; for indeed, whatever duties to courses they may also be discharging, they are, as I say, composing themselves. They are islands of consciousness, of conscientiousness; yet as these separate cells become more profoundly involved and more complicated, they somehow come together as a federation of concern. The record of mental effort on hand at a library is staggering. The conservationist faith a library represents, enriched by the past yet aimed at a better, better reasoned, future, is thoroughly uncynical, and more satisfying than any scout troop or Sierra Club. What a wholesome addiction! I defy you to recall any news bulletin about a serial killer found dead by his own hand which ended with "Police reported the discovery of a library card on the premises."

Guides to college life regularly include sections on how to meet like-minded people and suggest campus locales with the most promising deposits. Consider the library first. Sure, there are bars and ballgames to stalk, rock concerts and mixers to trawl, but think of the woman for whom the confines of the library are no confinement. Think of her capacity for bemusement as she fingers the recent acquisitions. Think of the regal scope of her appreciation as she inspects the parliament of current periodicals, stopping to handle one, then another, like a mother giving her knowing approval to the children decked out for church. Think of the lingering commitment of her eyes, hands, and thoughts as she caresses a concept. You want a woman to treat you like a book, not like a beer.

I had a dream once about being left in the stacks of an impossibly large library after closing. I was a spelunker in its infinite depths, where rumors of trapped albino bibliophiles hung in the bookish dark. I was a specialist in the digestive processes of the place, the complex of pneumatic tubes and databases, the shelving carts and dumbwaiters, the lovely guts where all words churned. Borges's fantastic Library of Babel, at once orderly and infinite, would be gobbled down whole by my dream archive; one of the Seven Wonders of the ancient world, the Library of Alexandria, would be as a footnote to my marvelous embowelment, the Library of Congress barely a morsel to this gargantuan readers' digest. It was a veritable paradise of passages. Need I mention that this was an erotic dream?

There is talk of the library's obsolescence. A gloomy future looms for documents, we read, for reading still goes on in the hills, where the counterrevolutionists hunker down, in their bookish remove, keeping the esprit-de-core collection alive. Though they breed assiduously, journals, we hear, are going the way of carrier pigeons. All the while unsightly chat piles are swelling on the Internet, where contact is constant and antiseptic, and the once-weighty Word slides over the screen's glowing surface, as Sven Birkerts derisively puts it in *The Gutenberg Elegies*, like a leaf on a river.

But the value of libraries exceeds nostalgia. Friends of the Library do not come together to eulogize a lost companion but to honor and sustain its constancy. And that is the splendid paradox of libraries: they simultaneously preserve and progress, protect and promote, and probably balance off other felicitous alliterations as well. So keeping to the *P*'s, in deference to Library of Congress logic (that is where they stack the books of literature, and where you'll occasionally find me browsing,

running my hands over their spines like some rogue chiroprac-
tor), in libraries Whitman winks at James, the Frost collects
before the Hawthorne, Updike idles—Updike, who said that he
aims in his mind as he writes not at New York but at some vague
spot a little to the East of Kansas where a young reader unwittingly happens upon his unjacketed book on a library shelf, and
here we are, John, here we are—and Joyce Carol Oates prolifer-
ates through some magical parthenogenesis or meiosis of the
manuscript so that it seems as though her volumes multiply
overnight. And don't think that I fail to seek out my own books
and essays when I visit a new library in a new city, hoping that
they have been welcomed into the community.

Just as I look for such a fellowship with you. When I was
doing my dissertation, I happened upon a book about marine
symbolism in British literature. My request was placed into a
coppery cartridge and sucked into the pneumatic intestinal tract
of the University of Illinois Main Library—reason enough to
work there—and I waited for my number to yellow up on the
big board. When it did, I was given this slender book, a wizened
first edition dated 1919, and which still had glued to its first
page the original due-date slip. This was 1978, and when my due
date was stamped in, that made a total of five of us who had
checked out the book in sixty years—one in 1919, when it made
its pristine debut; one in 1929, perhaps to escape economic realities for the sublimities of literary criticism; one in 1946, fresh
from proof of our naval ascendancy in the wake of World War
II; one in 1960, possibly inspired by the legend of Kennedy's
keeping his cool and his hair intact on PT-109; and now me,
eighteen years later, nibbling about the edges of a hoped-for
academic career. I thought of putting out an ad for missing per-
sons. The five of us had this common denominator. Whether
browsers or researchers, we were shareholders together.

Novelist David Foster Wallace has defined himself as the sort
of person who likes to get into a taxi and say, "The library, and
step on it." He is one of us. The writer-hero of Truman Capote's

Breakfast at Tiffany's responds to the challenge of giving high society call girl Holly Golightly an experience she has never had and
will never forget by taking her to the library. He is one of us, too.
(For her part, Holly takes him to Tiffany's, where he wishes to
buy her a memento of their day but can find nothing but a silver-
plated telephone dialer—and who remembers telephone dialers,
much less telephone dialing—that he can afford. Assured by the
clerk that he can have something engraved, he pulls out a plastic
ring. "You didn't purchase this here, did you?" the clerk asks, eyeing the prize. "No, it came in a box of Crackerjack," the writer
tells him, sheepishly. "Hmm. They still put prizes in
Crackerjack?" "Yes, sir." "Very reassuring, somehow," the clerk
urbanely and bemusedly replies, and that urbane and bemused
clerk was played by John McGiver, an urbane and bemused character actor who made a living out of such roles, and you can look
it up right here!) Neil Klugman works in a library in Philip Roth's
Goodbye, Columbus, where he is fascinated by a poor black boy who
lurks beneath the shelves supporting modern art. "Man, that's the
... life," the boy tells Neil, as together they rummage among the
pages for their own likes and likenesses. Set a place for both of
them at our table as well.

   Kurt Vonnegut makes the distinction in his novel *Cat's Cradle*
between a *granfalloon* and a *karass*. A *granfalloon* is a false relationship or merely coincidental connection—his examples of *gran-
falloons* include the Elks Club, Hoosiers, and families. A *karass*,
meanwhile, is a deeper, abiding kinship. Those who have
earnestly touched books and been touched by them in turn surely constitute a karass. I can imagine no more prestigious populations than books and those who give them residence. My apologies to Shakespeare's Polonius, but in terms of the library, one
should *both* a borrower and a lender be. In supporting the library,
you support my sharper appetites; in befriending the library, you
not only become some of its most precious holdings, you leave
a light on for me as well.

soldiers of fortune

It is a clear night tonight, and the neighborhood is dotted with fathers. They are conducting upwards for their rapt kids, sweeping their arms, pointing at lights light-years off, orchestrating the dark. They are spreading the news that some Grand Designer has accessorized the sky as if for this night's premiere. The stars have come on and hit their marks, and some of the fathers say that the most brilliant anchor the Bear. Ursa Major emerges from the cave of night each night to continue the most obvious prowl in the universe. No need to be afraid, they promise—that rough beast slouches toward us but does not bite.

Meanwhile, holding forth from other lawns, other fathers are insisting that through some Ovidian trick the very same seven stars have become the Big Dipper. See the bowl the bear breaks into? See the handle that was its haunch? Instead of viewing the stars as ellipses, think of runway lights. Think of synapses firing in the gaps.

With equal confidence, opposing squads of fathers bracket the air. There it is, that design and indenture, there, right there! You have to imagine the connections among "the queer elisions of the mist and murk," as Richard Wilbur says. Start with "that one star's synecdochic smirk," he advises, although the rhyme may verify the murk instead of dissolve it. In "The Dubious Night," it is open to question from which direction the doubt comes.

I hang on these gestures, but all of that congested essence is lost on me. I can't get what they're getting at. Rather than follow a certain signifying finger out to its implications, I stay riveted to the fist the way a dog would. I want to learn, honestly—I am a father, too, with my own lawn and my own comparable obligations—but no matter how earnestly they slice the sky at its invisible joints, I still don't get the picture. Or the figure slips from bear to dipper and back again like the duck-rabbit drawing that psychologists use to make the mind strobe. The Great Dipping Bear. Also known in some countries as the Plough. Also known as the Wagon. Does that help? The fathers head back inside, their palms smoothing the hair of their daughters, their arms encircling the shoulders of their sons, while I remain in the dark.

❏ ❏ ❏

We are not happy with the fortune cookies. We don't know what overhaul has taken place at the factory or what malign influence has entered the premises. Possibly some disgruntlement has entered at some point between the front office and the ovens. Possibly it's a labor dispute being played out in peevishness because the union has refused to act. In any event, it is obvious to all of us that the fortune cookies have changed, and changed for the worse.

Truth be told, the fortunes used to be fortunes. This is no nostalgic delusion, or if it is, we have all succumbed to it. We recollect the cookies served up on a plate with the check, shivering like brittle bivalves when the waiter set them down on the table as the last exoticism to swallow. We remember crushing them in sticky palms, detonating their yellow powder—like punching thumbs through old parchment or breaking into tombs—to extract and compare our destinies. And they *were* destinies, however vaguely articulated. They touched on loves

postponed or impending, arrivals of distant relatives or better
luck; they apprised us of the pits we could fall into or saw money
coming like clement weather. They risked prediction and, in
brief little bursts, impacted. They dared to dare us. Pulling out
the slip of paper could be like pulling the pin on a grenade.

But now some new strain of fecklessness or political correctness has broken out in the baked goods. Whatever the reason,
now it is all truism and bromide in our fortune cookies, all goofy
chiasmus and edgeless sense. It is as if they did not trust the children with the real utensils but consigned them to the squeak and
clatter of plastic knives and forks that could not cut. *The wise man
knows what to take from fools. Love is the gift one gets by giving. One learns
to trust by trusting to learn. Open a patient eye.* It is insulting, really, to
have the fate one's a function of pulverized into a baby's formula.
Who knows how deeply it eats into the tips?

□ □ □

You could smash the television set, it is that exasperating. The
lottery gets so swollen that not even taxes can snatch back
enough to keep any family—We have a winner, ladies and gen-
tlemen!—from fattening forever down the generations. You wish
it could be you and yours—no crime in that, no sin—but more
power to them. And then you find out that the winner won by a
lapse of memory (he got his kids' birthdays confused or misread
the Ouija board); or worse, he's earth's perfect clod, determined
to keep his job at the plant despite the fact that he's now rich
enough to exact any revenge he wants. "The money won't
change me," he announces, proudly impaled on his principles.
He intends to divide the prize money into a series of deferred
payments, a plan he'd devised a long time ago, just in case.

There must have been a misdeal in the tarot, you decide, or
no one thought to cut the deck. A momentary misalliance
among the stars—how else can you make sense of it? And yet,
there was also the guy in New Jersey who'd fought with his wife

the night before the drawing. Because they were not speaking to each other, they did not consult the next morning about who was going to play the numbers they had agreed upon when he was sober or before her mother had dropped in on them unannounced. You would suppose that the lottery would have been the last thing on their furred, infuriated minds, but there was no telling when the jackpot might swell to that size again (whereas they could always argue about his drinking or Mom's prying). The inevitable upshot was that he duplicated her purchase and thus duplicated her winnings, which left them rich enough for liquor, distance from the in-laws, or divorce. So much for communication being the key to happiness!

   And isn't that the way it always is? Dumb luck finds its own level, the windfall falling upon the dumbest lucky. It takes a dope, apparently, to dope out the cosmic logic that decides which seed gets soaked and which starves in the same rain. All over the country this evening, the schmucks are dining on unjust deserts. The only thing that stops your holler, that stays your hand from hammering the offending set, is that *you* can't *afford* to act out, especially not with the kids around, who hear everything.

                          ❑   ❑   ❑

The Leakeys of Kenya are well into their third generation of excavation. Louis, the son of missionaries who first migrated to Nairobi in 1902, married Mary, to whom was born Richard, which occasioned no significant interruption in the dig. Richard, who one day presented his mother with a complete skull of Australopithecus ("It's beautiful!" she cried), married Maeve, who currently works in the paleontology wing of the National Museums of Kenya, and who brought her daughter, Louise, to Kenya two weeks after she was born. (Continuity—that's the key.) Now mother and daughter discuss the facts of life in the Great Rift Valley. They divvy up shifts as if the layered eras simply made for one awful laundry day. "She works up to three million, or one and a half to three," Maeve explains. "And I work from three million to four million."

The courtyard of the National Museums of Kenya features a statue of Louis Leakey, who so notoriously gorged on the Olduvai. He is preserved forever in a happy hunch over a pile of bones. A photographer for the *Washington Post* has asked the great man's daughter-in-law and granddaughter to pose next to the statue of their famous ancestor—branching off the trunk of the family tree, as it were. Maeve interrupts the picture to pick a particle of lint that no one else can see from her daughter's blouse.

Paleontology, it seems, is as much an art as it is a science, and a modernist art of fragments and gaps at that. The transparencies you recall from high school made a cutaway section of the planet look like a club sandwich, but in reality there are breaks and absences that need to be filled in, much the way that individual pieces of discovered skull are puzzled, glued, and extrapolated with clay. It was in high school, too, that you saw films about the Leakeys. You best remember images of the archaeological team having at it with pickaxes and shovels, but you may be interested to learn that most of their exertions today require dental probes and fine brushes.

As the species ascends through thirty thousand centuries or so, there is bound to be some static on the line. Scientists are the first to admit that human telemetry requires a few leaps of faith. A case in point: there is ongoing speculation regarding a branch of "robust" australopithecines. The debate has to do with their disappearance after a relatively brief period of time (genealogically speaking). All at once defunct, they seem to have been supplanted by the lake-dwelling tool-users whose echoes we appear to be. On the other hand, many experts maintain that the fossil record is too incomplete to support this conclusion. For now, at least.

Another question surrounds three sets of footprints dating back half a million years before "Lucy." According to the pattern of the stride and the nature of the arch—yes, there are stride experts, there are arch experts—the scientists surmise that they were walking closely together. Possibly they were a family, possibly holding hands. This compels on several levels, of course. However, as Annie Dillard notes in *For the Time Being*, one of the sets of footprints does break off from the others. Mary Leakey's interpretation was that "a remote ancestor experienced a moment of doubt." This, too, compels on several levels.

Whether those creatures traveling toward their rendezvous with Mary Leakey's team were more human than ape or vice versa has yet to be determined. They are still strobing, you might say. At present, they are being referred to as "hominids." Terminology is critical at every stage of analysis.

For instance, we do not refer to a surviving stream of creatures as "lucky"; we call them "successful."

Meanwhile, the Leakeys show no sign of letting up. There is much to be done, and, fortunately, their current work near Lake Turkana continues to show results. It also gives them a feeling of peace, for, as Maeve says, what they are learning is "part of this longer, bigger system. That we're not very significant in terms of the whole process, but we can understand it. And that's where our significance is."

◻ ◻ ◻

The human body is a flimsy consortium of leaks, crusts, danders, and blats. Each of us is a Cagney no cell can hold for long. We are nothing if not deciduous, and most of what we dust is our dust.

Ghosts compound above and below. Our posterity and our graves are embedded in the heavens and beneath our feet. We were all of us once the stuff of stars—our atoms, the scientists say, are that itinerant and old; soon enough we'll build the soil back up as our children's children's children tamp us down. And so we reside for a time between astronomy and mulch. Not for long, genealogically speaking. You have to look quickly to catch us in the transition, or at all.

"We grow accustomed to the Dark," wrote Emily Dickinson. "Either the Darkness alters— / Or something in the sight / Adjusts itself to Midnight— / And Life steps almost straight." *Almost*—Dickinson's disclaimer is hidden in fine print at the bottom of the poem. Our sight is perpetually under construction, and even poets have to step cautiously around if they hope to get from day to day, much less from star to star.

Look out the window at midnight just right, and you won't see anything past your reflection trapped in the glass.

The sky awaits my paraphrase tonight like every night. No galaxy lags behind the interpretive curve or balks the zodiac. You need to learn the firmament by heart, including the cracks in the ceiling. There, in the western sky: a falling star: a sudden tear, which immediately heals. A paper cut in Creation. A lesion in the field of inquiry. Did you see it slip by like the flash of the pea in a roulette wheel? (Players, place your bets!)

But you know that a falling star is not a falling star but a meteor. Or it is a signal flare. You might make out a career, a code, or a thrown clot in the brain of God. You have to supply a little imagination to catch on.

Take the example of George Adamski, who disclosed in a piece in *Life* that he has had numerous contacts with aliens. One of these occurred on December 13, 1952, at Palomar Gardens, California. His photograph of the "iridescent glasslike craft," which is reproduced in the magazine, has been variously identified as a surgical lamp, the top of a vacuum cleaner, a chicken feeder, and a tobacco humidifier. It's not distinct enough to tell for sure.

In fact, the sky is full of bright fatalities, like an eternal series of deferred payments. All of it is my portion tonight, as far as I can see.

The stars bear down on us. Tell the children. Take them in.